DATE DUE			
M.H.C. JUL 9 '76 LIBRARY			
GAYLORD			PRINTED IN U.S.A

TEACHING
YOUNG CHILDREN
TO READ
AT HOME

TEACHING YOUNG CHILDREN TO READ AT HOME

WOOD SMETHURST

THE PAIDEIA SCHOOL, ATLANTA, GEORGIA
AND
DIRECTOR OF THE READING CENTER
EMORY UNIVERSITY

McGraw-Hill Book Company

New York   St. Louis   San Francisco   Düsseldorf   London
Mexico   Sydney   Toronto

Copyright © 1975 by Wood Smethurst. All rights reserved. Printed in the United States of America. No part of this publication may be reproduced, stored in a retrieval system, or transmitted, in any form or by any means, electronic, mechanical, photocopying, recording or otherwise, without the prior written permission of the publisher.

Library of Congress Cataloging in Publication Data

Smethurst, Wood.
   Teaching young children to read at home.
   Bibliography: p.
   1. Reading (Preschool) 2. Domestic education.
I. Title.
LB1140.5.R4S42   372.4'1   75-5854
        ISBN 0-07-058443-5

123456789 BPBP 74321098765

The editors for this book were Thomas H. Quinn and Cheryl Love, the designer was Christine Aulicino, and the production supervisor was Milton Heiberg. It was set in Primer by Progressive Typographers, Inc.

Printed and bound by Book Press.

To my parents,
Frank and Margarette Smethurst,
who taught me to read

Contents

Acknowledgments — ix

PART ONE

1. An Overview of Home Reading Instruction for Preschoolers — 3
2. Teaching Young Children to Read at Home: A Brief History — 10
3. The Research on Home Reading Teaching — 49
4. Some Conclusions from History and Research — 84

PART TWO

5. What to Do If You Decide to Teach Your Child Beginning Reading at Home — 105
6. Teaching Beginning Reading Skills: A Step-by-Step Program You Can Follow at Home — 109

A Buyer's Guide to Teaching and Learning Materials for Home Instruction — 202

A Reading List for Parent-Teachers — 213

References — 216

Index — 225

Acknowledgments

This book has been seven years in the making, and many people have helped at one stage or another. I want to thank at least some of them now.

First, my family has been helpful, tolerant, and for the most part resigned to my writing projects. To my wife, Lucy, and our sons, Frank and William, I owe more thanks than I can express.

I need to thank my teachers, too. Professor Jeanne Chall, my doctoral adviser at Harvard, has put up with me since 1967, and is surely one of the greatest teachers anywhere. I am indebted to practically everyone I knew in the Harvard years, but I especially want to thank my doctoral adviser in curriculum, David Purpel, and Professor Courtney Cazden, who was a very supportive third member of my thesis committee. I also want to thank my teachers who encouraged my interest in early reading (and to absolve them of blame for any mistakes I might have made): Robert Anderson, Arthur Blumenthal, Helen Branch, Milton Budoff, Tom Fillmer, Elliott Galloway, Richard Henderson, Gerald Lesser, Helen Popp, Douglas Porter, Blanche Serwer, Israel Scheffler, Burton White, and Sheldon White.

I am grateful also to the succession of students, friends, editors, and colleagues who have read and commented on the manuscript in one or another of its several stages of preparation.

I owe much indeed to my close friends and typist-editors—Anne Smith, Bette Turlington, and Joan Wager. They have helped me give the book such shape and organization as it has.

Grateful acknowledgment is made for permission to use excerpts from the following copyrighted material:

The quotation on pages 11 and 12 from Robert Claiborne and the Editors of Time-Life Books, *The Birth of Writing*. Copyright 1974, Time, Inc.

The quotation on page 20 from Philippe Ariès, *Centuries of Childhood*, translated by Robert Baldick (Alfred A. Knopf, Inc.). Copyright 1962.

The table on page 68 from Dolores Durkin, *Children Who Read Early* (Teachers College Press). Copyright 1966 by Teachers College, Columbia University.

The quotation on pages 40–42 from Eda J. LeShan, *The Conspiracy against Childhood* (Atheneum). Copyright 1967 by Eda J. LeShan. All rights reserved.

The quotations on pages 92 and 93 from Glenn Doman, *How to Teach Your Baby to Read* (Random House). Copyright 1964.

The quotation on page 33 from Leonard Bloomfield and Clarence L. Barnhart, *Let's Read: A Linguistic Approach* (Wayne State University Press). Copyright 1961, by special permission from Clarence L. Barnhart. All rights reserved.

The quotation on page 20 from Winston Churchill. Reprinted by permission of Charles Scribner's Sons from *My Early Life: A Roving Commission*, by Winston Churchill. Copyright 1930 by Charles Scribner's Sons.

The quotation on page 9 from John Culhane, *The New York Times Book Review* (Mar. 10, 1974, p. 8). Copyright 1974 by the New York Times Company. Reprinted by permission.

The quotations on pages 53 and 54 from Irving Anderson and Walter Dearborn, *The Psychology of Teaching Reading* (Ronald). Copyright 1952.

The quotation on page 26 from Nila Benton Smith, *Reading Instruction for Today's Children* (Prentice-Hall, Inc.). Copyright 1963. Reprinted by permission of Prentice-Hall, Inc.

The quotation on page 8 from Martha Dallmann et al., *The Teaching of Reading* (Holt). Copyright 1974.

The quotations on pages 55 and 56 from J. L. Evans, "Teaching Reading by Machine: A Case History in Early Reading Behavior," *Communication Review*. Copyright 1965. Reprinted by permission of the Association for Educational Communications and Technology.

The quotation on page 27 from Jean-Paul Sartre, *The Words*, translated from the French by Bernard Frechtman; reprinted with the permission of Fawcett, Crest Books. English translation copyright 1964 by George Braziller, Inc.

The quotation on page 58 from Carol Chomsky, "Write First, Read Later." Reprinted with permission from *Childhood Education* (vol. 47, no. 6, March 1971, p. 296). Copyright 1971 by the Association for Childhood Education International.

TEACHING YOUNG CHILDREN TO READ AT HOME

... what is the real basis of our present belief that children should be taught how to read *in school*? Originally, reading was taught as an apprenticeship skill by one who could read to one who wanted to learn. It was only when societies wished to change the proportions of literacy within a generation that schools were needed in which the children of non-literate parents could be taught in bunches. But today America's is an almost completely literate society. Why shouldn't mothers, who spend all day with their children, teach them to read, to understand money, to think about numbers, to understand the calendar, the clock, time, space? Now that these are the necessary requirements for a full humanity, just as walking and talking and understanding kinship relations and the local terrain were once the requirements for a full humanity, why can't all such essentials be taught at home? Do we know why not?

MARGARET MEAD (1961)

PART ONE

ABC

CHAPTER 1

An Overview of Home Reading Instruction for Preschoolers

Throughout the five thousand years or so that people have been reading, many children have been taught to read at home. Their teachers have been parents, siblings, relatives, servants, masters, governesses, tutors, or playmates. In some societies this sort of teaching has even been commonplace. Perhaps reading is, as Margaret Mead suggests, an apprenticeship skill—a social necessity which is appropriately taught to children at home in the same way that other apprenticeship skills are taught, such as dressing and toileting oneself, getting about, social graces, and kinship patterns. A first-grade classroom is by no means the only place for a child to begin reading—and maybe it is not even the best place to begin.

I am a classroom teacher, and I don't want to attack the schools here or discount the importance of good teaching. I certainly don't plan to argue in this book that *all* children should learn to read outside school (I don't think they should). All I'm saying is that, for some children, home may be a good place to begin the highly individual process of learning to read. In fact, children who have already made some sort of beginning at home seem to do at least as well—or better—in first-grade (and later) reading as classmates who have begun first grade without such a head start.[1]

The conventional wisdom of the last 50 years about parental teaching at home has been essentially, "Don't teach them." Parents were urged to leave children alone as far as reading instruction was concerned. Teaching children letters, sounds, and words was often thought to be best left to the professionals in first grade.[2] Parents who taught their children anyway were usually aware that they were bucking established practice.

All this may be changing. Following the success of "Sesame Street," we see letters, sounds, and words taught on network-TV children's programming; few educators object. First-grade teachers with whom I talk expect several of their pupils to come to them in September already reading. (This seems especially noticeable in areas where Montessori and other preschools teach beginning reading skills.) Montessori schools have taught young children to read in many countries and have gained wide acceptance in America since the late 1950s.[3] The so-called "childhood education establishment" has opposed the teaching of reading to young children, but their opposition seems not so vigorous as it used to be.[4] More and more kindergartens and day care centers in America and elsewhere teach beginning reading skills—letter names, sounds, sight words—without apology. The International Reading Association has published a set of guidelines for reading instruction in child care centers.[5] Reading teaching kits, records, and books are sold through the mail as well as in toy stores and supermarkets.[6] ABC books are back, with a vengeance. There is a whole line of "Sesame Street" products with Big Bird, Bert, and Ernie all helping children learn letters, numbers, and so on.[7] Walt Disney Productions now offers (and advertises on television and in supermarkets) an entire program of "read-it-yourself books specially created for children 4 to 8," and beginning with an ABC book that features Donald Duck (Disney, 1973). It's a new day.

Historically, this can be seen as a return to attitudes about home teaching that prevailed before 1920 or thereabouts. In the 1920s and 1930s parents began to be advised to leave the teaching of letters and such to the professionals, and it has taken fifty years or so for the tide to turn.

In America today, there seems to be a growing number of parents interested in helping their preschoolers learn about reading: This book is for them. I am writing expressly for parents who are considering teaching their children to read and who want to find out more about it. *At no time will I try to persuade any parent to teach any child.* The choice is entirely yours: if you want to, if your child wants to, I can suggest several ways to go about it. I will try to review the historical evidence and analyze such research as exists in the field. In addition, I will give a rather detailed reading list for anyone who might want to pursue the matter further. A buyer's guide to available teaching materials is included in Part Two, giving publishers' names and ordering information. I also include a specific, step-by-step program of my own to follow if you wish, which uses materials you can make at home with magic markers, index cards, and large drawing paper or poster board.

As a reading specialist who is also a teacher of young children (and a father of two), I am regularly asked by other parents for help and/or advice about reading and preschoolers. Most of the people who seek me out are deeply concerned about their children and are worried lest they, the parents, do the wrong thing. Many of these parents tell me that their kids have already begun asking them about letters, words, sounds, and reading; these parents aren't sure how to respond or what to do. Other parents who seek me out feel that their children will benefit intellectually from an early start in reading, but they worry about doing too much too soon, as well as about doing the wrong thing. This book is an attempt to answer their questions, which I think are altogether legitimate ones.

Some Definitions and a Warning

Before talking about how children learn to read at home, we need to be clear about some definitions. I believe that there are at least five specific skills that are basic to reading competence. I call these "beginning reading skills." These five certainly aren't all the skills needed, but I believe that competence in each of them is fundamental to any child's ability to read well.

The skills are:

1. Naming capital letters
2. Naming lowercase letters
3. Associating appropriate speech sounds with selected letter forms
4. Combining certain sounds to form short words, such as *man, pin, hot,* etc.
5. Recognizing some common words at sight, such as *the, are, some, said,* etc.

Two of the most important attitudes which seem to me to underlie the ability to learn to read are:

1. A positive attitude toward books and reading generally (shown by curiosity about books, enjoyment in being read to, and interest in looking at books, magazines, etc.)
2. A desire to learn to read (or to learn the letter names, sounds, words, or any of the other beginning skills)

It is hard to teach someone to read who does not have these two attitudes.

Let me define some of the terms I will use.

I use the phrase "young child" or "young children" throughout this book to refer to children less than six years old.

A "nonprofessional reading teacher" is defined, for the purpose of this work, as a person of any age who instructs another in reading but who has taken no professional education courses in the teaching of reading. Thus, a veteran high-school algebra teacher, a neurosurgeon, and a ninth-grade baby-sitter might all be considered nonprofessional reading teachers in our discussion.

The term "home teaching" is used, admittedly rather loosely, to describe reading instruction that is conducted outside the school. Thus the child who learns to read by watching "The Electric Company" on a neighbor's TV is receiving home instruction, just as is a child being tutored by his/her mother in the kitchen of their home.

"Formal" and "informal" are terms that badly need defining in a discussion of this sort. ("Formal instruction" is a widely used straw man for writers on early education—it almost always implies repressive and authoritarian instruction, and the writers are almost always against it.)

I will use "formal instruction" to refer to teaching that closely follows a prepared text, manual, or organized sequence and that is pursued on a regular basis. Formal instruction does *not* imply oppressive or authoritarian instruction, in my usage.

"Informal instruction" will refer to teaching which is occasional in character, which follows no textbook, workbook, or teacher's manual, and which uses the child's experiences or materials at hand in the child's environment for instruction. Just as "formal" does not necessarily mean bad and repressive, "informal" does not necessarily imply good and/or supportive.

My Beginning Reading Skills home instruction program, which I include in Part Two (p. 109), contains both formal and informal elements. It seems to me that both kinds of instruction have a useful place.

One more thing. In these suggestions, as in the program to follow, I have often used the he/she formulation where a pronoun was called for—and the sex was indefinite—everywhere that the writing would permit. In places this gets cumbersome, though. Consider this sentence:

"If his or her interest wanes, give him or her a book he or she can read himself or herself."

Too much? I believe so.

But using he, him, or his alone is sexist and offensive, I think, and "es," "te," "herm," "himmer," etc., are distracting at best. I have therefore taken the liberty of alternating pronoun reference throughout this book when I talk about "your child." It will be "he" in one passage, and "she" in a later place. I have tried to keep it consistent within passages, to hold down the confusion. I hope it works.

There is one flat, emphatic warning which will appear repeatedly in this book. It concerns the use of pressure—emotional or other stress—as a teaching device with young children. I strongly oppose pressuring young children, and I will not recommend or be associated in any way with any system using pressure.[8] The warning:

Do not push[9] your child to learn to read; avoid instructional systems or strategies which employ pressure.

Teaching your child to read should be fun for both you *and* your child, if you do it properly. If it is not fun, you shouldn't do it. Enjoy.

NOTES

1. Evidence is very scarce, but enough exists to suggest that some reading-achievement advantage may exist for early readers in elementary school. (See Chapter 3 for reviews of the major studies.)

There is less evidence for the persistence of any early-reader advantage in reading achievement through high school and college. What we have is retrospective interviews with good readers (Terman, 1925; Hildreth, 1958; Kasdon, 1958), who often state that they learned to read before beginning school, and a great many case histories and anecdotes about the education and later life of early readers.

In my opinion, not enough evidence of advantage exists to justify teaching a preschool child to read—if gaining this advantage is the only reason for the teaching. It *seems* reasonable that there would be an advantage, and there is some evidence for it, but the point is by no means proved.

I believe the best reason to teach a young child to read is that the child is interested and wants to learn. Parents wishing to teach a preschool child to read are advised to consider first ways to arouse the child's interest in reading before launching into a course of instruction. In the program in Part Two, pages 105–162, I give a number of suggestions for arousing a child's interest, such as reading stories aloud, trips to the library together, playing letter and word games, writing stories and letters, etc.

2. Durkin (1968, p. 6) quotes a curriculum bulletin of the New York City Schools which seems to state this position clearly: "Parents are asked not to teach their children to read because there are many methods of teaching reading. A child is taught by one method in school and his parents, by introducing another method, may serve only to confuse him" (Board of Education, 1952, p. 6).

Martha Dallmann et al. address this question in their textbook for teachers of reading. "Another contention of many first-grade teachers is that parents should not help boys and girls of preschool age with reading because a parent may use a different method of teaching reading than the one that will be employed in the school. The child may, the argument continues, encounter greater difficulties in reading at school than he would be likely to meet if he had not had parental guidance. However, it seems difficult to imagine that a child taught at home by, let us say, a whole-word method would be handicapped if later at school he were taught by a phonic method, or vice-versa" (Dallmann et al., 1974, p. 56).

3. A good discussion of Maria Montessori and the Montessori movement in America may be found in Pines's book *Revolution in Learning* (1967). Those who are interested further are encouraged to go on to Dr. Montessori's own works, which are (in my opinion) among the best books written about children's learning. La Dottoressa had her biases and blind spots, but for empathy with children, insight, and common sense she is hard to match.

4. I review some of this opposition in later sections of this book. For a fuller discussion, see Chapter 2, pages 38 to 43.

5. Durkin et al. (1973), "Day Care and Reading." ". . . guidelines thought to be helpful for any who have responsibilities in day care centers" (p. 2). These guidelines were published in *The Reading Teacher* in February 1973 and are available from the International Reading Association, Newark, Delaware 19711, upon request.

6. See pages 36–38 for a brief description of some of these materials. The Buyer's Guide, pages 202 to 212, contains descriptions and ordering information on a selection of teaching materials that interested parents can buy.

7. Electric Company's latest series of inexpensive books for home use by beginning readers deserves serious attention. *The New York Times Book Review* called the series "a publishing milestone." The books are currently being sold in drugstores and elsewhere at 39 cents each—a reasonable price indeed. The *Times*'s reviewer, John Culhane, said:

> The greatest strength of the Electric Company Easy Readers is that there aren't many good books with designedly limited vocabularies available at 39 cents.
>
> So, getting down to the nitty-gritty, what is an Electric Company Easy Reader Golden Book?
>
> A *real deal!* [*The New York Times Book Review*, Mar. 10, 1974, p. 8]

8. "Pressure" is usually the withholding of your affection or approval in order to persuade your child to learn to read; actually, any sort of parental force applied to induce the child to learn can be called "pressure."

9. I define "pushing" a child as follows: Urging the child to read, to listen to reading, or to work on beginning reading skills when the child does not want to.

CHAPTER 2

Teaching Young Children to Read at Home: A Brief History

Teaching children to read at home is a phenomenon which has occurred throughout the history of reading instruction. There is evidence that children have learned to read outside schools for thousands of years, in many languages and in many different cultures.

Oftentimes children who have learned to read at home have been under six years old when they began their instruction, and sometimes they have been well under six.

In this chapter I will try to review briefly the history of home reading instruction from antiquity to the present. I will conduct this review by taking first a panoramic view of the history of home reading instruction; then my focus will narrow to the history of teaching young children to read at home, in English.

Teaching Reading at Home in Many Cultures, from Antiquity to the Present

There are a good many instances of home reading teaching in the ancient world, and there are places in the world today where children are customarily taught reading at home, starting when they are quite young. Parents who are considering teaching their own youngsters to read may find this information reassuring.

Sumeria

Historians think that people learned to read and write in Sumeria around 3500 B.C.—between five and six thousand years ago. The earliest Sumerian clay tablet which we have dates to 3100 B.C., and there is some reason to believe that the art of pictographic writing existed there considerably earlier (W. N. Smith, 1955; Claiborne, 1974).

At first, reading and writing in Sumerian culture seems to have been the property of the priests. The skill was developed over centuries by temple scribes, and probably grew out of their need to keep accounts and to communicate in the increasingly complex Sumerian society.[1] It is interesting to note that home teaching seems to have been used from the very beginnings of the reading skill. In Sumeria, literacy was at first passed from father to son. Later, it seems to have been taught to favored children in temple schools, by a priest whose duty was instructing the novitiates.

As commerce grew in Sumeria, there arose a class of clerks, less prestigious certainly than priests, but who also knew how to read, write, and keep accounts. These clerks did much of the record keeping—writing with a stylus on clay tablets, some of which have survived to this time. It seems likely that these clerks were taught to read outside schools, as apprentices. Cheira, writing in 1938, thought that this might be the case: "Especially those preparing for the minor clerical positions must have acquired the art of writing privately from scribes who were not connected with temple schools. They apparently apprenticed themselves to the scribes and became known as their sons" (p. 1). Claiborne (1974) offers this view of the early days of Sumerian writing:

> In the early days of writing, professional scribes may well have passed their demanding craft on to their sons—and occasionally their daughters, for the names of a few female scribes crop up in ancient documents. But any other youngster seeking to learn the scribe's trade would find no one interested in taking him on as an assistant—unless he or his parents paid the instructor for the time and trouble. And that sort of relationship, in which A is paid to convey information and skills to B, is the school embryo. For the first scribes who gave private lessons, it could hardly

have taken very long to make the discovery that they could multiply their incomes by teaching students in groups rather than one at a time. Almost as soon, other scribes must have realized that it was far simpler to send their own sons off to school than it was to teach them at home. [p. 91]

Other Ancient Societies
In the ancient civilizations of the Indus Valley, in what is now India, reading and writing seem also to have been a priestly monopoly. According to Keay (1918), "During the earliest stages, Brahman education appears to have been administered by the father—each experienced priest teaching his own sons—and its purpose was obviously to train priests."

A tutorial tradition also existed among the aristocracy in the ancient civilizations of China and Japan (W. A. Smith, 1969). It is not clear how general this tutelage was, or how far down the social scale it extended, however.

Writing was a priestly and scribal monopoly in Egypt and Persia and in the high civilizations of Central America. We know little about the Phoenicians because they did their everyday writing on papyrus, which has not survived. We simply do not know how they taught their children. All we know is that many generations of Phoenicians learned to read and write (Edey, 1974).

The Hebrews
Perhaps because reading and literacy are important factors in the observance of their religion, Jewish girls and boys for centuries have been taught to read as very young children. From biblical times, the Hebraic tradition has placed the responsibility for children's learning to read and write upon the father:

> With the rise and spread of literacy came the need of teaching the young to read and write. However, apart from the facilities for the training of professional scribes and chroniclers, there are no indications of schools for this purpose. Indirect evidence supplied by the Old Testament points to a fair degree of literacy among the young in pre-Exile times, and it leaves no doubt whatever but that the obligation of teaching reading and writing—to the extent that these skills were deemed essential—devolved upon the father. [W. A. Smith, 1969, pp. 238–239]

It was under such a constraint that the great Rabbi Israel abn al-Nakov ruled, in about A.D. 1250, that, in a conflict with the father's *own* need to study, the father's need had priority, and the child should preferably be sent to a tutor (Baron, 1942).

It seems likely that such a tutorial tradition had great antiquity among the Hebrews. Literacy, at least among the wealthy, seems to have been common at the time of David, about 1000 B.C. (Swift, 1919). Many Jews could read, according to Swift, by the time of *Deuteronomy*, about 620 B.C. They were taught, he believes, either at home or by private tutors, since there is no evidence of schools as such.

Centuries later, according to one of the books of the Christian Apocrypha, there is a story of the child Jesus being taken by his father to such a tutor.[2]

In the centuries after the Diaspora, Jews, scattered all over the world, seem to have held tightly to the tradition of early reading instruction. In Europe, until fairly recent times, Jewish children were taught as infants to recognize the Hebrew letters and, as soon as they were toilet-trained, sent to *dareki kheyder*, or infant schools, and there taught to read (Baron, 1942; Zborowsky & Herzog, 1952).

In present day Israel, some kibbutz children are taught to read Hebrew in the nursery. Israeli kids outside the kibbutz are often taught beginning reading in preschools, or at home.

Ancient Greece

We know that the Mycenaeans and Cretans could write, but it is difficult for us to figure out what they wrote. As more Minoan writings are translated, we will perhaps learn when and how the very early Greeks learned to read and write (Claiborne, 1974).

Children were probably being taught to read in Athens by the seventh century B.C. The Athenian law requiring fathers to teach their sons to read (or to have them taught) dates from Solon, in the sixth century B.C. The exact text of the law has not survived, but it is known to have required fathers "to give their sons an elementary education, in letters, lyre playing, and gymnastics" (W. A. Smith, 1955). There is no mention in the law of the education of girls, though there were many women of education and culture in Athens. As in other societies, Athenian girls were taught at home, either by their parents or by tutors. Athenian children at home probably worked with wax tablets and stylus, and there may even have been an alphabet song, according to Mathews (1966, p. 5).

The Athenians seem to have gone from an informal tutorial method of teaching reading rather early in their history, perhaps by the fifth century B.C. or sooner, to the creation of schools. Home teaching seems to have survived, however, especially for girls. It is also likely that young children continued to be taught informally at home.

Aristotle, in the *Politics* (Book 7), urged that children of both sexes begin to learn at home at age five, and start school only at seven.

There was a Greek aristocratic tradition of the *paidagogos*, a personal slave whose duty it was to guard, teach, and supervise the wealthy child's upbringing. These pedagogues reportedly enjoyed high status in early times in Greece, but in later years their status seems to have sharply declined (F. A. Beck, 1964).

The pedagogue-slave was, of course, not usually available to poor families. There is considerable evidence, however, that most Athenians could read as early as the fifth century B.C., though schools were not yet common (F. A. Beck, 1964), and most children were taught at home.

> Most Athenian citizens were literate. Apparently even uneducated people could read, and when an Athenian wanted to describe a complete ignoramus, he used the proverbial phrase 'He can't read, he can't swim.' The Spartans were alleged to be not as literate as the Athenians, but, contrary to an old legend, many Spartans were literate. In classical Greece there was no mystique surrounding the craft of writing such as we find in the civilization of the East. [Cipolla, 1969, p. 38]

There was a serious catch to all this emphasis on reading, however. Athenians, because of their literacy, were themselves greatly prized as slaves in the ancient world. Athenians were especially in demand as tutors for children of the rich in Greece, and later throughout the Mediterranean, during the Classic Period and afterward. An Athenian missing in battle was said to be, from as early as 415 B.C. on, "either dead or teaching the ABC's" (Mathews, 1966, p. 9).

With Alexander, Hellenistic civilization (and literacy) spread widely, and Athenians and other literate Greeks—both slaves and otherwise—continued to be used as tutors throughout the Mediterranean, until well into Roman times.

Rome

Roman society, with its emphasis on the family, relied on home instruction in the basic subjects—including reading—especially for children of the middle and lower classes:

> Although there may have been an occasional early *ludus,* or private elementary school, native Roman education was carried on almost exclusively in the household under the direction of the paterfamilias . . . custom, buttressed by ancient Roman morals sufficed to insure that the father would shoulder his responsibilities seriously. Apart from religious and patriotic observances and the daily routine of living in which the young played the roles of apprentices, the content of native education was extremely limited, embodying little more than the minima of reading, writing and counting. [W. N. Smith, 1955, p. 135]

Smith goes on to point out:

> . . . the prevalence of teachers of Greek (grammatici) has led some to assume that the grammar school had already come into existence at this time (ca. 170 B.C.). There is, however . . . not a shred of solid evidence in support of this. The so-called grammatici of this period were nothing more or less than private teachers in the households of important families. The work of these teachers was none the less thoroughly effective. [p. 187]

Pliny, writing of the virtues of Roman education, said, "Every child had his father for schoolmaster." Gwynn quotes Tacitus eloquently describing the virtues of Roman household education (and please note that Tacitus has the mother or another woman doing the teaching):

> Of old our children were born of chaste parents and were reared, not in the chamber of some hired nurse, but in the lap or at the breast of their mother, whose chief glory was thus to stay

home and be the servant of her children. Choice was made of some matron from among the family's relatives, to whom were entrusted all the children of the same household. Of well-proved virtue, her influence was such that none dared utter before her an unseemly word or venture on an unbecoming action. Her presence, commanding awe and reverence, was there to check the children not merely at their lessons and serious duties, but even during their games and recreations. Thus, tradition tells us, did Cornelia train the Gracchi. . . . [Tacitus, Dial. 28, as quoted by Gynn, 1926, p. 14]

Roman society, according to Cipolla (1969, p. 38), "appears to have been tolerably literate, and the Roman legionary was not uncommonly a literate soldier." Cipolla also points out that "in Roman towns laws were posted on boards in public places and it was assumed that the majority of citizens would read them" (p. 38).

Quintilian, an amiable Roman schoolmaster, in the first book of his 12-volume treatise on the education of orators, considers at length the proper age and manner by which reading should be taught to young children. He weighs and rejects the claims of others (including Eratosthenes) that children should not begin to read until they are seven years old. Quintilian prefers a much earlier start, provided, however, that the work is easy and gentle and pleasant. He urges beginning with the child's learning to recognize and name the letters, and even suggests some learning aids.

> I quite approve of a practice which has been devised to stimulate children to learn by giving them ivory letters to play with, as I do of anything else that may be discovered to delight the very young, the sight, handling and naming of which is a pleasure. [Butler translation, 1920, p. 33]

But best of all, I find Quintilian giving, nineteen centuries ago, a sober warning that is equally appropriate today.

> I am not however so blind to differences of age as to think that the very young should be forced on prematurely or given real work to do. Above all things we must take care that the child, who is not yet old enough to love his studies, does not come to hate them and dread the bitterness which he has once tasted, even when the years of infancy are left behind. His studies must be made an amusement. [Butler translation, 1920, p. 29]

Europe in the Middle Ages and Afterward
There is a tradition that from about the fourth century on learning declined in Europe and that schools, teaching, and literacy were almost exclusively in the hands of the clergy (Thompson, 1960, p. v). Painstaking research has been devoted to showing that many educated people lived during those times, that schools *were* kept, and that the ability to read (though not necessarily to write) was more widely distributed than heretofore has been believed (Pirenne, 1934; Adamson, 1946; Thompson, 1960).

Much of the instruction seems to have been in the household, though Anglo-Saxon England had flourishing schools until the time of the Northmen, and perhaps later (Adamson, 1946). Girls were probably admitted to these schools—our evidence is fragmentary—and both girls and boys were almost certainly taught at home, either by parents or tutors.

Especially in England, the custom of having children tutored at home has persisted among the middle and upper classes.

John Hart, an Englishman, published a guide for these tutors in 1570, called *A Methode or Comfortable Beginning for All vnlearned, whereby They may bee Taught to read Englishe, in a very short time, with pleasure.*[3]

In 1717 the poet-diplomat Matthew Prior drew lyrical attention to an interesting practice in English reading instruction, which some have called "the gingerbread method."

> I mention'd diff'rent Ways of Breeding,
> Begin We in our Children's Reading.
> To Master John the English Maid
> A Horn Book gives of Ginger-bread:
> And that the Child may learn the better,
> As he can name, he eats the Letter;
> Proceeding thus with Vast Delight,
> He spells, and gnaws from Left to Right.
>   [Prior, 1717, Canto II, as quoted by
>   Smith, N.B., 1965, p. 7]

In Germany, there is also a solid tradition of home instruction going back for centuries and continuing into the present. A German, Ickelsamer, published a primer in 1527, directed to parents as well as teachers (Mathews, 1966, p. 15). In the eighteenth century, another German, Gedike, inveighed against the pressure and boredom visited on three-year-olds learning ABCs and syllables from unqualified teachers. Gedike devised his own less painful method of teaching reading; using it, he claimed to have taught his five-year-old daughter to read in two months. He eventually published a primer, whose title, translated, is *Children's Book for the First Practice of Reading without the ABC's and Spelling* (1791).

Glenn Doman's book entitled *How to Teach Your Baby to Read* has been translated into German and has sold successfully in Germany (Doman, 1968). Other programs for home-reading instruction in German are commercially available to parents.

Sweden has a long history of home teaching and literacy:

> Charles X and Gustavus Adolphus did for Sweden and their generation what America, with all her achievement has failed to do since—made education so common that in the year 1637 (the year of the founding of Harvard) "not a single peasant's child was unable to read and write." [Boone, 1889, p. 4]

Much of that education was in the home.

Summary
On looking quickly over nearly six thousand years of reading instruction, it seems safe and reasonable to conclude that, over the centuries, reading in many languages has been taught to children outside of schools; and the children who have been so taught have sometimes been under six years old.

Tutorial systems of education have flourished in many societies, and, indeed, have sometimes been the primary means of basic education in the society.

Teaching Children to Read at Home and in English

There are not one but several branches or traditions of home reading instruction in the English-speaking world—beginning perhaps in Roman and Anglo-Saxon England and continuing in America and throughout the old British Empire.

Although these branches often overlap and occasionally merge, I will list them as if they were quite distinct:

1. The aristocratic tutorial tradition
2. Parental teaching
3. Children who learn early with little teaching
4. The educational movements which involve home reading instruction
5. Reading instruction via the communications media in the 1960s and 1970s

1. The Aristocratic Tutorial Tradition
As mentioned earlier, in England there is a venerable tradition of home tutelage of young children, whether by family, nanny, or governess—it depends somewhat on the social class of the child in question. An elaborate literature is available advising such tutors what to do.

An excellent sample of this tutorial literature is provided by Miss Elizabeth Appleton in her text *Early Education: On the Management of Children Considered with a View to Future Character* (1821). Miss Appleton was also the author of a much-used book on teaching older children at home, *Private Education* (1815). I am indebted to this lady for one of my favorite quotes on teaching reading to young children outside schools, from *Early Education:*

> There are many schemes and plans for teaching little children to read in a very short space of time; but we never find, I believe, that children so taught are, in the end, wiser or cleverer than those gradually and gently initiated into the mysteries of the horn-book. [Appleton, *Early Education*, p. 350]

Many other books were written to guide the would-be teacher of young children.[4] One of these was called *Reading without Tears*, by F. L. Bevan (1857), and we are told of at least one child of the English aristocracy who did not take kindly to this particular program of home reading instruction. In his boyhood Winston Churchill was notoriously inept as a scholar, and from his own testimony things seem to have gone badly from the very beginning. This account of his nurse's attempts to teach him to read at home is from Churchill's book *My Early Life* (1934):

> Mrs. Everest produced a book called *Reading without Tears*. It certainly did not justify its title in my case. I was made aware that before the Governess arrived I must be able to read without tears. We toiled each day. My nurse pointed with a pen at the different letters. I thought it all very tiresome. [p. 17]

2. Parental Teaching

Parental teaching and teaching by masters to their apprentices seems to have been common in the seventeenth, eighteenth, and even nineteenth centuries.

One of the first reading texts in English, Edmund Coote's *The English Schoolmaster,* was addressed explicitly to parents and masters of apprentices. It is described by Philippe Ariès (1962) in his classic study of the history of childhood:

> In 1596 Edmund Coote published *The English Schoolmaster,* a manual of seventy-nine pages in English, not Latin, which was remarkable in that it was not addressed to professional pedagogues, nor even to educated readers. It went through twenty-six editions between 1596 and 1656. . . .
>
> . . . Coote declares that his book is addressed to "such men and women of trade as tailors, weavers, shopkeepers, seamsters, and such others as have undertaken the charge of teaching others." And he describes in a few words these humble workshop schools: "Thou mayest sit on thy shop-board at thy books or thy needle, and never hinder any work to hear thy scholars, after thou hast once made this little book familiar to thee." Thus we can see that without leaving his work, an artisan would sometimes gather some apprentices around him . . . and teach them a few elements of reading, writing. . . . [Ariès, 1962, p. 298]

Ariès describes how, fortified by Coote's primer, the amateur teacher could go on to become professional, accepting pupils on a regular basis (p. 299).

In the early days of the Massachusetts Bay Colony, parent teaching or its equivalent was required by law, much as it had been in classical Athens. In 1642, the General Court of Massachusetts assigned selectmen to "take account" of the education of children in their districts, and to ascertain if all children were being taught (at home or elsewhere) "to read and understand the principles of religion and the capital laws of this country." The selectmen were empowered to fine parents and masters who failed to provide the necessary instruction (Cubberley, 1919; Cremin, 1970).

In Cubberley's view, the law of 1642 was:

> ... remarkable in that, for the first time in the English-speaking world, a legislative body representing the State ordered that all children should be taught to read. This was a distinctively Calvinistic contribution to our new-world life, and a contribution of large future importance. [1919, p. 17]

Other colonies passed similar laws holding parents responsible for the education of their children.

> Connecticut passed similar legislation in 1650, requiring that children and servants be taught to read English, that they be instructed in the capital laws, that they be catechized weekly, and that they be brought up in husbandry or some trade profitable to themselves and to the commonwealth. New Haven followed suit in 1655, New York in 1665 . . . , and Plymouth in 1671. And, in 1683, an ordinance of the new colony of Pennsylvania provided that all parents and guardians of children "shall cause such to be instructed in reading and writing, so that they may be able to read the Scriptures and to write by the time they attain to twelve years of age; and that then they be taught some useful trade or skill, that the poor may work to live, and the rich, if they become poor, may not want; of which every county court shall take care." [Cremin, 1970, p. 125]

The famous "Old Deluder Satan" ordinance of the Massachusetts Bay Colony in 1647 was the first law requiring compulsory education and setting up schools in the colonies:

> It is therefore ordered, that every township in this jurisdiction, after the Lord hath increased them to the number of 50 householders, shall then forthwith appoint one within their towne to teach all such children as shall resort to him to write and reade, whose wages shall be paid either by the parents or masters of such children, or by the inhabitants in generall. . . . [Johnson, 1904, p. 2]

The law also required parents and masters, where there were no schools, to "teach their children and apprentices perfectly to read the English tongue." Johnson (1904) states that "instances are not rare" of parents and masters brought to court for violation of this law (p. 2).

In Colonial and frontier times, parent tutelage was commonplace, perhaps more the rule than the exception:

> The household was also the scene of a good deal of sustained and systematic instruction. In the first place, there was reading, which was as commonly learned at home as anywhere, both in England and in the colonies. "My younger days were attended with the follies and vanities incident to youth," John Cotton's grandson Josiah (1680–1756) noted in his diary; "howsoever I quickly learned to read, without going to any school I remember." The experience was characteristic in an age when it was assumed that a youngster ready to undertake formal classwork would have a certain rudimentary ability to read in the vernacular. Once again, the evidence is fragmentary, but there is every indication that individual reading, responsive reading, and communal reading were daily activities in many colonial households, and that reading was often taught on an each-one-teach-one basis by parents or other elders, or by siblings or peers. For youngsters growing up in homes in which no one was equipped to teach reading, there was frequently a neighboring household where they might acquire the skill. [Cremin, 1970, p. 128]

A continuation of Cremin's discussion of household reading instruction during Colonial times may be found in the notes for this chapter on page 46.[5]

The early American primers were written for use by parents as well as teachers, as the advertisements and introductions make clear (Johnson, 1904). The enormous distribution of Webster's "Blueback Speller" (which was actually a beginning reader entitled *The American Spelling Book,* published in 1783) gives some indication of the extent of this tutelage. The book had sold 24 million copies by the time of Webster's death in 1842. Mathews cites an estimate made in 1947 that "Ole Blueback's" total sales "must have approached the *hundred million mark*" (Mathews, 1966, p. 101; italics mine). These early readers were printed by several publishers and were sold directly to parents as well as to schools. It was common for frontier parents who could read to teach their own children, and also perhaps to teach other neighboring children whose parents could not teach them. Home teaching continued long after public schools were established:

> A curious condition in this country was that in some of the cities where public schools had been established, by one agency or another, no provision had been made for beginners. They merely followed the older New England practice of expecting the pupils to be able to read when they came to school. They were supposed to obtain the elements of reading at home, or in the dame schools. In Boston, for example, where public schools were maintained by the city, no children could be received into the schools who had not learned to read or write. This made the common age of admissions somewhere near eight years. The same was in part true of Hartford, New York, Philadelphia, Baltimore, and other cities. When the monitorial schools were established they tended to restrict their membership in a similar manner, though not always able to do so. [Cubberley, 1919, p. 96]

Indeed, the phenomenon of home teaching can still be observed where frontier conditions continue to prevail. In Australia's outback and in Alaska, children are commonly taught to read by their parents, with the added help of mail-radio communication with educators. There are, in fact, noncommercial organizations and correspondence schools which provide materials and directions to parents who for some reason need to teach their children at home. The Calvert School of Baltimore is an accredited, nonprofit, independent school which has been providing such mail-order instruction to thousands of children since 1906. Their prime clients are missionaries, the parents of sick children or shut-ins, and traveling, isolated, or frontier families—currently, their enrollment includes children on oil rigs, ranches, and in fishing fleets, as well as children of diplomats, touring actors and actresses, and Americans working in foreign countries.

In America and abroad, Calvert's reading and other courses are often used by parents to supplement the offerings of local schools. Calvert's staunchly traditional emphasis is on phonics, handwriting, composition, and other no-nonsense academics:

> From 1897 to 1972 Calvert School, through decades when such old-fashioned stuff was widely scorned, has persisted in empha-

sis upon the Three R's, upon phonics, and upon drill. Composition, with concomitant good usage, good spelling, and good handwriting, has always been one of the two basic subjects of the School, reading being so integrated with writing as to make a single subject in the early years. Arithmetic—understanding, drill, and proficiency—is the other basic subject. [A. Hart, 1972, p. 117][6]

The Calvert home study courses are highly detailed, with carefully written step-by-step procedures for the parent-teachers to follow. An integral part of the Calvert instruction is correspondence between the Calvert home study teacher and the parent.

This school has flourished and for years has filled a real educational need. There are thousands of graduates of Calvert home teaching courses, and the Calvert certificate is widely respected.

Not all parent teaching, of course, is as controlled as Calvert home study lessons, or as leisurely as might be hoped. Parental teaching has occasionally been carried to extraordinary lengths. Perhaps the best example is that of John Stuart Mill:

I have no remembrance of the time when I began to learn Greek. I have been told that it was when I was three years old. My earliest recollection on the subject is that of committing to memory what my father termed Vocables, being lists of common Greek words, with their signification in English, which he wrote out for me on cards. Of grammar, until some years later, I learned no more than the inflexions of the nouns and verbs, but after a course of Vocables, proceeded at once to translation; and I faintly remember going through Aesop's fables, the first Greek book which I read. . . . What he [my father] was himself willing to undergo for the sake of my instruction, may be judged from the fact that I went through the whole process of preparing my Greek lessons in the same room and at the same table at which he was writing: and as in those days Greek and English lexicons were not, and I could make no more use of a Greek and Latin lexicon than could be made without having yet begun to learn Latin, I was forced to have recourse to him for the meaning of every word which I did not know. This incessant interruption, he, one of the most impatient of men, submitted to, and wrote under that interruption several volumes of his History and all else that he had to write during those years.

The only thing besides Greek that I learnt as a lesson in this part of my childhood [before eight] was arithmetic: This also my father taught me: It was the task of the evenings, and I well remember its disagreeableness. But the lessons were only a part of the daily instruction I received. Much of it consisted in the books I read by myself, and my father's discourses to me, chiefly during our walks. [Mill, 1873, p. 4]

Another parent who really got personally involved in teaching her child was Mrs. Winifred Sackville Stoner. Mrs. Stoner taught her daughter, Winifred, Jr., to read following her own method, which she described in *Natural Education* (Stoner, 1914, 1916). An energetic and strong-minded woman, Mrs. Stoner's account is full of games, materials, and teaching routines which she used with Winifred. Mrs. Stoner was an argumentative and controversial figure of her times, but she seems also to have been a perceptive and lively teacher for her little girl. Winifred was reading, according to her mother, at sixteen months. Mrs. Stoner's efforts were by no means confined to teaching Winifred to read: she taught her Latin, Esperanto, and mathematics as well, and followed an imaginative program of intellectual stimulation with the child. The two often lectured together. Winifred's first book of verse was published when she was seven and she went on to write many more books and to join her mother in *Who's Who*. She married Count Charles P. deBruche.[7]

Still another parent who stepped in to teach her child was John Wesley's mother, at least according to Ronald Morris:

It is related of John Wesley's mother that when she became aware one day that her Johnny at the age of four was unable to read she decided forthwith that something should be done about it. Accordingly she taught him his letters that day and on the next had him working successfully at the identification of individual words in a familiar text from the Bible. [Morris, 1963]

Looking over the abundant accounts of parents teaching young children to read at home, one finds wide variations in the apparent sensitivity and imagination with which the teaching was done. The cases I have cited are a few examples of parental teaching; there are many others. I find rather more glowing accounts than otherwise, but then people are more likely to write about teaching that has turned out well.

3. Children Who Learn with Little or No Teaching

Many children are reported to have learned to read with little or no instruction. For the most part they appear in anecdotes told by or about the subjects, who are usually precocious or successful or both.

A textbook written for the training of teachers of reading by Professor Nila B. Smith describes the way one young child of her acquaintance learned to read at home with little instruction:

> When Cathy was three, the writer, together with other guests, frequently spent an evening in her home. As the guests arrived, Cathy would gather up half a dozen books, seat herself under a lamp, and sit there oblivious to conversation of the guests, literally devouring her books for long periods of time.
>
> When turning four, Cathy began asking what certain words were; she would sit by herself and read orally from books, largely from memory but recognizing a word here and there. When she was about four and a half she was in a ten-cent store with her mother one day. While the mother was busy shopping, Cathy amused herself at a counter covered with books. Suddenly she discovered a paper-covered booklet with pictures in it and a word under each picture. She ran to her mother, begging her to buy this book. With the use of the book Cathy taught herself to read all the words under the pictures. When she entered the kindergarten at five, she was reading fluently. [N. B. Smith, 1963, p. 449]

There are some interesting individual accounts, too, by early readers who describe their experiences. My favorite is Jean-Paul Sartre's; if the objection is raised that Sartre learned to read in French and we're talking only about English, I can only say that his emotional response is probably universal. Also, I will balance Sartre's story with the account of C. S. Forester, who was about as English as anyone can get, and with Harry Truman, who supplies the necessary common touch.

In his autobiography *The Words,* Sartre gives an account of how he learned to read before he went to school:

> ... I got my hands on a work entitled *Tribulations of a Chinese in China* and went off with it to a store-room. There, perched on a cot, I pretended to read. My eyes followed the black signs without skipping a single one, and I told myself a story aloud, being careful to utter all the syllables. I was taken by surprise—or saw to it that I was—a great fuss was made, and the family decided that it was time to teach me the alphabet. I was as zealous as a catechumen. I went so far as to give myself private lessons. I would climb up on my cot with Hector Malot's *No Family,* which I knew by heart, and, half reciting, half deciphering, I went through every page of it, one after another. When the last page was turned, I knew how to read. . . .
>
> I was wild with joy. [Sartre, 1964, p. 48]

C. S. Forester, author of *The African Queen* and the Hornblower novels, among others, was another early reader who says he learned by himself. In the story of his early life, *Long before Forty* (published posthumously in 1967), he describes his learning to read as a child in Egypt:

> It may be that those early years in a hot climate conduced to precocity; or it may be that as the youngest of five I tended to copy my seniors, but however it was at three years old I could read with ease and could make some sort of show at writing. I was never taught either—I learnt to read by studying the big bound volumes of *Chums* which my brothers read. . . . [Forester, 1967, p. 11]

Harry Truman was another early reader. This is his account, quoted by Merle Miller in *Plain Speaking* (1974).

> *Mr. President, can you remember a time when you haven't read?*
>
> "No, I can't, not unless I was sick, and even then if I could manage it, I'd prop a book up and read on the sickbed. I read the Bible clear through twice before I went to school. My mother taught me to read, and my father, too, of course. I guess I read the Bible because the type was large, but then it devel-

oped about the time I was six years old, it was then that we first noticed it, that I had flat eye balls. So my mother took me to a doctor, and he tested my eyes and gave me a pair of glasses, and I've worn them ever since.

But glasses or not, I never stopped reading. I've never regretted it either, and I suppose considering the fact that I became President of the United States, it wasn't time wasted. [Miller, 1974, p. 52]

The best account, though, probably comes from fiction. Scout, Harper Lee's narrator in *To Kill a Mockingbird*, gets at the truth of the experience better than any other source that I know. Scout is by no means the only early reader to encounter an unsympathetic first-grade teacher. This is a classic misadventure:

. . . Miss Caroline came to the end of the story and said, "*Oh, my, wasn't that nice?*"

Then she went to the blackboard and printed the alphabet in enormous . . . capitals, turned to the class and asked, "Does anybody know what these are?"

Everybody did; most of the first grade had failed it last year.

I suppose she chose me because she knew my name; as I read the alphabet a faint line appeared between her eyebrows, and after making me read most of *My First Reader* and the stock-market quotations from the *Mobile Register* aloud, she discovered that I was literate and looked at me with more than faint distaste. Miss Caroline told me to tell my father not to teach me any more, it would interfere with my reading.

"Teach me?" I said in surprise. "He hasn't taught me anything, Miss Caroline. Atticus ain't got time to teach me anything," I added, when Miss Caroline smiled and shook her head. "Why, he's so tired at night he just sits in the living room and reads."

"If he didn't teach you, who did?" Miss Caroline asked good-naturedly. "Somebody did. You weren't born reading the *Mobile Register.*"

"Jem says I was. He read in a book where I was a Bullfinch instead of a Finch. Jem says my name's really Jean Louise Bullfinch, that I got swapped when I was born and I'm really a——"

Miss Caroline apparently thought I was lying. "Let's not let our imaginations run away with us, dear," she said. "Now you tell your father not to teach you any more. It's best to begin reading with a fresh mind. You tell him I'll take over from here and try to undo the damage——"

"M'am?"

"Your father does not know how to teach. You can have a seat now."

I mumbled that I was sorry and retired meditating upon my crime. I never deliberately learned to read, but somehow I had been wallowing illicitly in the daily papers. In the long hours of church—was it then I learned? I could not remember not being able to read hymns. Now that I was compelled to think about it, reading was something that just came to me, as learning to fasten the seat of my union suit without looking around, or achieving two bows from a snarl of shoelaces. I could not remember when the lines above Atticus's moving finger separated into words, but I had stared at them all the evenings in my memory, listening to the news of the day, Bills to Be Enacted into Laws, the diaries of Lorenzo Dow—anything Atticus happened to be reading when I crawled into his lap every night. Until I feared I would lose it, I never loved to read. One does not love breathing. . . .

I knew I had annoyed Miss Caroline, so I let well enough alone and stared out the window until recess when Jem cut me from the covey of first-graders in the schoolyard. He asked how I was getting along. I told him.

"If I didn't have to stay I'd leave, Jem, that damn lady says Atticus's been teaching me to read and for him to stop it——"

"Don't worry, Scout," Jem comforted me. "Our teacher says Miss Caroline's introducing a new way of teaching. She learned about it in college. It'll be in all the grades soon. You don't have to learn much out of books that way—it's like if you wanta learn about cows, you go milk one, see?"

"Yeah, Jem, but I don't wanta study cows, I——"

"Sure you do. You hafta know about cows, they're a big part of life in Maycomb County."

I contented myself with asking Jem if he'd lost his mind.

"I'm just trying to tell you the new way they're teachin' the first grade, stubborn. It's the Dewey Decimal System." [Lee, 1960, pp. 21–23]

Clearly, Scout qualifies as a self-taught early reader.

In the review of research studies in Chapter 3, there is a report by Jane Torrey of her careful investigation of another such case of apparently self-taught early reading, a little boy who used television in much the same way Scout used her father's reading of the *Mobile Register*.

4. Educational Movements Which Involve Home Reading Instruction

Several times in America during the past two centuries people have advocated home teaching as a remedy to some perceived shortcomings in the public schools.

The first of these that I am able to discover is the Fireside Education Movement, centered around Boston in the years from 1830 to 1860, and inspired by Bronson and William Alcott, among others. These writers generally deplored the impersonality, tedium, and danger of bad influences to be found in the public schools. The place for children during their tender formative years, the Alcotts said, was at home, and their proper teachers were their parents and older siblings (Alcott, 1843). Strickland (1973) describes Bronson Alcott and his daughter Anna romping about, imitating the letters of the alphabet with their bodies (p. 35). William Alcott maintained:

> . . . that the MOTHER, whether wise or ignorant, learned or unlearned, healthy or sick, pious or impious, is the most efficient educator. [Alcott, 1836]

The beginnings of reading were already commonly taught to young children at home in New England. The Fireside Education Movement's writers—the progressives of their day—were more concerned with moral and philosophical development—giving the young child healthy and rewarding experiences—and most of these authors opposed the drill and pushing of young children commonly done in the homes of the time.

I quote below from Kuhn (1947) who retells a tale first told by Harriet Martineau (1837, I, p. 264), an educated English traveler in America:

> After visiting in a New England farmhouse during the 1830's, Harriet Martineau commented on the one way in which she and

her friends had made their "kind hostess" uneasy, and this was by their neglect of "Charley's book-studies." Charley was a six-year-old in Miss Martineau's party who had enjoyed the nineteenth century equivalent of a modern "progressive education." Miss Martineau, amused at the rural mother's reaction, explained that "Charley's little head was full of knowledge of other kinds," but that "the widow's children had all known more of the produce of the press at his age than he." This throws an interesting sidelight on midcentury concepts with regard to the early intellectual cultivation of children. The newer point of view, represented by the visiting British party, was also that of enlightened Americans, who were beginning to conceive of child growth and its objectives in broader terms. The mental development of children, formerly thought of as the acquisition of the three R's followed by as rapid mastery as possible of the weightier "produce of the press," was coming to have a much wider definition involving the social, moral, and physical as well as the intellectual training of children. The drier system of book learning with its emphasis on memoriter drill and its unhappy forcing of the growth process was in sharp disfavor among advanced thinkers of the day.

Despite the infiltration of broader concepts of learning, however, the traditional approach of the farmhouse widow was to persist in many areas throughout the midcentury, and to exert a tenacious hold upon conservative New England minds. [quoted by Kuhn, 1946, p. 98]

Most of the Fireside authors urged postponing reading instruction until age five or six, but keeping it in the home. They distrusted the infant precocity that had been so highly valued in the previous century (and still was widely held to be important and sought after), but they apparently distrusted the formality and pressures of the schoolroom as much or more. They expected parents to teach their children to read and write, and especially to value proper morality.[8]

The Natural Education Movement was spearheaded by the energetic and determined Mrs. Winifred Sackville Stoner, or Mother Stoner, as she was known to her followers (see page 25 above). Her book entitled *Natural Education* (1914) describes home teaching of reading in considerable detail, but reading instruction was only incidental. The main thrust of the movement was to realize maximum physical, ethical, and intellectual development through "play-to-a-purpose," all centered in the home.

A home-teaching movement apparently flourished in the 1920s and later led by the League of Teacher-Mothers. The League claimed seven thousand members and had an illustrious Advisory Committee that in 1923 included, among others, the then-current U.S. Commissioner of Education, as well as a former U.S. Commissioner of Education, the superintendent of the Pennsylvania schools, the headmaster of Penn Charter School, the editor of *The Journal of Education*, a former president of New York University, and the superintendent of the Atlantic City public schools. Their basic publication *Educating the Child at Home* (Lynch, 1914) was sold by mail to interested parents for $1.50, and a complete kit with instructions, a four-month supply of practice paper, and "Bookless Lessons for the Teacher-Mother" was offered for $5. Teacher-mothers could begin teaching children as young as four or five (see Lynch, 1931).

In the 1950s and 1960s there was a "back to phonics"* movement, in reaction to the prevailing "whole-word"† method of teaching reading. This is not the place to delve into the details of the phonics/look-say controversy—for these the reader is referred to Jeanne Chall's lucid, evenhanded account entitled *Learning to Read: The Great Debate* (1967).

The "back to phonics" movement had its own organization, the Reading Reform Foundation, which was started in 1959. Another organization, the Council for Basic Education, sponsored a book called *Tomorrow's Illiterates*, and has been consistently critical of the reading instruction found in America's schools.

A number of books were published in those years deploring look-say or whole-word teaching methods.[9] Several of these are of great interest to our discussion, because they bear

---

* Phonics is defined as the set of rules governing letter-sound association, spelling, and pronunciation.

† The whole-word or "look-say" approach to reading usually teaches children to recognize words as wholes before beginning systematic phonics instruction.

directly on home instruction. The most important was *Let's Read*.

Let's Read is a quiet, scholarly book, written, amazingly enough, by perhaps the most eminent American linguist of the time—Leonard Bloomfield—and his collaborator, the noted lexicographer Clarence Barnhart.[10] The Bloomfield-Barnhart program appeared in 1961, although the materials had been devised by Bloomfield much earlier (Bloomfield, 1942). Bloomfield's materials had been circulated "underground" for years in mimeographed form among colleagues and friends who used them to teach their preschoolers to read. The materials had also been used with success in Chicago-area parochial schools during the 1940s.

"Leonard Bloomfield created this system of teaching reading so that he could teach his boys to read before the boys started school . . . ," begins Clarence Barnhart's introduction to *Let's Read* (Bloomfield & Barnhart, 1961, p. 3). Barnhart maintains that Bloomfield:

> . . . devised these reading lessons so that any child who knows how to talk may learn to read in the most efficient way. . . . His school work will come easier to him. . . . If you teach your child to read, you will share with him his first great intellectual experience. You will see him safely launched and able to develop his capacities to their limit. . . . You need to spend only ten or fifteen minutes a day. . . . [pp. 3, 4]

Because it was labeled "a linguistic approach" to reading,* and because it was so radically different from Dick and Jane, Bloomfield was unable to find a publisher for his book. After Bloomfield's death, Barnhart finally found a publisher who would print the book: Wayne State University Press. A description of Bloomfield's method may be found on pages 90–91.

Another important book was a bombshell. A Columbia Teachers College Ph.D. named Rudolf Flesch wrote a book called *Why Johnny Can't Read*.

Flesch's book (1955) roundly damned the whole-word approach to teaching reading. Flesch blamed everything wrong

---

* A "linguistic approach" emphasizes the regularities in the sound and spelling patterns of the language.

with readers on "look-say" and his book provoked a lively controversy. Educators generally (and sometimes indignantly) rejected Flesch's book, pointing to some overstatements, quotes out of context, and questionable interpretations of research, although some parents and educational critics took up his cause.

However, the whole title of Flesch's book was *Why Johnny Can't Read—and What You Can Do about It*. The "what you can do about it" part, according to Flesch, was to teach your child phonics at home—before starting school preferably, but during school if need be. The last part of Flesch's book is a straightforward primer, a phonics reading course for parents to use in teaching their children at home.[11] This 83-page section at the back of his book includes reading material and instructions for the parent-teacher.

Flesch's book made real waves, and it has sold millions of copies. It is hard to estimate how many preschoolers have actually learned to read because of it.

5. Reading Instruction via the Communications Media in the 1960s and 1970s

In 1961–62 the Denver Public Schools conducted a project, using educational television to determine "how effectively parents can prepare their preschool children for reading" (Brzienski & Hayman, 1962).

Some 1,040 Denver preschoolers were involved, and the project was generally successful and widely commented upon. (It will be reviewed in some detail in Chapter 3 along with other research studies.)

Somewhat later, Channel 2 in Boston, WETV, had a phonics program which some parents used to help teach young children to read at home. While doing my thesis research at Harvard, I encountered several children from the Boston area who had learned to read through this televised instruction (Smethurst, 1970). I will discuss in Chapter 3 the case of another child who apparently learned to read from watching television commercials.

One of the major events in American education was the

appearance of an imaginative television program for young children called "Sesame Street," which taught beginning reading skills, among other things.

"Sesame Street" was the name given by the Children's Television Workshop (CTW) to the program which emerged in 1969 from two years of planning and research. It revolutionized the use of media in teaching. A team headed by Harvard psychologist Gerald Lesser and Producer Joan Ganz Cooney (and funded by the federal government and foundations) analyzed existing children's television and tried to do better. Better they did. Millions of American households welcomed Big Bird, Oscar the Grouch, the Cookie Monster, and their friends. "Sesame Street" was a hit—a colorful children's program using live actors, puppets, animation, and spritely visual and sound effects. Dr. Lesser and his Harvard colleagues found themselves very much in show biz[12] (Lesser, 1972, 1974).

After being generally hailed in its first year, "Sesame Street" began to draw more critical fire (including a broadside from John Holt) in the second year (Holt, 1971; Lesser, 1974). The CTW group under Joan Ganz Cooney has, I believe, profited from the criticism, improved the show, and pressed on. No one really knows how many preschoolers have learned beginning reading skills from watching these programs, but the number must be very great (Ball & Bogatz, 1970; Bogatz & Ball, 1971; *CTW '72*, 1972; Lesser, 1974).

Next to appear was another CTW show, this one frankly about reading and aimed at an audience of schoolchildren, called "The Electric Company." Working with animation and live actors (in the "Sesame Street" tradition), "The Electric Company" provides a bright, fast-moving television experience as well as solid instruction in reading. It seems to be watched by children from two to ten or so, in school and out. Evaluations have demonstrated considerable success in teaching reading concepts (Cazden, 1973; Ball & Bogatz, 1973; Ball et al., 1974). An assortment of funny, vivid, and quite inexpensive "Electric Company" reading books is commercially available and constitutes "a real deal" in the early

36 · *Teaching Young Children to Read at Home*

reading field (*New York Times Book Review,* Mar. 10, 1974, p. 8). I will discuss the research on "Sesame Street" and "The Electric Company" in Chapter 3.

The television networks were quick to follow CTW's lead. In 1971 NBC began to run Caleb Gattegno's *Pop Ups* film loops, each one a minute long, teaching Gattegno's idea of the essentials of reading (Gattegno, 1970). These spots were run every Saturday morning during regular children's programming.

Network and local kiddie shows have come to deal regularly with written letters and words as well as other reading concepts. American children are exposed to written language in abundance on television and elsewhere.

Other communications media besides television—books, newspapers, magazines, radio—have been active in preschool reading.

Glenn Doman's book entitled *How to Teach Your Baby to Read* caused a sensation in 1964. A shorter version had appeared in the *Ladies Home Journal* in May 1963, and the book was serialized in newspapers. All of this exposure called down the wrath of childhood educators and reading authorities on Doman—his book is littered with unfortunate overstatements and claims without evidence, and his critics were quick to point this out. Despite the vigorous disapproval of educators, Doman's book was widely read by parents, and enough of them tried teaching their children to keep Doman's ideas under discussion for a decade. I describe his program on pages 91 to 93.

One of America's more politically conservative newspapers, *The Chicago Tribune,* was responsible for an ingenious and innovative use of media in teaching young children via the comic strip. Joan Beck, the *Tribune*'s child care columnist, created a comic strip called "Short Cuts to Reading You Can Teach Your Child." This was adapted from Dorothy Taft Watson's *Listen and Learn with Phonics* (1961).

The comic strip ran in the *Tribune* from August through November 1964. A public service promotion device, it was extraordinarily successful. Since 1964, more than 200,000 reprints of the comic strips have been sold by the *Tribune*

(J. Beck, 1969). The comic strip has now run a third time in that newspaper and has again received considerable response. It is clear, colorful, and seems easy enough to use (see the Buyer's Guide for information). If any systematic evaluation of the program's effectiveness has been made, I am not aware of it.

In April 1974, *The Reading Teacher* published an account of Julie Chan's radio and newspaper work with American parents in Germany.* Ms. Chan made a year-long series of ten-minute Armed Forces Network radio broadcasts entitled "Getting Your Child Off to a Good Start in Reading." In these broadcasts she is interviewed by an announcer, and gives advice on how to read to your child, what books to select, when to begin reading aloud, etc. The newspaper articles are published in *Stars and Stripes*, the military newspaper.

Since the program is aimed directly at parents in the United States armed services, considerable attention is given to parental reading help for children moving from one school system to another. Though there is no explicit reference in the article to parents teaching young children to read before they start school, it will be interesting to see if many of Ms. Chan's listeners go on to teach their preschool children to read.

Reading-teaching kits are offered for sale in toy stores and through the mails. Americana Interstate advertises their preschool teaching kits widely in Sunday newspaper supplements. Their ads show a smiling young girl in a library, with the caption, "At four and one-half she's reading second grade books."

The Great Reading Turn-on, by Joan Beck and Marjorie Hopper (1972), is sold in gift and other stores. This attractive paperback takes a low-key, easy-going approach to teaching children the names of letters, sounds and some words. Well-illustrated and clearly written, this book should have considerable influence.

Montessori Motivational Toys, Inc., produces teaching kits and records for home teaching in the Montessori tradition. These materials are sold through toy and department

---

*"Tuned in to Parents, Reading Hits the German Airwaves," *The Reading Teacher*, vol. 27, no. 7, pp. 676–679.

stores. The "reading readiness" records, according to their jackets, are for "teaching children ages two and one-half to seven to read using the world-famous Montessori Method." These records give historical and explanatory Montessori background as well as how-to instructions for parents. The records may be used with or without the kits, which are sold separately.

It is clear that parents of preschool children are exposed via the communications media to a variety of products and offerings which promise to help their children learn beginning reading skills. The effect of all this on their children is less clear, however.

The Opponents of Early Reading Instruction
There has long been opposition to teaching children to read early, whether the teaching was done at home or not. The arguments of these opponents contain four main objections:

1. The possibility of physical and/or psychological harm to the child from early reading
2. The possibility of interference with the child's schoolwork
3. The inappropriate *manner* (high-pressure, boring, inexpert) of instruction given to young children
4. The fundamental inappropriateness of reading to the lives of young children

It may be helpful to consider the objections one at a time.

1. The possibility of physical and/or psychological harm to the child from early reading

There is *no* evidence of negative physical aftereffects from early reading (see pp. 85 and 100). To say that there is no evidence, of course, is not to say there can *never* be any evidence. Caution is warranted always, I think, and parents who worry about possible physical difficulties from early reading should talk to their child's pediatrician or ophthalmologist.[13] Bad emotional or psychological aftereffects *are* possible—perhaps even likely—where parents use threats, punishments, stress, or emotional pressure to force children to learn to read.

When children learn willingly through play, games, and voluntary teaching they seem to do well, without negative aftereffects traceable to early reading. For more than a century, thoughtful writers on childhood education in England and America have urged parents against forcing precocity on their children. I agree with that position.

    2. The possibility of interference with the child's schoolwork

"She'll be bored in first grade" is the way this objection is usually phrased. I think it has a certain amount of validity. Certainly this boredom can happen, but my own impression is that first-grade teachers are coming more and more to expect a few "early readers" each September. These children can be accommodated readily by placing them in a top reading group, by setting them to help other children, or by just giving them a book and letting them read.

At any event, as other children learn to read, the danger of boredom lessens. Certainly, the research does not bear out these fears of widespread first-grade boredom, though it may happen.

According to the studies, early readers (perhaps even *bored* early readers) generally do well in first grade and later (see especially my review of the research on pages 68, 72–73, and 101). But early readers in the studies are not your child in your school situation. Whether or not to teach a child is always an individual parent's decision, just as how to deal with first grade is an individual parent's decision.

It is also worth noting that, although learning to read comes to mind when you think of first grade, actual reading instruction takes up a relatively small part of the school day. It seems unlikely to me that a child who can read would be bored by math, science, art, or show-and-tell. Quite the contrary, in my experience.

    3. The inappropriate *manner* of instruction (high-pressure, boring, inexpert) given to young children

Objections to inappropriate instruction seem to me altogether valid. Certainly it is better not to teach a four-year-old to read at all than to force him to learn—and thereby possibly teach him to dislike both reading and instruction generally. (I have stated my opposition to the use of pressure in reading instruction on pages 7–8, and I will do so again in many places throughout this book.) Teachers of reading in school and out certainly should know what they are doing, and their teaching should, I believe, be interesting and lively and creative—not boring. But early reading instruction *does not have to be* high-pressure, or boring, or inept. It can, in fact, be pressure-free, and it can also be entertainingly and appropriately done.

Several critics of "hardnosed" early reading instruction like Huey (1908), Bettelheim (1966), and Hymes (1971), and even Ilg and Ames (1972) can sometimes accept home reading instruction that is informal and pressure-free: These authors go on to warn of dangers in "formal" reading instruction for young children.[14]

In his pioneering text entitled *The Psychology and Pedagogy of Reading* (Huey, 1908), still perhaps the most sensible, readable book about reading, E. B. Huey took the position that a child should be brought gradually into reading at home. This process was a natural one and started very young with parents reading aloud to the child, teaching letters, singing songs, etc. Huey felt, however, that formal school instruction in reading should not come until the child was eight years old, by which time he or she was probably already reading.

Other early opponents objected to the pressure and inhumanity of boring drills for little children (Gedike, 1791; Dewey, 1898), and modern writers make similar complaints (Hillman, 1963; Bettelheim, 1966; Hymes, 1970; LeShan, 1967). Some critics of early reading instruction, notably LeShan, will have none of it. Regardless of how it is done, apparently:

> There is no reliable evidence that children who can read words at two are better readers by the time they are in the sixth

grade. There is no reliable evidence that children who learn to read in kindergarten do any better later on than children who are not good readers until third or fourth grade. Furthermore, there is no evidence that children who were considered poor readers until fifth or sixth grade are necessarily poor scholars, or that early reading skills have any correlation whatsoever with whether or not they may be brilliant intellectuals in adulthood. . . .

. . . Despite all the current hullabaloo, a child who is surrounded by written language, who enjoys being read to and who sees the people around him enjoying this experience, will learn to read in his own good time, without having to feel harassed or pushed or frightened. He will eventually, if he has pleasurable experiences with reading, read well. When reading is presented to him as a gradually expanding adventure that can provide him with many satisfactions, he can learn to read with almost no instruction at all. Millions of people have done just that, in the course of history. Any normal, healthy child growing in an atmosphere of approval, in which there is also challenge and opportunity for exploration, will want to make sense out of the world he finds himself in; he will want to fit things together, he will want to correct his errors—he will want to grow and to learn. Unless we permit children the freedom to explore and to make corrections on their own, they will get the idea that nothing should be attempted unless it can be known ahead of time that it will be right—and the only way to be sure is to ask a grown-up. Only a small percentage of child experts are concerned with teaching babies to read. The majority continue to believe that so long as we provide our children with an exciting and interesting and accepting environment, we do not have to worry about reading. A child who learns to read when he wants to, because he wants to, does so better and faster than by any method we could invent.

The problem is not one of being for or against a standard of excellence in thought, for or against the fullest enjoyment of learning, of intellectual development. It is rather the question of how to help babies grow up in life so that they can become *persons,* not computers—can become warm, feeling adults, gleeful to be alive, free to love and be loved and to find work that uses them and entrances them—that adds to a sense of aliveness, a joy in discovery and in *being. It simply does not matter* if a baby learns to read. He is too young to enjoy reading or to gain anything from it. He has other more important business just exploring the first feeling and sensations of being alive. [LeShan, 1967, pp. 52, 62–63]

  4. The inappropriateness of reading to the lives of young children

LeShan, in the passage quoted above, makes this objection about as strongly as it can be made. LeShan is right when she states that we have no reliable evidence of early-reader advantage after sixth grade. But there isn't any evidence, either, that the possible early-reader advantage in first through sixth grades goes away—there simply isn't any conclusive evidence either way. There are a few suggestions in the work of Kasdon (1958) and others, but nothing you could hang your hat on. We simply don't know.

I agree with most of LeShan's assertions about children when it comes to an approving and stimulating home environment, and I agree, too, that it simply does not matter if a baby learns to read.

However, babies aren't four- or five-year-olds, and such evidence as I can find from history and research seems to me to suggest that it *can* matter quite a lot if a young child learns to read. I think it can matter in at least two important ways. Learning to read *can* be a good activity for parent and child to share together, and learning to read can give the child a powerful tool to help him understand and cope with his world. Surely these are important considerations, especially if your child is *interested* in learning about letters, words, and reading.

James L. Hymes, a respected early childhood educator and a critic of much early reading instruction (1963*a* and *b*), puts matters in perspective in what I believe is a cautious and reasoned statement. In a widely read and quoted article entitled "Teaching Reading to the Under-Six Age: A Child Development Point of View," Hymes reaches the following conclusions:

> Our title says: "A child development point of view." From the vantage point of one who tries to watch children, to stay close to

children, to study children, how they see the world, the answer has to be: "Yes, of course." One has to teach reading to the under-six child. To the under-six five-year-old. To whatever under-six age we may have in school, or have in our homes. A child development point of view cannot lead one to say: No, don't teach . . . postpone. It has to say: Teach, and teach as much as each child is comfortably, naturally, easily, rightfully ready for. [Hymes, 1973, p. 132]

Reading Readiness
It seems reasonable to close this chapter with a brief discussion of "reading readiness" since a certain amount of confusion is created by the concept as it has been used in schools.[15] Largely based on faulty and enthusiastic interpretations of a research study done in the early 1930s (Morphett & Washburne, 1931), a conventional wisdom grew up about reading readiness to the effect that children become ready to begin learning to read at a mental age of six and one-half. This conventional wisdom on readiness was solemnly repeated for decades afterward in reading textbooks and elsewhere. Almost ignored was Gates' 1937 caution that "reading is begun by very different materials, methods, and general procedures, some of which a pupil can master at the mental age of five with reasonable ease, others of which would give him difficulty at the mental age of seven" (Gates, 1937, p. 508).

In the years since then, readiness tests and programs have been developed and used widely in kindergartens and first grades—even though as early as 1939 Gates and others after him found low correlations between success on reading readiness tests and actual success in learning to read (Gates et al., 1939; Durkin, 1970).

The usual reading readiness program concerns itself with things like:

    Left to right progression
    Identifying objects as "the same" or "different"
    Discriminating between letters
    Learning letter names
    Learning letter-sound associations, especially initial consonants, like "T is for table"

Being able to tell whether a letter form is oriented properly, i.e., Ǝ or E

Putting pictured events into logical sequence reading rebuses or picture stories

There are other activities in different readiness programs. Some concentrate on developing perception and small motor skills; others concern themselves with coordination, kinesthetics, and psychomotor activities—crawling, feeling the letters, putting puzzles together, etc.

There is little argument to be made with a child's pursuing any of these tasks in some appropriate teaching setting. Most of the "readiness" tasks have at least some logical connection with learning to read, and two of them—learning letter names, and learning letter-sound associations—are listed in my own canon of beginning reading skills.

It has to be remembered that "reading readiness," as the term is used by the schools, means "readiness for formal school instruction in reading." This has nothing to say about a child's readiness to learn, informally and at home, the letter names or letter-sounds, or how to write her own name, or any of the beginning reading skills.

In my view of the matter, a child is ready to learn about letters and words when he or she becomes interested in them, without a tutor's resorting to pressure or any other sort of force. Plenty of two- to five-year-olds couldn't care less about letters and reading—while others are deeply interested and eager to learn.

So, if your child is interested and you're willing to spend some time, he can be considered ready. If he *isn't* interested, even in letter learning games or posters or whatever, relax and enjoy him in the assurance that, sooner or later, a time will probably come when he *is* interested.

Jack Holmes, an educational psychologist at the University of California at Berkeley, looked specifically at the question of early reading and mental age (1962). He concluded that normal children can be taught to read before six, and even as early as age two or three (the *advisability* of teaching them was another matter). He also concluded that the earliest age at which a child can learn to read depends upon the amount of time or help that the teacher can give (Holmes, 1962, p. 239).

Norma Rodgers states approximately this view in a 1971 article entitled "What Is Reading Readiness?"

> Learning to read is a complex mental process and as we have seen the belief concerning an optimum mental-age of 6-6 should be attained before beginning reading, was held by many educators in the past and into the present. However, more recent studies suggest that the necessary mental-age will vary with the materials, the teaching methods, the size of the class, the skill of the teacher, and the availability of special personnel. [Rodgers, 1971, p. 4]

Dolores Durkin deserves the last word on this subject, however.

> Whether or not a child is ready depends upon his particular abilities, but also upon the reading instruction that will be offered. . . . There is no room for thinking that there is one best age for starting reading; no room for thinking there is one best methodology and one best set of materials. Nor, certainly, is there a place for thinking that all children must accomplish the same learning at the same time. [Durkin, 1970, p. 564]

NOTES

1. Various fanciful accounts exist of reading's origin—the goddess Inanna got Enki, the Lord of Wisdom, drunk and persuaded him to give her writing (along with many other gifts) for the benefit of her people. Or, if you prefer a livelier though considerably less authentic version, the skills of civilization were given Sumerian priests by gods who descended from the heavens in a chariot of fire. Once the priests had learned what the gods had to teach, according to this version, the godlike tutors got back into their chariots and ascended into the heavens (von Däniken, 1972). Readers interested in the Sumerian legends surrounding the introduction of writing (and other "civilized" skills) into their culture are referred to W. N. Smith, 1955; Mathews, 1966; and Kramer, 1967; for authoritative accounts. Of particular interest is Sumerian scholar Samuel Noah Kramer's (1967) description of the painstaking detective work which goes into the translation and reconstruction of the Sumerian myths from fragments of clay tablets scattered about in the world's museums. His stories of the adventures and misadventures of the goddess Inanna are especially interesting, though all too brief. The recent Time-Life book entitled *The Birth of Writing* (Claiborne, 1974) provides a lucid explana-

tion of the Sumerian development of writing from pictographs to cuneiform script. The Claiborne book is a genuine treat: easy to read, clearly written, and beautifully illustrated. The reader interested in pursuing this topic is advised to begin with Claiborne's book.

2. *The Hebrew Gospels,* Christian Apocrypha.

3. It is interesting to note that in the sixteenth century Hart was as discontented with the English spelling system as some modern writers have been, and that he proposed a reform of the spelling and writing of English. Like other such reformers after him, he had little success (Mathews, 1966, p. 26).

4. To give some indication of the scope of this literature on home education, Harvard University's Widener Library shelf lists contain more than 50 volumes devoted to this subject, all published before 1875. A few of these are American; most are English.

5. Cremin continues: "And, indeed, when an occasional New England goodwife decided to teach reading on a regular basis in her kitchen and charge a modest fee, she thereby became a 'dame school'; or, when an occasional Virginia family decided to have a servant (or tutor) undertake the task for its own and perhaps some neighbor's children, the servant became a 'petty school.' Such enterprises were schools, to be sure, but they were also household activities, and the easy shading of one into the other is a significant fact of the seventeenth century.

"In the teaching of reading, a family might use a textbook like Edmund Coote's *The English Schoole-Maister* (1596); or a simple hornbook or ABC, which presented the alphabet, a prayer or grace, usually the Lord's Prayer or the Apostle's Creed; or perhaps some combination of hornbook or ABC and primer or catechism, a primer being an elementary book of religious material usually including the Lord's Prayer, the Apostle's Creed, and the Decalogue, a catechism being a series of questions and answers setting forth the fundamentals of religious belief. *The English Schoole-Maister* was the most formal: It was addressed 'unto the unskillful, which desire to make use of it for their own private benefit: and unto such men and women of trades (as tailors, weavers, shopkeepers, seamsters, and such others) as have undertaken the charge of teaching others'; and it went systematically from letters, syllables, and words, to sentences, paragraphs, and colloquies. The hornbook, ABC, primer, and catechism, on the other hand, were the most characteristic: They were addressed to the same untutored audience as *The English Schoole-Maister,* but they were explicitly tied to the oral tradition of the liturgy, the characteristic thing about them being that they taught the art of reading using passages with which the learner was probably familiar" (Cremin, 1970, p. 129).

6. The story of Calvert's school-by-mail is fascinating. Interested students are referred to Archibald Hart's two volumes, *Calvert and Hillyer* (1947) and *Calvert and Brown* (1972). Both books are published by The Calvert School, Tuscany Road, Baltimore, Maryland 21210.

7. Mrs. Stoner died Nov. 10, 1931. Winifred apparently dropped from view after 1928, the date of the last full *Who's Who* entry I can find (p. 1997). Her husband Count Charles P. deBruche died not long after their marriage in 1921.

8. Kuhn makes the point that this trend away from precocity influenced the family profoundly: "First, it helped to break up the patriarchal family pattern in which the father was responsible for the intellectual culture of children. His efforts in behalf of the youngest members of the family were seen to be actually damaging in their effects. The picture referred to above, used by Goodrich in his text *Fireside Education,* shows an attempt to restore this family pattern, but it should be noted that the father is depicted as instructing an older child, while the younger ones are receiving their 'cultivation of the heart' at the hands of the mother. Secondly, the reaction against precocity was accompanied by a demand for a substitute form of intellectual culture which, in its emphasis upon gradual and constant unfoldment of the mental powers from infancy upwards, was of necessity the function of the one most closely associated with the young child, the mother." [p. 102]

9. A number of books attacking the way reading was taught appeared in the years just before and after Sputnik. Most of these seem to me to make approximately the same points Flesch made, with perhaps less audience. The reader interested in pursuing this literature is referred to Mortimer Smith, 1949, 1956; Bestor, 1953; McCracken, 1959; Terman and Walcutt, 1958; Rickover, 1959, 1962, 1963; Walcutt, 1961; Trace, 1962, 1965; Walcutt et al., 1974, and especially Conant's unsuccessful effort to resolve the squabble (Conant, 1962). A response to the educational critics and a spirited defense of Flesch is found in Terman and Walcutt (1958).

10. This has obvious echoes of Noah Webster, the premier lexicographer and linguist of his time, who wrote a revolutionary reading program in "The Blueback Speller." Royalties from "Ole Blueback" supported Webster and his family for 20 years while he was working on his dictionary.

11. Flesch apparently got much of his inspiration from Bloomfield's ideas and used them to teach his own child: "Several years later, Bloomfield took time out to prepare an alphabetic-phonic primer, based on strictly scientific principles. It was an excellent piece of work, carefully designed to teach children quickly and painlessly.

"The introduction to this Bloomfield primer was published as an article in the *Elementary English Review* in April and May, 1942. I ran across that article eight or ten years ago and that's what started me on this whole business. Taking the ideas of that article and applying them in homemade fashion, I taught my eldest daughter Anne to read when she was five years old" (Flesch, 1955, p. 9).

12. Readable accounts of the "Sesame Street" experience are given in Lesser's article "Learning, Teaching, and Television Production for Children," *Harvard Educational Review,* May 1972, with illustrations by Maurice Sendak, and in Lesser's book *Children and Televison,* Random House, 1974.

13. Durkin in her text *Teaching Them to Read* (1974, p. 138) offers a thoughtful discussion on the question of the possible impairment of vision in early readers, and of our lack of evidence on the subject. A long-standing controversy over "close work and myopia" exists among ophthalmologists—a common sense position is that it is possible, certainly, that extensive "close work" in early childhood *might* contribute to visual problems later in the child's life. At present, this is not borne out by evidence. Obviously, if proof *were* to develop of harmful visual effects of early reading on young children, reason

would exist to modify or avoid early reading instruction. Again, if you are concerned about your child's vision, you should consult your ophthalmologist.

14. "Much, in fact rather too much, has been written about the formal teaching of reading in the preschool years. Certainly any mother will quite naturally let her child go as far as his spontaneous interests suggest along these lines. Research has shown, however, that most efforts at setting up formal reading instruction in the preschool years do not succeed in teaching the child to read. Even if they do, such a child's advancement over his contemporaries is usually not maintained. Other bright members of his class group will very quickly catch up or even surpass him once the class has reached the customary time for learning to read. Play is the preschooler's work. Let's not worry that he is wasting his time.

Allowing a child to learn is one thing. Formal teaching in the preschool years is another. It is unfortunate when a parent thinks only of teaching a child. He then loses the quality of living, the experiencing together that is the stuff of their relationship" (Ilg & Ames, 1972, p. 324).

15. As she has done with most other topics in the area of early reading. Dolores Durkin has written a clear and scholarly summary of reading readiness as a concept. The interested reader is referred to Durkin's 1968 article "When Should Children Begin to Read?" See also Durkin (1974), chap. 3, "Readiness to Learn to Read," which describes in some detail the growth and development of the reading readiness concept. Still further, see Durkin (1974), the second edition of her text for teachers of reading, *Teaching Them to Read,* and "Reading Readiness," a 1970 article for *The Reading Teacher.*

CHAPTER 3

The Research on Home Reading Teaching

Despite the fact that much has been written about teaching children reading at home, there has been little actual research. The research that does exist is very helpful to us, but one wishes that there were more.

In the succeeding pages of this chapter, I will review all the research I could find on the home teaching of reading to young children.* For those not much interested in the details of educational research, I will try to summarize the material in a few paragraphs.

---

* This review will be limited to the literature of early readers who are instructed outside schools. O. K. Moore's work with preschoolers and the "talking typewriter" is of great interest, but it falls outside the purview of this book (Moore & Anderson, 1967).[1] The restriction to nonschool learning also eliminates Fowler's 1965 study, in which he taught reading to a group of three-year-old twins and triplets in a nursery-school setting. Other landmark studies in early learning to read that are thus eliminated include Brown (1924), Davidson (1931), and Durkin (1969b), as well as all the "reading in the kindergarten" studies (Durkin, 1966) and most of the "reading readiness" studies. Also eliminated, regrettably, are Maria Montessori's accounts of her work with young children in the Casa dei Bambini and elsewhere, and accounts of Montessori schools in America.[2]

These research studies were not excluded lightly. The restrictive definitions which I have drawn are for the explicit purpose of concentrating on the teaching of reading to young children at home.

A Summary of the Research

The research falls into several categories:

Other reviews of the research literature
Individual case histories
Retrospective studies
Empirical studies
The "Sesame Street" studies

Other authors reviewing the research on early reading conclude that some children do indeed learn to read before school, and that it is possible to teach reading in preschools (Olilla, 1971; Blanton, 1972). Both reviewers whom I have cited raised, but did not answer, questions of whether reading *should* be taught young children.

The case histories which I have included were, typically, reports of individual early readers who came to the attention of psychologists or educators. Most of these case histories include testing and observational data.

The case studies give us useful information about children who learn to read early—occasionally beginning as young as two and three, but more often at four and five. Most of these closely observed early readers have been bright or very bright, with IQs commonly above 120, and now and then from 160 to 200. Parents (to judge from these cases) rarely acknowledged much teaching, and it is possible to speculate that these children sometimes gleaned a good bit of instruction from their environment and often learned casually from people around them.

The large-scale studies show that parents can help their children, and occasionally do, in learning beginning reading skills. These studies also seem to show that children who learn to read before they begin school do at least as well in first grade reading (and afterwards) as nonearly readers, and often they read better (Durkin, 1966; Brzienski & Hayman, 1962; Morrison et al., 1969).

Among many other things, the "Sesame Street" research demonstrates that many children watching the program learned beginning reading skills. In the studies, children who watched most seemed to learn the most beginning reading skills—though this finding can't be interpreted to mean that watching the show was *the reason* they learned more.* "Sesame Street" research also indicates that both privileged and underprivileged children learn effectively from the show. Also, avid "Sesame Street" viewers seem to do well in school, according to follow-up studies, and there is the clear suggestion that "Sesame Street" had a positive effect on the attitudes of children toward school, as well as toward other people's race. Finally, the research suggests that it may be helpful for a child and parent to watch the show together and discuss it afterward (Ball & Bogatz, 1970; Bogatz & Ball, 1971; Lesser, 1974).

In all the studies of early reading, no evidence of physical ill effects such as impaired vision was found by any researcher. (This is not to say that the visual effects of early reading are nonexistent—it is just that none has ever been shown to exist.)

Emotional difficulty is occasionally reported in young children who were pushed hard by parents, tutors, or preschool teachers. Readers are cautioned to remember my warning from Chapter 1, with which I will close this summary, because it is my own conclusion from reviewing the research.

Never push your child to read. Avoid instructional systems or strategies which employ such pressure.

REVIEWS OF THE RESEARCH

The most ambitious review of the research was published by William E. Blanton in 1972, entitled *Preschool Reading Instruction: A Literature Search, Evaluation, and Interpretation. Final Report.* The U.S. Office of Education in 1971 gave a grant to Blanton and the University of Indiana to conduct a thorough review of the research existing on teaching children to read early (Blanton, 1972). They concentrated heavily on the "reading in the kindergarten" studies, but the work is still of interest to us.

In Volume I of the published report, Blanton, the senior investigator, discusses the research on preschool reading,

---

* They may have learned more for the same reason they watched more—curiosity, say, or interest, or some other factor entirely.

52 · *Teaching Young Children to Read at Home*

then gives his analysis and recommendations. He concludes that some children can and do learn to read before age six, and calls for more research.

Volumes II and III (the report is in three volumes, totaling more than 500 pages) are written for preschool teachers and parents respectively.

Blanton's review is a valuable contribution, although in my judgment he gives Durkin's pioneering work too little attention, and there are several omissions.

Despite my reservations, I am indebted to Blanton for learning about several studies, especially those of Keele and Harrison (1971) and Evans (1965). I will refer to Blanton's review at several points in this book, and I include it in the Reading List (page 214).

Published through ERIC (the U.S. Government-sponsored Education Research Information Clearinghouse), the Blanton review is obtainable on microfilm, microfiche, and Xerox. It is a pity that the work is not better known, because it is of genuine usefulness.

Another scholar, Lloyd Olilla, reviewed the research on early reading in a paper given at the International Reading Association's 1971 conference. Olilla's paper was entitled "Pros and Cons of Teaching Reading to Four- and Five-Year-Olds." As with Blanton's, Olilla's survey was not confined to home teaching, but also considered early teaching done in kindergarten and nursery school settings. Olilla took it as demonstrated that children can be taught to read at ages "five, four, and even three."

For Olilla, "Today the controversy has moved from 'can children under six learn to read' to the following questions: 'Why should they read earlier?' and 'What are the benefits of early reading?'" (Olilla, 1971, p. 19).

CASE HISTORIES

Martha
Lewis Terman, one of the major figures in American psychology, wrote the introduction to the earliest case history I am both able to find and prepared to classify as research (and even that classification is a bit shaky).

Martha was a bright and talented girl in Palo Alto and one of Terman's subjects when she was twenty-six months old. Her father, a lawyer, had taught both Martha and John, one of the older brothers, to read as preschoolers. His education of his daughter so impressed Terman that the father was persuaded to write up his experience for the *Journal of Applied Psychology* (Terman, 1918). Martha's father taught her to recognize letters, then whole words, and finally to read sentences. At nineteen months she could recognize and name all the capital letters; at twenty-four months she had a reading vocabulary of over two hundred words; at twenty-six months she was able to read from first-grade readers, and had a reading vocabulary of over seven hundred words (Terman, 1918, p. 226).

Terman's description of his first encounter with Martha is of interest:

> Martha's father brought her to my home and allowed me to observe her reading ability. Her performance was quite beyond anything I had deemed possible for a child a little more than two years old. She read from any primer fluently and with better expression than most first grade children are capable of. Her pronunciation, however, was babyish as one would expect in the case of a child who had only talked one year. Given primers which she had never seen, she read from any starting point without hesitation. Whenever she came to a word she did not know she said, "What's that?" In one little lesson she was given to read, four new words were encountered and pronounced for her. An hour later she was able to recognize all of these even when they were shown to her in word lists at the back of the book. I did not undertake to measure her reading vocabulary, but from what I heard of her reading I am convinced that it is larger than that of the average child who has spent ten months in the first grade. [Terman, 1918, p. 219]

Tom

Anderson and Dearborn, in a highly respected textbook, *The Psychology of Teaching Reading* (1952), report a case of another very bright early reader. Tom, four years nine months old, was said to be "reading everything." Tom's grandmother believed in starting to read aloud to infants when they were only "a few months old, and thus capturing their natural curiosity." (Anderson and Dearborn report that the grandmother claims to have produced several precocious children in this way.)

Tom was given intelligence and reading achievement tests. On the Stanford-Binet, his IQ was reported as 168. He also took the Metropolitan Reading Test for grades 3-4-5, and, the examiner's report states, it "was so far below his capacity mechanically, and also so far below his interest level, that it offered little challenge. . . .Mechanically, he can read smoothly on a fifth- or sixth-grade level, and his powers of word analysis are on an even higher level" (Anderson & Dearborn, 1952, pp. 62, 63).

Cindy

Mayme Cohan, a former primary-grade teacher, taught Cindy, then two and a half, to read 40 of her "own words" printed in manuscript on 4 × 6 inch cards (Cohan, 1961). Beginning with the words "Baby" and "Cindy," Mrs. Cohan added two words per day, until in a two-week period Cindy learned the following list:

egg	dog	Daddy	root beer
Janice	drive	Mom	baby
bell	car	nursery school	Cindy
cow	play	dance	banana
bicycle	swing	Michelle	apple
wagon	table	shoes	
see	chair	penny	
purse	cooky	I	

Words were chosen which:

> . . . were those which had considerable meaning to the child and which were related to her recent or continuous experiences. A few of them were suggested by Cindy herself. It is doubtful whether she would have learned the words as easily if they had been relatively remote form her own experiences. [p. 507]

Cindy's interest in reading waned after a while. The learning activity was mostly confined to working with word cards, although a scrapbook using the words was also included. Mrs. Cohan's primary concern seems to have been to investigate the learning capacity of a two-and-one-half-year-old in a subject area—reading—in which children Cindy's age are not often instructed.

No tests or follow-up data were offered—I am now trying to discover what has become of Cindy, and how she has progressed as a reader since her first lessons in 1960.

K.E.

In 1965, James L. Evans published "Teaching Reading by Machine: A Case History in Early Reading Behavior." This is an account of how Evans taught his little girl, K.E., to read, beginning instruction shortly after her third birthday. Evans, who was vice-president of a teaching machine company, tried the materials and equipment that he was developing on "K.E." His account is of considerable interest because it covers two and one-half years, during which he kept careful records of time spent, administered tests at regular intervals, and encouraged his pupil with all sorts of good things like pennies, prizes, candy, and praise.

Evans used a teaching machine called the Multi-Max. K.E. spent a total of five hours and 42 minutes working with the machine over a period of approximately four months, at the end of which time:

> K.E. was reading phonic material with considerable proficiency. A list of 223 short phonetic words, such as "pot," "rag," and "sat," were prepared, of which K.E. was successful in pronouncing 218 correctly. Special phonetic primers were prepared and negotiated successfully as well as commercially available phonetic material.

To support the machine's teaching Evans did other things with her which he calls "additional motivational and maintenance activities," but he does not specify what these activities were.

After the machine course, and a washout attempt to give her a reading readiness test,* Evans began working with K.E. on the Scott, Foresman pre-primer, which features Dick, Jane,

---

* She couldn't draw the lines right.

Spot, and sentences like "Oh, Dick. Look and see. See Spot jump down" (Gray et al., 1956).

K. E. and Evans managed to negotiate all this quickly—Evans says she used an "acceleration" procedure, turning pages rapidly and moving on (Evans is right up there with the best in his unswerving attention to the teaching task):

> As indicated . . . , this "acceleration" procedure permitted covering 102 pages in one 90-minute session, with no overt signs of fatigue or loss of motivation by the student. (This session was terminated by the insistence of K.E.'s mother that it was an hour past the child's normal bedtime.) [Evans, 1965, p. 306]

Once she finished about half of the Scott-Foresman series, "K.E.'s reading was spontaneous for one to two hours a day, and has continued at that level for the past two years."

Evans thereafter kept on supplying her with reading matter:

> The chief function of the experimenter since that time has been that of librarian, to provide appropriate reading material on an *ad lib* schedule. Particular favorites have been Dr. Seuss, *Highlights for Children* (a children's monthly), comic books, and standard library selections. (Cartoons from *Playboy* are also unaccountably popular.) [1965, p. 307]

Evans began testing K.E. in earnest shortly before she was four years old, at which time she was reading at third grade level. He tested her at six-month intervals until age 5.5, at which time she scored well into fifth-grade level.

Robin

In an unpublished article entitled "Reading in the Crib," Danny and Miho Steinberg, two psycholinguists from the University of Illinois, Champaign-Urbana, report on a program they devised for teaching their son. They describe it as a "psycholinguistic account of a successful effort to teach a child to read." Beginning in the prespeech stages of infancy, the Steinbergs taught their son "Robin" first to be familiar with the letters, then to identify them by pointing, then to recognize words printed on cards, and eventually to read books on his own.

The effort, presumably, was a successful one—the Steinbergs report favorably on Robin's progress:

> The child, our own, is now 4½ years old. He is a happy boy who delights in reading. He has about 100 books of his own which he reads fluently, with feeling, and with complete comprehension. A few months before his 4th birthday he joined the Urbana Public Library. Since that time he has been reading, on the average, 8 or 9 library books a week. Reading test norms place him beyond the 3rd grade level. [Steinberg & Steinberg, 1970, p. 2]

No intelligence measurement is reported, and there is little in the way of anecdotal, or observational, matter concerning the teaching/learning process itself.

Robin was tested at the age of four years eleven months at the University of Illinois, Champaign-Urbana, Reading Center. The tester reports (as quoted by the Steinbergs) that he was "self-assured and very responsive to requests, to test-directions, and to general conversation with Reading Center personnel."

Various reading tests were administered, including the Gates-MacGinitie tests and Wide Range Achievement Test. On the Gates-MacGinitie Form A tests his scores were as follows:

Vocabulary: Grade level 3.6
Comprehension: Grade level 2.5

On a comprehension retest using Gates-MacGinitie Form B, Robin scored at grade level 3.6. On the reading section of the Wide Range Achievement Test, Robin placed at the 4.3 grade level.

The Steinbergs' instructional methods depended on the child's acquiring reading competence at the same time that he acquired spoken language. Their instructional techniques seem quite simple and are derived from a theoretical analysis of learning to read that is of considerable interest.[3] These and other aspects of the Steinberg approach will be discussed again later on, together with other accounts of early readers and proposed methods.

It seems reasonable to assume that Robin was a very

bright child; in any case, extrapolating from his experience to the general population of children is hazardous. Several questions suggest themselves. Could a less intelligent child, for instance, learn in the same way in which Robin is reported to have learned? How long would it take? Would parents need the linguistic sophistication of the Steinbergs? The Steinbergs maintain that parents would not, but the question must be regarded as legitimate in the absence of other evidence.

Harry

In an article entitled "Write First, Read Later," Carol Chomsky (1971*b*) described her preschool son's progress with writing words *before* he was able to read. Harry invented his own spellings—for instance, *w* was substituted for *r* to match his pronunciation. Harry's closely observed work with the written language—and Chomsky's account of it—is of value because of the linguistic and human insights it offers. It is valuable as well because of the echoes in this brief account of the experience of Montessori, working with poor children in Italy, where children began making words with movable letters as soon as they knew some sounds. Also, it is helpful to recall the many "pencil and paper kids" in Durkin's samples who wrote from the beginning. Harry's spelling is remarkably like the "spelling systems" investigated by Charles Read (1971).

The opening paragraph of Chomsky's article is of considerable interest, I believe.

> Children ought to learn how to read by creating their own spellings for familiar words as a beginning. This task is not as hard or as exotic as it sounds. Once they know the letters of the alphabet (sounds, not names), they should spend time putting letters together to make words of their own choosing. They can use a set of plastic letters, for example, or alphabet blocks. It is a great thing to put together a word by figuring out for yourself what comes first, what comes next, and so on until you have the whole word laid out in front of you. And what better way to *read* for the first time than to try recognizing the very word you have just carefully built up on the table in front of you? [Chomsky, 1971*b*, p. 296]

Velia

From September 1955 through May 1956, as an experiment for his doctoral thesis at the University of Chicago, the psychologist William Fowler taught his two-year-old daughter to read. The little girl, Velia, turned out to be an apt student, and Fowler's thesis was later published as a *Genetic Psychology Monograph* (Fowler, 1962b).

In teaching Velia, Fowler worked with her five days a week and occasionally on weekends. Sessions varied in length from 5 to 10 minutes at the beginning to an hour or more toward the end. He also gave her "supplemental reading stimulation," such as reading to her at mealtimes when, in his description, "her enjoyment in eating and her settled position seemed to provide an excellent motivational setting" (p. 195).

Velia encountered difficulties in adjusting to a nursery school, which she began in April 1956, and this showed up in her reading also. "Some evidence appeared of both psychosocial disturbances and reduced intellectual performance which could be linked to the reading stimulation" (p. 277). Her father records all this in considerable detail—the monograph is quite long—and Fowler's abilities as an observer, both of himself and his pupil, make it a valuable document.

In the end, Fowler found that it *is* possible for a two-year-old to "make considerable progress in learning to read" (p. 276). The value of the research lies not so much in this finding as in the documentation Fowler provides of a specific kind of teaching—and motivation.

The question remains of Velia's emotional difficulties. As her father indicates, she was beginning nursery school the week the trouble began. Velia had been doing well in her reading instruction but suddenly seemed to lose interest and to resent being asked questions. Fowler continued the instruction, although he altered the format and frequency of the lessons:

> Contrasting markedly with the first 7½ months of training (when S [Velia] had always recovered from downswings of interest in reading—nearly concomitant with changes in technique, attitude, and instructional pace and complexity instituted by E [Fowler]) were the final 1½ months of the experi-

mental period. Motivation for reading lessons fell off and an undercurrent of hostility developed and intensified, at times becoming decidedly overt. S's productivity gradually declined in quantity, although the fate of her skill level was less clear. Reductions in the amount, rate, and complexity of the stimulation presented failed to reverse the process. Lessons were scheduled less frequently but were often lengthy, as S sought out the play relationships, while rejecting the reading stimuli, as such.

Coinciding with this pattern and period of decline, to the week—if not the day—was Velia's attendance at a nursery school (beginning April 18), where she exhibited a chronic but subdued reluctance to participate until the final week, when her protest and withdrawal became more acute. There were few signs of psychological deterioration in other areas through the month of May and early June. Relations with peers in the neighborhood, with adults, and interest and creativity of play apparently remained adequate and definitely improved over her status as of the beginning of training. There were certain exceptions, namely, an increase in fear response (to trains, planes, dogs, and unfamiliar situations) and signs of dependency (e.g., leaving parents to go with other adults), most of which were not evident until the training was over. [Fowler, 1962b, p. 267]

For 19 months after the conclusion of Fowler's experiment Velia made little progress in reading achievement in any dimension. She forgot many sight words but seemed to remember letters; and later, when she was five, her interest began to grow again until she was reading in third-grade texts. "Follow-up tests and observation to age 8.5 have repeatedly revealed Velia to be reading avidly with comprehension and facility 2–3 grades above level." Her IQ tests "between 150 and 170" (Fowler, 1962a, p. 132). Fowler also states that Velia has maintained "moderately good social adjustment" since that time (Fowler, 1962a, p. 141).

John
This study was made by Jane Torrey of the reading and family background of "John," a five-year-old early reader who had apparently learned with little or no direct teaching. John lived

in the black community of Atlanta with his parents, grandmother, and four siblings in a "new three-bedroom garden apartment" that was "well kept and had the normal equipment such as washing machine, TV, Hi-Fi, and so forth" (Torrey, 1968, p. 551).

The study is of special interest to this book because it is the best-documented account of an early reader who seems to have learned to read from the writing in his environment—television, library books, and can labels, principally, according to his family. Neither his mother nor his grandmother could recall his having had any help in reading. Since John at five read better than both his older sibs, Torrey assumed that they did not help him either; both said that they had not. Further, Torrey states:

> John's mother reported that he had not begun talking especially early, but that he had been able to read almost from the time he could talk. She said no one read to him or taught him to read. . . .
> The principal difference between John's case and the others [Durkin's] is the absence of any report of his receiving help. His mother insisted, even under cross-examination, that he had learned by himself. All reports of his reading from her or from his grandmother were simple accounts of their surprised discovery of something he could already do. His grandmother had been unprepared for his spelling and reading can labels and written TV notices. His mother had been worried about damage he might do to the library books his sister brought home. She said she often took them away until one day he read aloud to visitors all of what she described as a 'third-grade library book.' [pp. 551–552]

If one assumes from all the foregoing that John's available help with reading was at least limited, his obsession with television commercials is of some interest as a possible source of instruction.

> His mother once said that he must have received the gift directly from God. . . . The only plausible earthly source of instruction she was able to mention was television commercials. She reported that when he was younger he had known all the commercials by heart and recited them as they appeared on the

screen. She said she could never get his attention until the commercial was over. [p. 551]

Torrey's check of television programming indicated that "an average of 40 words per hour are simultaneously shown and pronounced" (p. 551). Torrey continued the argument on behalf of television as a reading source for John:

> The one known source of instruction remains television commercials. It has already been mentioned that John watched and memorized them. Commercials are frequently repeated, so that whatever a child fails to learn in one showing can be drilled ad nauseam in subsequent days and weeks. Commercials are designed to get attention, so they are usually loud, lively, and simple. Memorizing of short sentences is facilitated by catchy tunes. Many common words are shown and the unfamiliar brand names (e.g., 'Ban,' 'Sominex') are usually short or easy to pronounce. It seems possible that from commercials a child could get a start on a basic vocabulary and make a few inferences about phonics. [p. 552]

Torrey also reported that John liked to write and spent much time printing words and numbers. She described him as "something of a loner, a Mama's boy" (p. 551). She reported that he took great interest in identifying words and numbers.

It seems altogether possible that John could have directed his own learning, with help from television, his sister's library books, and perhaps occasional indirect help from adults and older children in answer to his questions.

Retrospective Studies

A final fillip to the case histories are the retrospective studies, most notably those done by Terman and his colleague, Catherine Cox, and the premiere student of gifted children, Leta Hollingworth. These seem to me to add to the insights provided by the case studies.

In Volume I of his major work *Genetic Studies of Genius,* Terman (1925) reported that 250 of a group read before beginning school. These figures were drawn from responses to a questionnaire given parents. The age of learning was reported as follows, for 156 children:

> 113 of these children learned to read before age five
> 34 of these children learned to read before age four
> 9 of these children learned to read before age three

In *Children above 180 IQ* (1942), Hollingworth gives case studies of twelve highly gifted children, all of whom were early readers. In ten of these twelve cases, the child was the first-born. Median age of reading is reported as three years, though one child, "D," seems to have learned at 18 months: ". . . [W]hile sitting on his mother's lap as she sat before a typewriter, he learned to read by looking at the letters. . . . At the time he should have entered kindergarten D could read fluently and perform complicated arithmetic processes."

Hollingworth's book is a treasure house of anecdotes about the early learning and subsequent educational experience of extraordinarily bright children. This tale of Hollingworth's child "C" is illustrative of the flat disbelief with which early readers are so often greeted.

> When he was 4 years old, C went one day into a store with his father. While the latter was making his purchases the child took a book from the shelf and began to scan it. The shopkeeper noticed the child looking attentively at the book and said, for a joke, "Boy, if you will read me that book, I'll give it to you." Instantly C began to read fluently and carried the book away from the astonished merchant. [p. 66]

There are also accounts of extraordinary tutelage and involvement with their children by parents in the child's education. "E"'s mother:

> . . . devoted a great deal of attention to his education and welfare, keeping records of his development, supervising his health, and acting as his teacher. She often accompanied him to school, sometimes registered for courses with him, or herself took courses calculated to make her more useful in his training. She gave an exceptional amount of attention to his formal educational program and cultivated with him numerous extracurricular intellectual activities. During E's college career the two were often seen together on the campus. [p. 85]

In addition to her 12 case studies, Hollingworth summarized the 19 other cases from the literature about children who were then known to have tested IQs of 180 or over. Of these cases, only 13 give the age of beginning reading; all report it to be 3.5 or 4 years.

The ease with which these very bright children learn to read at home is of interest to our discussion. One parent reported that the ability to read seemed to have been "born in" the child, another that "B was taught to read by her mother at age 4, by the 'picture-story' method. She knew the alphabet long before. A few lessons only were given her and thereafter B read and has continued to read independently" (p. 58).

Still another: "At the age of three he learned his letters untaught by anyone, apparently, and was spelling words. It was felt that this would interfere with his learning to read later on, so he was taught to read by the phonic method" (p. 38).

In Volume II of *Genetic Studies of Genius,* Cox (1925) attempted to estimate the childhood IQ for each of three hundred eminent men. Although this seems a dubious procedure at best, Cox nevertheless persevered through a great deal of biographical research on her subjects to find evidences of their high intelligence in childhood. The retrospective IQ scores she assigned to these men may not have much meaning, but her assembled information on the early childhood of geniuses is of considerable interest. Davidson (1931) working with the Cox data for an article entitled "An Experimental Study of Bright, Average, and Dull Children at the Four-Year Mental Level," selected the names of all those who were definitely stated to have learned to read before age five.

Figures in parentheses are Cox's estimated IQs and mental ages at the time of learning to read; quotes are from the summary in Engelmann and Engelmann (1966, pp. 41–42).

> *Jonathan Swift* (125: 3–9). At the age of three he could read any chapter in the Bible. He had learned to spell by the age of three or four.
> *Alexander Dumas* (140: 5–7). Learned to read when he was four "through a curiosity to discover the history,

customs and instincts of the animals whose pictures he saw in Buffon's *Natural History*."

Thomas Hobbes (140: 5–7). Attended school from the age of four. Was learning Latin and Greek at six years.

Charles Dickens (145: 5–7). "Charles' mother began when he was four to teach her son English and the rudiments of Latin, awakening his passion for reading and knowledge."

Ralph W. Emerson (145: 4–4). "A week before young Emerson's third birthday his father recorded that he 'did not read very well,' but the lad progressed in favor from that time."

Louis Alfred De Musset (160: 4–9). "At the age of three, Alfred began lessons in reading and writing, subjects which he pursued with great ardor in order to gain sufficient skill to carry on a correspondence with a beloved cousin."

Count De Cavour (150: 6–0). "At four Camillo was taught by his mother to read, but although he soon learned to read and write with ease, the passion for study did not appear until later."

Voltaire (170: 5–1). "Instructed in a desultory way by the Abbé Châteauneuf, little Arouet (aged three) learned to read from La Fontaine's Fables."

Macaulay (180: 5–4). "At three Macaulay did not care for toys but was fond of taking his walk and telling interminable stories from his reading or from his imagination. . . . At three young Thomas read incessantly and his memory retained without effort the exact phraseology of the book."

John S. Mill (190: 5–8). "He began to learn Greek at three, and from then on to his ninth year he studied Greek classics. . . . Mill read Greek and history from his fourth year onward; Plato at seven. . . ."

In a study of "reading autobiographies" collected from a group of 54 junior-high-school students with IQs of 120 or higher, Ruth Strang (1954) reported that approximately half had learned to read "when they were five years old or younger."

In her book, *Teaching Reading* (1958, p. 587), Gertrude Hildreth discusses the reading histories of 100 highly intelligent children. There are 50 boys and 50 girls in her sample. IQs of the group ranged from 145 to 203. Hildreth reported that nearly 80 percent of these children could read by the time they began first grade.

In the *Journal of Educational Research* in 1958, Kasdon published the results of his investigation into "early reading background of some superior readers among college freshmen." He asked about the reading histories of 50 superior readers and reported that 27 read before entering first grade. Of these 27 early readers, 18 reported that a member of their family taught them to read. Kasdon concluded that the importance of a child's environment to reading success should be emphasized more by educators.

EMPIRICAL STUDIES

I am able to find five of these studies. The first two which I will discuss are the ones most frequently cited, the two longitudinal studies by Dolores Durkin. Third is the prophetic work of Brzienski and Hayman (1962) in the Denver Television Project. The fourth study to be discussed is a small and little-known adjunct to a very large and well-known study, the CRAFT Project (Morrison, Harris, & Auerbach, 1969; Harris et al., 1968). The fifth is a doctoral thesis by H. N. Perlish (1968).

Dolores Durkin (1966)
Professor Durkin's book *Children Who Read Early* is a carefully written, detailed account of two longitudinal studies of early readers in Oakland, California, and New York City. The studies span six years, from 1958 to 1964: The California study came first in 1958; the New York study began in September 1961 and ran through May 1964.

The California study was begun by Durkin after her 1958 encounter, in the course of other work, with a first grader named Midge who came to school already reading. The following fall Durkin and her co-worker tested the whole entering first grade in the Oakland schools—5,103 kids—and found 49 children who were already reading. These 49 early readers were given individual Stanford-Binet IQ tests, and they and their families were interviewed. For the next six years the early readers were tested each May. (They were also tested in September of their second-grade year.) Upon comparison of the early readers' reading achievement scores with those of nonearly readers, Durkin found that the average early reader's achievement was significantly higher than that of equally bright classmates who had not learned to read early.

The California study also did a great deal to shed light on questions of possible academic, physical, or social injury to the early reader: None was found. Durkin's family interviews revealed that all the 49 early readers had received help with reading, and she collected useful information about the background and personalities of these children and their parents.

In 1961 Durkin began a second study, this time in New York City, in which she sought to answer some of the questions raised by the earlier study and used more elaborate testing and experimental controls. The California study had not collected comparative data on children who do *not* read early, so that only tentative conclusions could be reached about factors which appeared to foster early reading. Durkin also wanted to investigate personality characteristics of both early readers and nonearly readers. Also, in the California study the measures of reading achievement and intelligence used in comparing early readers and nonearly readers all came from school-administered tests. Would more closely controlled testing yield more valid data? The California study could be considered a broad attack on the problem—an attempt to define it and to find out what the questions were. The New York study to follow would try to get at the answers.

For the second study, 4,465 children in 40 New York City schools were tested, and 157 early readers were identified and given Stanford-Binet IQ tests. A special experimental group of 30 early readers was selected and individually matched for intelligence and first-grade teacher with other individuals in a group of 30 nonearly readers—that is, each early reader was matched with a nonearly reader in his first-grade class. There were 19 boys and 11 girls in each group: children were predominantly from middle and upper socioeconomic status[4] (SES) Jewish homes. Durkin interviewed the families of children in both the special experimental and control groups. Personality tests were given both groups. Reading achievement tests were given all the early readers and the nonearly readers in May of 1962, 1963, and 1964.

Among Durkin's conclusions were these:

> ... First, the average reading achievement of the early readers was significantly higher than that of the nonearly readers, over a three-year period; ... secondly, the advantage in achievement seems especially pronounced for the early readers who were accelerated. [p. 84]

Comparisons of the early readers and nonearly readers in her New York study seem to indicate that, for early readers of lower intelligence, there is an advantage in beginning to read early. I quote Durkin's table 22:

Advantage of a Head Start in Reading in Relation to Intelligence

INTELLIGENCE QUOTIENT		NUMBER OF EARLY READERS	MEAN DIFFERENCE SCORES, IN YEARS		
Range	Median		May 1962	May 1963	May 1964
99–124	119.5	10	+0.52*	+0.61	+0.98
126–134	132.5	10	+1.02	+1.03	+0.90
135–170	146.5	10	+1.46	+1.21	+1.14

* Positive difference scores indicate early readers showed higher achievement than the nonearly readers with whom they were paired.
SOURCE: Durkin, *Children Who Read Early*, Teachers College Press, Columbia University, New York, 1966, table 22, p. 86.

A limitation is that the children being compared are extremely bright—so much so as to restrict the usefulness of generalizations from this data to lower IQ ranges. However, there are two points to be made:

> The first is about the difference scores, examined one year at a time. Looked at in this way, difference scores indicate that, among bright children, the higher the IQ, the greater is the advantage of earlier reading.

. . . The second observation is about the same data when they are examined over a three-year period. Looked at over time, the data indicate that the advantage of a head start is increasing for the less bright, but decreasing for the brightest children. [Durkin, 1966, p. 86]

Although restricted by intelligence range sampled, this finding seems highly suggestive for new research. One would like to see replications in which comparisons are made of early readers and nonearly readers across the range of observed intelligence in which Durkin found early readers (IQ 82–170), with special attention to children with IQs below 100.

In the California study, Durkin found that a majority—26 of 49—of her early readers came from "upper-lower" socioeconomic status (SES) families, using W. L. Warner's index of social-class scale (Warner et al., 1949). This finding was not repeated in the New York study, in which the early readers were largely middle and upper class. Still, however, seven of the selected group of 30 early readers in the New York study were characterized as lower SES.

Durkin also was able to draw interesting comparisons between the families of early readers and those of nonearly readers. She found that parents of the early readers showed greater willingness to help and that they showed less tendency to believe that reading should be taught by a trained person. Especially important was her family interview data, which indicated that "most of the parental help which led to a child's early reading ability was given in response to the child's questions and requests for assistance" (1966).

The studies ended in 1964, and, unfortunately, no follow-up has been published since that time. Some minor quibbles have been made about Durkin's extraordinarily intelligent sample, but in my view her research is sound and meticulously done.

There are, however, serious difficulties involved in dealing with Durkin's interview data. Durkin's family interviews and case studies of early readers and their families are the most extensive ever done. But interview data can only be what the person interviewed was willing and able to tell. On some questions this may be of no concern; on others it may produce serious distortion. A related difficulty is that the data were taken by a single interviewer, Durkin, who also drew the conclusions from the interview data and then wrote the book explaining them. Durkin obviously tries to control her bias, and her reportage seems fair and even. Still, it is important to recall these points when using the data from her interviews.

Joseph Brzienski and John Hayman, Jr. (1962)
Brzienski and Hayman reported on a research study using educational television, conducted in 1961–1962 by the Denver Public Schools, to determine "how effectively parents can prepare their preschool children for reading" (Brzienski & Hayman, 1962, p. 1).

Aims of the study were to find out if parents can teach children basic beginning reading skills, such as letter names and associated sounds (Hurd & Rimmel, 1961). An interesting aspect of the study was the distribution of teaching materials to parents and the use of television teaching to show parents and children how to use the materials. There were 1,040 Denver preschool youngsters three and four years old in the study.

The experimenters used a sophisticated statistical procedure to analyze their data. An analysis of covariance design was employed which permitted determination of the significance of four secondary effects—sex, mental age, chronological age, and the number of minutes the child was read to. On analysis, it was found that categorizations by sex, mental age, and the number of minutes the child was read to all produced significant differences.

The study ended after sixteen weeks and did not attempt to test the children beyond their knowledge of letter names and letter-sounds. The *parent* materials and the instruction went beyond this, however.

Brzienski and Hayman found that parents could teach preschool children "certain basic skills of beginning reading." They also found that practice of skills was important, surprisingly enough, and that children who were read to—whether they did the lessons or not—showed improvement. Children who did best, according to Brzienski and Hayman, were those who practiced more than 30 minutes a week and who also were read to more than 60 minutes a week. The authors concluded that reading to the child should be recommended also.

Morrison, Harris, and Auerbach (1969)
The CRAFT Project was a large-scale comparative study of two approaches to teaching beginning reading in twelve New York City elementary schools. These schools had pupil populations in 1964 that were almost 100 percent black. This study came out of that project and was published separately from the project report (Harris, et al., 1968). At the beginning of the CRAFT project in 1964 the authors found 58 children of the study population of 1,378 entering first graders whom they termed "early readers." They defined as an "early reader" any child who could "identify words in print, no matter how few" (p. 4), from a list of words on the Detroit Word Recognition Test.

The 1,378 children in the study population were taught to read by one of two approaches: "Skills Centered" or "Language Experience." All the children in the study were followed for three years to compare school achievement, and achievement test scores of the early readers were compared with the scores of children of similar ability who were not early readers.

At the beginning of first grade the children were given a Murphy-Durrell Diagnostic Reading Readiness Test, which has in it a speed-of-learning section. Children were not tested for intelligence (school regulations prohibited IQ testing).

By the end of the first grade the early readers scored significantly higher than the group total on all five subtests of the Stanford Achievement Test.

By the end of the second grade, early readers had an advantage over the larger group, which they maintained at the end of the third grade.

Morrison et al.'s definition of early readers presents obvious problems, as does their failure to test IQs and to control for sex, age, intelligence, SES, etc.

In the most useful aspect of their paper, early readers were matched with nonearly readers on the basis of scores on the Murphy-Durrell Learning Rate Subtest. It is not clear what general abilities are tapped by this learning rate subtest (Durrell, 1956, pp. 49–51, 70–74).

Nonetheless, the grade-level comparisons of achievement test scores of the matched groups of early readers and nonearly readers are informative; I quote Morrison et al., tables 32, 34, and 36:

Grade Equivalents for Matched Students on April Stanford Achievement Test, Grade 1

SUBTEST	NONEARLY READERS	EARLY READERS
Word Reading	1.6	1.9
Paragraph Meaning	1.6	1.8
Vocabulary	1.5	1.8
Spelling	1.6	2.0
Word Study Skills	1.5	1.8

SOURCE: Morrison et al., 1969, table 32.

Grade Equivalents for Matched Students on Pretests and Posttests, Grade 2

	NONEARLY READERS	EARLY READERS
MAT*–October		
Word Knowledge	1.5	2.1
Reading	1.9	2.4
MAT–April Posttests		
Word Knowledge	2.8	3.2
Word Discrimination	2.7	3.5
Reading	2.6	2.9
Spelling	3.0	3.6

* Metropolitan Achievement Test.
SOURCE: Morrison et al., 1969, table 34.

Although the appropriateness of the matching criterion is open to question, the early readers seem to enjoy a clear advantage over the "matched" group of nonearly readers on all reading subtests.

Grade Equivalents for Matched Students on Pretests
and Posttests, Grade 3

	NONEARLY READERS	EARLY READERS
MAT – October		
Word Knowledge	2.7	3.3
Reading	2.6	3.0
MAT – Posttests		
Word Knowledge	3.4	4.5
Reading	3.4	4.2

SOURCE: Morrison et al., 1969, table 36.

Caution is in order in interpreting these findings. Matching students on the basis of a speed-of-learning test administered in the first grade leaves uncontrolled a host of variables.

Still, it seems indisputable that the early readers—for whatever reason—had an advantage in grade 1 that persisted in grades 2 and 3.

Morrison et al., in reviewing their own data from this study as well as the CRAFT Project study itself, draw these conclusions:

> What all of the foregoing suggests is that *some* disadvantaged children who enter first grade have some word recognition skill which they have acquired in the home, or from some form of preschool education other than public kindergarten. This finding appears to substantiate previous research studies on the subject of early readers. It also reinforces a finding by Durkin that some children coming from homes other than those identified as being in the middle or upper socioeconomic income level do enter first grade with measurable reading abilities.
>
> In addition, the present study indicates that, as far as the children in the CRAFT project were concerned, the advantages that they maintained at the beginning of the study persisted and grew throughout the three years of the study. Indeed, through the years early readers tended to increase their achievement advantage over the total CRAFT population, as well as over the matched group, indicating that reading skills taught prior to the time the child enters first grade are not detrimental to long-range achievement. . . . [1969, pp. 19–20]

Perlish, H. N. (1968).
Harvey Neil Perlish's doctoral research at the University of Pennsylvania was *an investigation of the effectiveness of a television reading program, along with parental home assistance, in helping three-year-old children learn to read* (the title of his dissertation).

Perlish developed a children's reading program for a Philadelphia educational television station, WFIL-TV, then went on to study the children who watched it. The program was called "Wordland Workshop," and it featured a hostess named Miss Irene, and a ticklish kangaroo—Wendy Wallaby—whose pouch yielded words to be read. There was also a magic word tree, plus word games, stories, poems, puppets, trips to the zoo, and what Perlish describes as "merry banter" between Wendy Wallaby and Miss Irene.

Perlish recruited a group of 134 three-year-olds in the Philadelphia area and had them watch "Wordland Workshop" from 7:00 to 7:30 A.M. five days a week, for 39 weeks. (He also had a control group of 162 three-year-olds in Binghamton, New York, who watched "Captain Kangaroo" instead of "Wordland Workshop.") We can only surmise what parents thought as they got up day after day before 7:00 A.M. so they could watch Miss Irene and Wendy Wallaby with their three-year-olds.

After 39 weeks of the program and parental reinforcement activities, the group of children who watched "Wordland Workshop" scored significantly higher on a test of reading performance than did the children who watched the Captain.* According to Perlish's dissertation abstract:

> Significant relationships were found between posttest reading performance and health, children's interest in program, parental competence [presumably competence in giving the "home assistance"], parental interest, and child's interest in home-conducted reading activities. [p. 2154A]

Perlish's conclusions are worth quoting.

> With children similar to those in the experimental group, a carefully produced television reading program, along with parental

---

* It is worth noting that only 70 of the 134 children in the experimental group completed the project. Perlish reports that 82 of the 162 children in the Captain's group finished. What all this implies I am not sure.

home assistance, may indeed be effective in helping them learn to read. A consensus of participating parents disclosed that the children had apparently enjoyed the TV reading program and their home-conducted reinforcement activities. [p. 2155A]

THE "SESAME STREET" STUDIES

When "Sesame Street" made its appearance in 1969, a significant amount of formative* research had already been done. Ingenious studies of children's behavior as they watched television guided the CTW group in their production (Palmer, 1974; Lesser, 1974), to achieve a television program which appears to meet the classical standard of excellence, "to delight as well as to instruct."

Classics notwithstanding, it was clear from the beginning that an outside evaluation would need to be done, and the Educational Testing Service (ETS) of Princeton, New Jersey, undertook the task. This sort of evaluation is called summative; it attempts to say how well the program met its goals and what effects it had. ETS designed a set of tests based on the specific cognitive objectives that "Sesame Street" was trying to teach. These objectives were arrived at after much deliberation, and featured a group of beginning reading skills. I quote these first-year objectives here in full because I believe they are of major significance.

The Instructional Goals of Children's Television Workshop
I. Symbolic Representation

The child can recognize such basic symbols as letters, numbers, and geometric forms, and can perform rudimentary operations with these symbols.

A. Letters

(Note: For most of the following goals, the training will focus only upon a limited number of letters. The entire alphabet will be involved only in connection with recitation.)

1. Given a set of symbols, either all letters or all numbers, the child knows whether those symbols are used in reading or counting.

---

* Formative research is done to help shape a set of instructional procedures or a program—it is more concerned with guiding decisions than with final evaluation.

2. Given a printed letter, the child can select the identical letter from a set of printed letters.
3. Given a printed letter, the child can select its other case version from a set of printed letters.
4. Given a verbal label for certain letters, the child can select the appropriate letter from a set of printed letters.
5. Given a printed letter, the child can provide the verbal label.
6. Given a series of words presented orally, all beginning with the same letter, the child can make up another word or pick another word starting with the same letter.
7. Given a spoken letter, the child can select a set of pictures or objects beginning with that letter.
8. The child can recite the alphabet.
B. Numbers . . .

[Lesser, 1974, p. 62]

By the second year these goals had expanded and had become considerably more ambitious—as well as much more explicit.

Statement of Instructional Goals for the 1970–71 Experimental Season of Sesame Street

I. Symbolic Representation
  A. Pre-reading Goals
    1. Letters
      a. *Matching* Given a printed letter, the child can select the identical letter from a set of printed letters.
      b. *Recognition* Given the verbal label for a letter, the child can select the appropriate letter from a set of printed letters.
      c. *Labeling* Given a printed letter, the child can provide the verbal label.
      d. *Letter sounds*
        (1) For sustaining consonants (f, l, m, n, r, s, v), given the printed letter, the child can produce that letter's corresponding sound.
        (2) Given a set of words presented orally, all beginning with the same letter sound, the child can select the letter associated with the sound from a set of printed letters.
        (3) Given a set of words presented orally, all beginning

with the same letter sound, the child can select another word with the same initial letter sound from a set of words.
  e. *Recitation of the alphabet* The child can recite the alphabet.
2. Words
  a. *Matching* Given a printed word, the child can select an identical word from a set of printed words.
  b. *Boundaries of a word* Given a printed sentence, the child can correctly point to each word in the sentence.
  c. *Temporal-sequence/spatial-sequence correspondence* (words and sentences are read from left to right)
    (1) Given a printed word, the child can point to the first and last letter.
    (2) Given a printed sentence, the child can point to the first word and the last word.
  d. *Decoding* Given the first five words on the reading vocabulary list (ran, set, big, mop, fun), the child can decode other related words generated by substitution of a new initial consonant. (Example: given the word "ran," the child can decode "man" and "can.")
  e. *Word recognition* For any of the words on the Sesame Street Word List, the child can recognize the given word when it is presented in a variety of contexts.
  f. *Reading* The child can read each of the 20 words on the Sesame Street Word List.

Sesame Street Word List

1. ran	8. danger	15. stop
2. set	9. exit	16. street
3. big	10. I	17. telephone
4. mop	11. is	18. the
5. fun	12. love	19. walk
6. bird	13. me	20. you
7. bus	14. school	

  g. *Spanish-English vocabularly* (to be determined)
B. Numbers Goals . . .

[From Appendix B, Bogatz & Gall, 1971]

The ETS tests attempted to see just which of these instructional objectives children had actually learned, and what sorts of other, unintentional effects there may have been. (For details of the rather complex and carefully designed testing and evaluation procedures, and of the tests themselves, the student is referred to the basic reports: Ball & Bogatz, 1970; Bogatz & Ball, 1971.) But it must be noted that children were not expected to attain *all* the goals.

For the purposes of this discussion, it will be sufficient to summarize the findings. The first season, ETS selected a sample of 943 children from Boston, Philadelphia, Phoenix, Durham, North Carolina, and a rural area in northeastern California. The sample included:

> ... disadvantaged children from the inner city, advantaged children from suburban areas, children from rural areas, and disadvantaged Spanish-speaking children. Overall, the research sample included more boys than girls and more lower class than middle class children. More of the disadvantaged were black than white; most of the children were 4 years old, although some were 3 and some were 5; and more of the sample's children viewed *Sesame Street* at home than at school. [Ball & Bogatz, 1970, p. 349].

This group of children was divided into four subgroups, or quartiles, depending on how often they had watched "Sesame Street." These quartiles ranged from children who rarely or never watched to children who watched the program more than five times a week.

The chart entitled *First Year Report Card* gives a graphic demonstration of the gains made by these groups in eight months. All groups gained, though those who viewed more gained more.

The figures quoted above for disadvantaged children were also borne out by studies of advantaged children (Ball & Bogatz, 1970).

For our purposes, it is important to observe that these studies show young children learning beginning reading skills (letter-sounds, words, etc.) at home with the assistance of television.

It is also important to note that poor children learned as

well as advantaged children, and that there is no "middle class monopoly" on learning with "Sesame Street" or in parent involvement. In this regard, Evelyn Davis of the CTW community staff said:

> One of the great misconceptions that people have is that because you are poor, because you are black, because you are Spanish, you are not interested in your child. We are asked at CTW "How do you get parents so involved in your activities?" We answer: "Because they are for their children." [Lesser, 1974, p. 209]

Report Cards Record Impact

These are summaries of test results in the Educational Testing Service samples of disadvantaged children showing how they increased their knowledge of certain basic skills taught during Sesame Street's first two seasons. ETS, a non-profit educational measurement and research organization, began its independent study of the impact of the series in 1969. In the first season (left) the white bars indicate the base-line which the 731 disadvantaged children in the nation wide test sample scored on a test conducted before the program went on the air. The dark bars indicate percent of gain by the same children when they were tested again after the season ended.

Percentage gains for the children included:

9% gains for children who watched seldom if ever.
15% gains for those who watched 2–3 times a week.
19% gains for those who watched 4–5 times a week.
24% gains for those who watched more than 5 times a week.

In the second season (right), about half the sample group of 283 disadvantaged youngsters was encouraged to view the series, while the remainder were not encouraged (neither group had seen Sesame Street's first year). Percentage gains among both groups are shown in black. In the second season, which was far more ambitious in scope and complexity due to the addition of new goals, ETS found significant gains in these categories: function of body parts, naming geometric forms, roles of community members, matching by form, naming letters, letter sounds, sight reading, recognizing numbers, naming numbers, counting, relational terms, classification (single criterion) and sorting.

An additional finding in the second study, which included a follow-up of 283 first-year viewers, was that the first "graduates" of Sesame Street were better prepared for school than their classmates who saw the show infrequently or not at all, according to an evaluation by their teachers. ETS also found that the Sesame Street "graduates" adapted well to the school experience. Another significant result reported by ETS was a gain in favorable attitudes toward school and toward people of other races among children who had viewed the program both years.

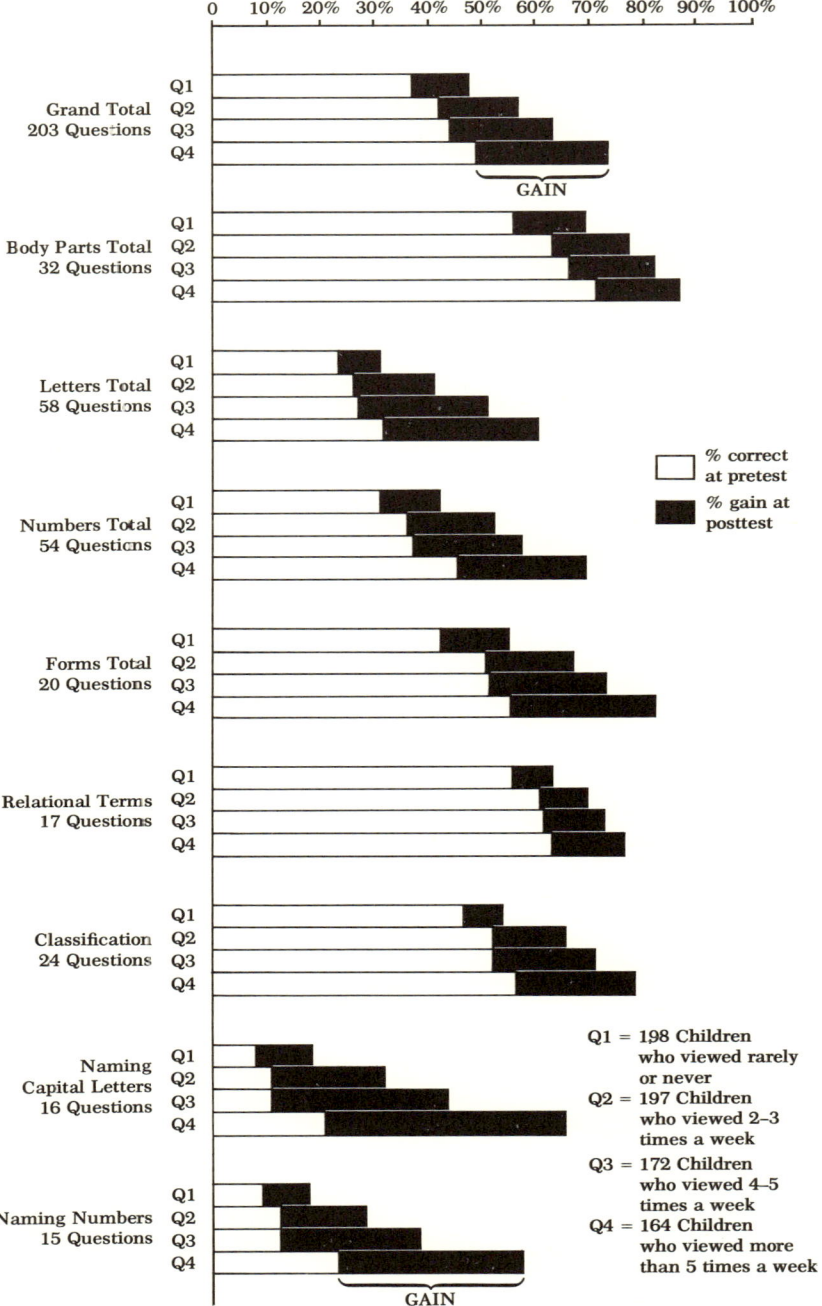

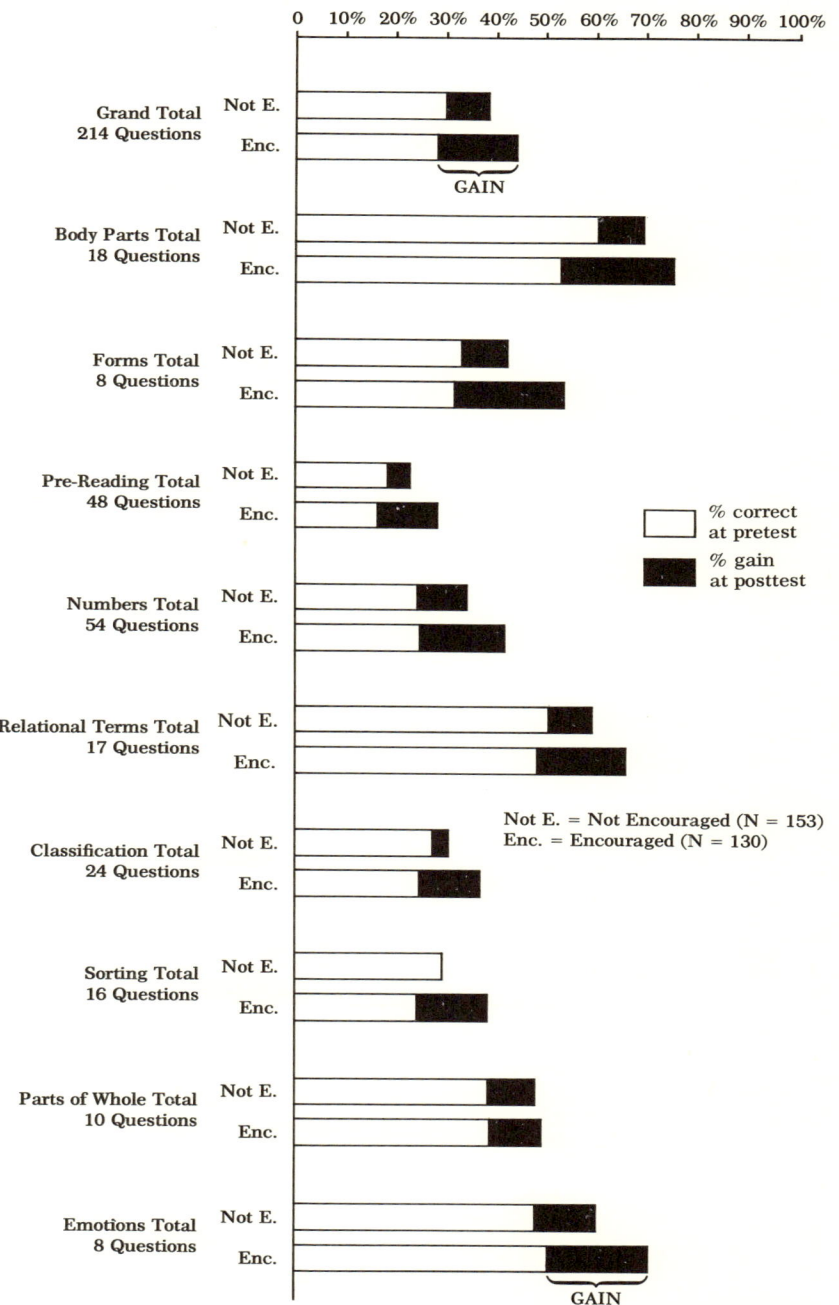

SOURCE: *CTW '72: Annual Report of the Children's Television Workshop*, CTW, 1972, pp. 13–14.

The second year of "Sesame Street" was more difficult to evaluate because it was hard to find children who had never watched the show. Accordingly, a different strategy was adopted. Some children were "encouraged" to watch the show through home visits and a variety of community, day care, and other activities. A matched group of children was not encouraged. (And as they predicted, the kids who were encouraged to watch, watched more, but the "not encouraged" kids watched a lot, too; so the data are not as clean as they could be.)

As is clear from the second chart, the Second Year Report Card, the group which was encouraged to watch gained more on all the tests.

Beginning reading skills which appear to have been effectively taught were: naming letters, recognizing letters, letter-sound associations, sight words, initial sounds of words, and "decoding."[5]

In all, the "Sesame Street" evaluations constitute an example for educators of careful and conscientious evaluation of instruction.

The interested reader is referred to the research itself— much of it fascinating but largely outside the scope of our interest in home teaching of beginning reading skills to young children.[6]

NOTES

1. Maya Pines has an excellent, readable account of Moore's work in *Revolution in Learning: The Years from Birth to Six* (1967).

2. For brief summaries of Montessori in America, see Pines (1967) and J. Beck (1967).

3. John Carroll, Carol Chomsky, Courtney Cazden, Arthur Gates, and others have addressed the parallels between the learning of written and spoken language. The interested reader is urged to see Courtney Cazden's *Child Language and Education* (1972) and John Carroll (1966).

Dr. Ed Coleman, at the University of Texas, El Paso, has done extensive work in what he calls "osmosis" learning—a sort of total immersion in printed language. I quote from an account in the *Reading Newsreport,* October 1972: "Using television, the newspapers, printed materials—literally every medium that is available—Coleman saturates the child's environment with the words he wants him to learn. The result seems to be a natural 'osmosis' learning. As Coleman puts it, 'Children can teach themselves printed language at about the same age and in the same natural way they teach themselves spoken languages . . .' " (p. 36). Harriet Iredell said substantially the same thing in 1898, in an article entitled "Eleanor Learns to Read."

4. As measured by W. L. Warner's index of social class (Warner et al., 1949).

5. In an interesting doctoral thesis done at Fordham University, Judith Minton (1972) investigated the impact of "Sesame Street" and the culture on reading readiness of kindergarten children. Minton compared the Metropolitan Reading Readiness Tests given kindergarteners during two pre–"Sesame Street" years (1968 and 1969) with similar tests given children in 1970.

Upon analysis, she found no significant difference in overall test scores, but she did find that 1970 children knew more letters and did significantly better on the alphabet subtest. Minton concluded that "Sesame Street" in 1970 was "an effective teacher of letter recognition to kindergarten children. . . ."

6. In an interesting study almost outside the scope of this account, Keele and Harrison (1971) trained groups of parent and high school tutors to teach kindergarten and first-grade children selected beginning reading skills. Tutoring appeared to be successful, and the authors found that the high school students were about as effective as the parents in this particular sort of tutoring.

CHAPTER 4

Some Conclusions from History and Research

Several conclusions seen to have been well established by research and corroborated in the historic and descriptive literature. Although some of these statements will seem less than earthshaking to you, they nonetheless have received the attention of serious historians and researchers and have been (indeed, still may be) contradicted widely in print and verbally by people who perhaps should know better.

1. Through much of the history of reading, children have often been taught reading at home. Parental teaching of reading is by no means new.
2. It is possible to find frequent instances of children under six who are reported (reliably or otherwise) to have learned to read outside schools.
3. There exist documented cases of children aged five years and under who have been taught to read by nonprofessional teachers outside schools (Terman, 1918; Cohan, 1961; Fowler, 1962a; Durkin, 1966).
4. Some American children—perhaps from 1 to 3 percent—begin first grade already knowing how to read (Durkin, 1966). It seems possible that these figures may be too conservative, since they are based on Durkin's work in the late 1950s and early 1960s. It may well be that with the influence of "Sesame Street" and "The Electric Company" increasing

numbers of early readers will enter first grade in the 1970s (Ball & Bogatz, 1970, 1973; Bogatz & Ball, 1971; Minton, 1972; Ball et al., 1974; Lesser, 1974).
5. Young children with IQs of less than 100 have been taught to read by nonprofessional teachers outside schools (Durkin, 1966).
6. Young children of lower SES families have been taught to read outside schools by their parents, siblings, or relatives (Durkin, 1966; Morrison et al., 1969).
7. Young children have been taught beginning reading skills outside schools by nonprofessional teachers who did not have a high school education (Durkin, 1966; Brzienski & Hayman, 1962).
8. No evidence has been found of harmful effects of early reading on physical development or visual acuity. However, Durkin (1974, p. 138) warns that, "in the absence of research on this question, caution is justified" (Fowler, 1962a, 1965; Durkin, 1966; McKee, Brzienski, Harrison, 1966; Morrison et al., 1969; Blanton, 1972).
9. No evidence has been found of harmful effects of nonprofessional teaching of reading to young children outside schools on subsequent school achievement (Fowler, 1962a, 1965; Durkin, 1966).
10. Parents can be successfully taught how to teach their young children beginning reading skills (Brzienski & Hayman, 1962; Keele & Harrison, 1971).
11. It appears that, among early readers in Durkin's New York study, children with IQs 135–170 have the greatest advantage in reading achievement over matched nonearly reader controls. This advantage seems to decrease over the first three grades.

    Also, it appears that, among early readers in this New York study, children with IQs 99–124 show an *increasing* advantage over matched controls in reading achievement (Durkin, 1966).
12. While young children with IQs below 100 apparently *can* learn to read, most young children who are taught to read outside schools by nonprofessional teachers tend to be above average in intelligence (Fowler, 1962a, 1966; Durkin, 1966).

13. All of Hollingworth's children with IQs of 180 and above learned to read before attending school; all apparently learned before they were five (Hollingworth, 1942).
14. Several highly intelligent children, who had learned to read early as a part of a program of intensive mental stimulation in infancy, showed difficulties in social adjustment in later life (Dolbear, 1912; Hollingworth, 1942; Fowler, 1962*a*, 1965; Goertzel & Goertzel, 1962).
15. Children watching "Sesame Street" have learned upper- and lowercase letter names, as well as certain letter-sound associations (Ball & Bogatz, 1970; Bogatz & Ball, 1971; CTW, 1972; Minton, 1972).

If these conclusions are justified, then teaching young children to read at home *can* be both possible and helpful—if it is gone about in the proper way.

Several Paths to Reading

From studying the resource literature and the accounts of early readers themselves, I have concluded that there are perhaps three broad paths to early reading. These are, in my view:

1. The informal path*
2. Direct teaching/code emphasis
3. Direct teaching/meaning emphasis

There are many combinations of these three, and it can be easily charged that I oversimplify. Probably I do. In my doctoral thesis I tried to describe five distinct paths, but that's too many to try to keep straight. I've combined three of them in one large catchall category—"informal"—for any child who learns to read without someone intentionally teaching him. I shall try to describe this and the two direct paths in some detail.

---

* See my earlier discussion of the terms "formal" and "informal" on pages 6 and 7.

1. The Informal Path
Following this path, the child seems to use many different elements of his environment to help him learn to read. Usually there is at least some teaching or what Dolores Durkin calls "direct help with reading"—playing school, explaining about letters or sounds, or writing, spelling, or identifying words. But, in the main, children who follow this path to reading instigate much of their own instruction and figure out much of reading for themselves. These are almost invariably children who *want* to learn about reading, writing, books, and words. A child who follows this path will probably exhibit several of the following characteristics; few, if any, children exhibit all of them. The child:

1. Shows pronounced interest in writing—goes from scribbling and drawing to copying letters and words to trying to write names and messages.
2. Is read aloud to frequently by adults or other children.
3. Lives in an environment where people read often and where books and magazines abound.
4. Plays games with adults and other children involving letters, sounds, and rhymes.
5. Asks to be told "what that word says" or "where it says Peter Rabbit" and so on, either while being read to or at other times.
6. Learns to write and recognize his or her own name and perhaps the names of others—family, playmates, pets, friends.
7. Learns to recognize specific words, usually words with some personal meaning: his or her own name, trademarks, interest words like *bomb* and *monkey*, product names like Coca-Cola, Barbie, Chevrolet.
8. Shows deep interest in one thing for long periods of time, e.g., cars, wildflowers, snakes, trains, cooking, birds, or fish.
9. Watches television—sometimes quite intensively—especially but not necessarily "Sesame Street," "The Electric Company," or other children's programs with reading content.
10. "Plays school" with other children.

Sybil Terman and Charles C. Walcutt, in their book *Reading: Chaos and Cure* (1958), described how a child proceeds along this path in a chapter entitled "The 'Born Reader'—and How He Grew." (Try to overlook their remarks about the "homes of most educated people.")

> This is the story of how one mother produced a family of good readers, forty years ago. The mother had had practically no books to read in her childhood and so had bought books constantly after she grew up. There were bookcases in every room containing several thousand volumes, including most of the English classics in complete sets and all the best children's classics, of which each child had his own share. Reading was regarded as a pleasure to be indulged after the day's work was done, and the parents spent every evening reading. Never for a moment had they any doubt that the children would have the same attitude toward books that they did.
>
> The old-fashioned method followed in this, as in most homes of educated people, until a generation or so ago, was to give a child a set of alphabet blocks when he was about two. He played with them and built things out of them. At first he disregarded the letters, but gradually he began to notice them as any child will notice detail. Eventually, he would ask some older person, "What's that?" and be told that was *A* or *D*. Perhaps the adult would indicate that the small *a* or the cursive *a* on the other faces of the same block were forms of the same letter, but the child started with the capitals, which are easily distinguished from each other. There is no danger of confusing *B* and *D* or *P* and *Q* in the capital letters.
>
> The child was at the age where one of his main activities and one of his chief delights was learning the names of things. He liked to point to an object and ask, "What is that?" At that age the child seemed to have no trouble associating the name with the object, and he was absorbed in this game for many delightful hours. He learned the names of the letters just as he learned the names *table, chair, shoe,* and *cup*. Since he enjoyed this sort of thing so much, his mother said, "Show me *A*," or "Show me *B*." He was delighted to do so. Sometimes he took the initiative and said, with great satisfaction, "That's *X*!" In order to learn the names of the letters, of course he had to be able to distinguish between them, and this he readily did. It was all a game—it was fun.
>
> This mother also read simple books to her child, holding him on her lap so that he could watch as she read. Eventually he observed that the letters on the blocks were on the pages of

the book. He also got the idea that mother was somehow turning these letters into a story that told about the pictures in the book. One of the books was an alphabet book: that was standard in every nursery two generations ago. Mother read this over and over again to her child, and eventually he learned to say it to himself. With the blocks and the alphabet book he could not fail to observe that letters represented sounds. "*A* was an apple pie. *B* bit it. *C* cut it. . . ." Intoning this with delight, he learned to connect the name and the form of the letter with the sound that it makes. The sound of *B* is contained in the name of the letter *B*. It became fun to recite the alphabet and even to sing it to a simple tune. Having learned them so thoroughly, the child could not fail to notice the letters on signs and boxes.

Eventually he would get a pencil or a piece of chalk and begin copying. In the corner of the nursery there stood a small blackboard with the letters on a scroll over it. From time to time he practiced copying the letters on the blackboard until he was able to write all four *A*'s—large and small printed letters and large and small written letters. By the time he was four these letters had become a part of him—old friends that he could never forget.

In the meantime, of course, he was using language as communication in all his waking hours—talking, asking questions, conversing with others. At bedtime he demanded that something be read to him, and probably before he was four the idea that he would like to read himself had occurred to him. In imitation of the grown-ups he would recite a well-known story while looking at the book in which it was printed. Finally he learned to print his name and a few other words on his blackboard. At this point he had what the modern educationists call "reading readiness."

Finally, he took the initiative, found a primer, managed to get the attention of an older sister, and got her to tell him the first words in the book. And thus he started reading without realizing he was taking any special step. Someone simply pronounced the words in a book for him, and since the visual images on the page were absolutely clear and distinct—being made up of his old friends, the letters—he had no trouble making the connection between the printed and the spoken word and he realized how the letters represented the sounds. It was so much fun, such a pleasant game, that he went on to learn more words, for he saw that new words were made of various words and syllables with which he was already familiar. When he knew *boy, toy* said itself at a single glance. [pp. 150–152]

2. *Direct Teaching/Code Emphasis*

In this path the parent or someone else sets out deliberately to teach the young child to read, following what could be called a "code emphasis approach" (Chall, 1967). In this kind of approach the thrust of the teaching is toward helping the child to master the elements and the use of the "code"—the letters and spelling patterns of the written language. The most noteworthy examples of these are the Bloomfield-Barnhart materials and Flesch's do-it-yourself pages in *Why Johnny Can't Read.*

It is not necessary, of course, that parents follow the Bloomfield, Flesch, or any other particular set of materials or directions—although there are many available. The materials used and the methods advocated diverge widely. It may prove helpful to consider one of them—Bloomfield's is perhaps the best.

Leonard Bloomfield, an eminent American linguist, disapproved of "sounding out" and "blending" letter-sounds, and instead sought to teach the spelling patterns of words. A parent following the Bloomfield system first teaches the child to name the letters, both upper and lower case. Once the child knows these, she is ready to begin reading. She then learns to identify regular short-vowel words, in a progression that takes her gradually through *a, i, u, e,* and *o.* Beginning with *can, Dan, man, fan, Nan, pan, ran, tan,* and *an* in Lesson 1, by Lesson 36 the child is asked to read, "Dad got on a bus."

Lessons are meant to be brief. The following excerpt from Bloomfield's directions will serve to illustrate the procedure. The parent or teacher is supposed to point to the word:

can

. . . or show[s] the word either on the blackboard or on a card. The child knows the names of the letters, and is now asked to read off those names in their order: *see, aye, en.* The parent or teacher says, "Now we have spelled the word. Now we are going to *read* it. This word is *can.* Read it: *can.*" [Bloomfield & Barnhart, 1961, p. 41]

In the first sessions the child is asked to do only two words; then the sessions grow longer as the child gets the idea and as there are more words to review. He will not go on to the second page until he has "overlearned" all the words on the first (Bloomfield & Barnhart, 1961, p. 51).

After he completes Lesson 36, the child enters a stage of "easy reading" and has progressed to "the commonest irregular words" by Lesson 98, in which he reads a story: "Bess Will Not Drink Tea without Milk in It."

The program goes on from there through Lesson 245, a story about Florence, a girl who "lived with her father and mother in a big apartment building in the city."

Now, it must not be imagined that all code-emphasis programs for teaching young children to read are like Bloomfield's. His is, I think, the least varied and most straightforward, smacking of good honest work, though Flesch is a close rival in this regard. Others use comic strips and games (J. Beck, 1964, 1967), the Montessori sandpaper letters and movable alphabet (Hainstock, 1968), flashcards and "activities" involving letter-sounds (McEathron, 1952; Hurd & Rimmel, 1961), or movable alphabet cards, activities, and games as in Watson (1965) or my own program beginning on page 109.

Although there are marked differences from program to program, the "code-emphasis" approaches concentrate on teaching the child the elements of the code first: either letter names, sounds, or both. Once the code is learned, these programs teach the child how to use it in reading. Most of these approaches teach the child the names of the letters as well as some of the letter-sounds. However, Montessori teaches only the sounds. Bloomfield and the Steinbergs teach only the letter names.

3. Direct Teaching/Meaning Emphasis

Perhaps the best-known whole-word or meaning-emphasis system for young children is Doman's, which starts children off at age two or, "if you are very clever," at ten months. Parents following the Doman procedures outlined in *How to Teach Your Baby to Read* (1964) are instructed to make large poster-board cards (or purchase a commercially available kit which has the cards in it, already prepared). These cards, which are printed plainly in large red letters, have words on them like *Mommy, Daddy, toes,* or *hand.* In the beginning the teacher shows the child the word card *Mommy* nine times in the first two days, and says, "This says 'Mommy.'" On the tenth trial, if the child actually shows he knows the word, there is, in Doman's phrase, "a celebration":

> If the child says, "Mommy," you must then be delighted and make a great fuss. Tell the child he is very good and very bright. Tell the child that you are very proud of him. Tell him that you love him very much. It is wise to hug him and express your love for him physically. [Doman, 1964, p. 112]

If the child does not get the word, the mother is cautioned not to show any disappointment and instructed to go ahead with the routine until the child *does* get the word.

Eventually the child learns to differentiate the words *Mommy* and *Daddy.* Then he is taught the twenty "self" words—such as *toes, hand, nose, leg, elbow,* and *finger*—which are introduced individually, on cards, with red lowercase letters four inches high. The "self" words are taught in the following way:

> We begin with the body-image word *hand.*
> Mother first takes the child's hand and says clearly, "This is *hand.*" She lets the child see the hand; she says hand again clearly; she then squeezes the hand.
> She then holds up the word *hand,* and again says, "This is hand."
> The parent then follows exactly the same procedure she did in teaching the words *mommy* and *daddy.*
> When Mother is sure that the child knows the word *hand,* and only then, she may proceed to the next word. [p. 119]

The next step is the "home" vocabulary—in red two-inch letters. This category includes words which name the objects around the child and contains four subvocabularies: members of the family, objects owned by the family, the child's own possessions, and "doing" words (for example, *sitting* and *running*). When the child has learned these, he is led by a series of steps to read a book, after first having learned all the words in the book. Once he has read the book, he is ready to learn the alphabet, which is also on cards.

Doman's method is highly publicized. His writing is lively and interesting. He has, however, what seems to be a penchant for making astonishing assertions ("Beyond two years of age, reading gets harder every year," 1964, p. 104) without offering any research evidence for them.

Nonetheless, it *is* a meaning-emphasis system, and a rather carefully organized one. It is also highly visible, current, and well known. Doman's book has been translated into ten languages besides English. It is clear that some children do indeed learn to read using Doman's method. Marilyn Segal (1966) tells, in *Run Away, Little Girl*, the moving story of how she taught her brain-injured child to read using Doman's materials.

In 1971 a parent and teacher named Felicity Hughes published an account of how she taught her two children to read using the Doman method. In her book entitled *Reading and Writing before School*, Ms. Hughes expands Doman's original program to include both phonics instruction and writing.

This book seems to me considerably more useful than Doman, but it pays no more attention to the research on early reading than his did. Moreover, Hughes treats as demonstrably true (and offers no research evidence for) a number of Doman's assertions which are at least open to serious question.*

Despite all that, any parent who decides to teach the Doman system would, in my judgment, do well to use Hughes's much more complete and detailed version, which supplies the writing and phonics instruction omitted by Doman, and which also contains many more teaching hints, games, activities, and the like.

Other meaning-emphasis systems meant for young children include the earlier mentioned works of Mrs. Scripture

---

* Some examples: "A written word is *exactly* comparable to a spoken word" (p. 23). . . . "For example, it follows that if the brain is doing exactly the same thing when it understands written words as when it understands spoken words, a child must be able to read as easily as he can understand the words he hears" (p. 25).

(1897), Stevens and Orem (1968), and Parke (1957; reprinted 1969). Fowler (1962b) used a meaning-emphasis system in teaching Velia. Parke's text *You Can Teach Your Child to Read* is sold in paperback at newsstands and department stores. Historically speaking, a nineteenth-century German pedagogue named Wackernagel probably took the meaning-emphasis method about as far as it can ever be expected to go. I quote Mathews's description of the Wackernagel program:

> The primer of Wackernagel was designed particularly for mothers to use with their children at home. The mother would read the selections over and over to the child, who looked on, until he memorized them and could then recite them by heart. This exercise continued until no matter where his mother opened the book the child could begin reciting. [Mathews, 1966, p. 42]

An Analysis: How Children Learn to Read at Home

This analysis will undertake to describe how children are said to have learned to read at home. I will try to discuss the following aspects of home teaching:

1. Materials used
2. Characteristics and backgrounds of pupils and teachers
3. Learning environments
4. Specific instructional procedures
5. Subsequent school and reading experiences of early readers
6. Evaluation of teaching and learning by both teachers and pupils
7. Problems and achievements of early readers after completing school
8. Physical and/or psychological aftereffects ascribed to early reading

1. Materials Used

Materials for learning to read can be almost anything that uses written language—including television, comic strips, workbooks, storybooks, magazines, signs, labels, and so forth.

These materials can be used by the child alone or by the child at the direction of his tutor. Many materials seem vital in the learning of some children, unimportant to the learning of others. An example might be picture dictionaries (which are described as quite helpful by Huey [1908] and by Durkin [1966]); yet not all children who learn to read early have picture dictionaries.

Materials cannot be thought of as static: Their effectiveness often must depend heavily on their use. A favorite storybook, read to the child in such a way that she can see the pages, as Huey suggests (1908), may be far more likely to be effective than the same book read in such a way that the child cannot see the pages. (See especially Durkin, 1966 [cases Arlene, p. 60, and Carol, p. 61]; and Chomsky, 1971a [case Harry].)

Durkin does not make any direct analysis of materials read to the children, although the high incidence of parents who report reading aloud to their children (all the parents in the California study, and all thirty of the selected group in the New York study) would seem to agree with Huey's idea of the importance of reading aloud to children. Perhaps a hint of the sort of material read may be found in the reports of library use by the mothers of early readers in the New York study: 70 percent reported that they took out books from the library (as against 53 percent of mothers of nonearly readers). Durkin reports a consistent edge in favor of homes of early readers in responses to the question:

Before your child ever learned to read, what kinds of materials were available to him?

MATERIALS	*Early readers*	*Nonearly readers*
Basal readers	23	30
Workbooks	33	27
Library books	70	53
Golden Books	87	77
Coloring books	70	63
Alphabet books	87	77

SOURCE: Durkin, *Children Who Read Early,* 1966, p. 162.

As may be noted, "basal readers" seem to be the only books in the table above which, it was claimed, were available to more nonearly readers than early readers. The difference is so slight (23 percent versus 30 percent), however, that even the most dedicated foe of basals would be hard pressed to make something out of it.

Materials for writing, or perhaps scribbling, seem to be of major importance in learning to read. In discussing the California study, Durkin took some pains to point this out:

> In general, then, the children identified as early readers in California were children who could also be described as "early scribblers." They were children who appeared to have advanced from aimless scribbling to the drawing of people and objects, and then to the making of letters copied most often from alphabet books, school papers of older siblings, and small blackboards. It is probably not an accident that in every one of the 49 families interviewed, a blackboard was available—often because it had belonged to an older child in the family, or because it had been purchased as effortlessly and cheaply as "up at the drug store for ninety-eight cents." [Durkin, 1966, p. 57]

In Durkin's New York study, 83 percent of parents of early readers listed the "availability of paper and pencils" as one of the things that interested their children in learning to read. A surprisingly large percentage (93 percent) of early readers were given help with printing. In the California study all but one of the forty-nine early readers knew how to print when they entered school, and the one exception "had been eager to learn before the first grade, but was not allowed to try because her mother did not know 'the right way to do it' " (1966, p. 57).

2. Characteristics and Backgrounds of Pupils and Teachers

It seems almost pointless to attempt generalizations about "what kind of child learns to read early" or "what kind of parent teaches his child to read at home." This also seems to hold true for socioeconomic status (SES). Early readers and their teachers seem to show a wide variation of education, personality, and SES (Brzienski & Hayman, 1962; Durkin, 1966). However, early readers seem to occur more frequently in middle- and upper-SES families. The relationship of a parent's educational level to the child's early reading is not clear.

High intelligence appears to be helpful in learning to read before first grade, especially for those children who begin at two or three (Fowler, 1962*b*, 1965), but high IQ is clearly not a necessity to learning to read early (Fowler, 1962*a*, 1965; Durkin, 1966; Torrey, 1968). Durkin (1966) had several early readers of below 100 IQ; John's IQ was 104 (Torrey, 1968).

Obviously, the teacher can be almost anyone: parent, grandparent, or other adult; sibling; cousin; playmate. There seems to be no limit on the variability, though most tutors (in Durkin's studies, anyway) seem to be mothers and older sisters.

3. Learning Environments

It seems to be a logical necessity that print—written language—be found in a child's environment if the child is to learn to read early, whether the child is self-taught or is taught deliberately by an adult.

The environment of most early readers seems to include books in plenty, blackboards and writing materials, TV, and usually one or more adults who read and value reading (Durkin, 1966).

4. Specific Instructional Procedures

Learning to read early apparently can be either the child's idea or the tutor's. The instruction can be whenever the child wants it or whenever the tutor wants to give it. Presumably, there is room for great variation. From the parent interviews of Durkin, at any rate, it would seem that in most cases it was some of both—the children wanted to learn and someone often wanted to teach them (Durkin, 1966).

This line of inquiry cannot be pursued very far, however, before the nature of reading instruction begins to blur. A five-year-old whose mother is teaching her to read might also spend a good deal of time puzzling out words in her picture books or trying to figure out where it says "Mattel" in the TV toy commercials. Very likely the reading instruction she has received will help her in these endeavors, but are they extensions of the instruction?

Often, children seem to have begun learning to read without a parent's ever doing much more than answering the child's questions or permitting instruction by an older child. In either of these events, the parent seems to have no real "go or no go" decision point at which he must decide whether or not his child is to learn to read before entering school. Many parents, especially those who value reading themselves and read aloud to their children frequently, may find themselves already in the process of reading instruction before they realize it, with children who ask the sounds of letters or want to be shown certain words on the page (Durkin, 1966; Pines, 1967).

Such parents, finding themselves with children who want to learn about reading, might well be expected to look for some guidance from educators in the form of materials and/or instructions they can follow.

5. Subsequent School and Reading Experiences of Early Readers

Our limited data suggest that early readers are generally successful in school, at least insofar as reading achievement is a measure, especially during elementary school.

6. Evaluation of Teaching and Learning by Both Teachers and Pupils

Some pupils, especially those whose fathers were driving, authoritarian teachers, complained of the lessons taken in early childhood (Mill, 1873; Wiener, 1953). Others appear to recall the event more pleasantly—there seem to be pupils whose learning experience was warm and affectionate, more like Scout's recollection in *To Kill a Mockingbird*.

Parent-teachers mostly seem to react quite positively. Many letters have come to Joan Beck about the experience of teaching children from the comic strip that ran in *The Chicago Tribune*. At my request, Ms. Beck sent me copies of more than fifty of these letters recounting parent experience to examine. This is a fairly representative one—there seem to be many like it:

March 12, 1969

Dear Miss Beck,

My four-year-old daughter and I have been enjoying your "Short Cuts to Reading" so very much. Every morning, her first question is, "What letter did we get today?" It just amazes us how much she has learned in just a little over three weeks and how avidly she looks forward to each new lesson.

We have made a scrapbook to keep all the lessons, and she is constantly coming to me with the book to review them over and over again. She is so much more aware of words in general now, and so often we hear her trying to sound out words she sees in books, even on sides of trucks, buildings, etc.

Making a "game" of reading has certainly been a big success at our house! I only wish the entire series could be published in book form so that more parents and children could share in its advantages.

Thank you so much!

In her book *Children Who Read Early*, Durkin quoted the response of two mothers who had taught their children to read. One mother in the New York study:

> . . . talked about the many things she and her young son had done together; and then she added, "Gee, I enjoyed that child." Another mother of an early reader said she sometimes wondered whether she herself was immature because she found the company of her sons so much more stimulating than the time she spent with other adults. Here she commented about the children's interesting questions and observations which, she said, "made it sheer joy to be with them." [Durkin, 1966, p. 110]

7. Problems and Achievements of Early Readers after Completing School

There is not much evidence at all on this matter. We know of many early readers who have been successful, but these are often geniuses, like Cox's subjects. There are others, for instance the good readers found in college by Strang (1954), as well as many of Terman's (1925) subjects and several of Hollingworth's (1942). It would, of course, be helpful to have follow-up data on Durkin's early readers as they continued through school, but such data are not available.

Not all early readers are successful, though. A small segment of highly intelligent children with IQs of 150 or over seem to find serious difficulty in adjusting to schools and peers (Fowler, 1962a, 1965; Goertzels & Goertzels, 1962). In some cases this social difficulty continued with the person through life (Dolbear, 1912; Hollingworth, 1942; Wiener, 1953; Engelmann & Engelmann, 1966). It seems unlikely that these social difficulties of some very bright individuals can be attributed to early reading or even early instruction alone.

Fowler, who had first-hand knowledge of social problems of early readers, discussed it as follows:

> It is also true that studies of bright children, who were highly stimulated at an early age, have uncovered a small proportion who experienced some disturbance in personality functioning. Cases have been concentrated in the extremely high IQ subgroup (e.g., Hollingworth, 1942). Significantly, problems have generally appeared to stem from the child's social role difficulties, arising from the manner in which society has tended to evaluate a child of this caliber—viz., "egghead." . . . Occasionally there is evidence that role adjustment problems of this type may not have been the sole source of disturbance. [Fowler, 1962a, p. 141]

8. *Physical and/or Psychological Aftereffects Ascribed to Early Reading*

There simply is no evidence of physical aftereffects at all. Psychological aftereffects of early intensive instruction in reading are reported; such cases as are available, such as Velia's (Fowler, 1962a, 1962b), are confounded by other factors.

It seems likely that early readers who later show anxiety and difficulty with social adjustment have in common (1) very high intelligence and (2) a history of parental pressure and intense tutelage in very early childhood (Dolbear, 1912; Hollingworth, 1942; Goertzel & Goertzel, 1962; Fowler, 1962b; Engelmann & Engelmann, 1966).

Social maladjustment seems to be the negative aftereffect most feared by the critics of nonprofessional teaching of reading to young children outside schools (Sheldon, 1963; Bettelheim, 1966). Although mostly negative aftereffects seem to be considered by both critics and advocates of early reading (J. Beck, 1967), positive aftereffects seem to me at least as plausible. The child who learns to read early is likely to be praised, respected, and listened to by adults and should have a good chance of being successful in school. All of these effects would seem promising for that child's future.

PART TWO

ABC

CHAPTER 5

What to Do If You Decide to Teach Your Child Beginning Reading at Home

The psychological, philosophical, and historical aspects of home teaching were discussed in the first part of this book. Part Two is about the practical aspects. In the following pages I will try to suggest what to do and how to do it as well as when and where—if you want to teach your child to read.

In this chapter I list a set of things that any parent can do, and I also suggest several published reading programs for those who want a highly structured approach. I don't think any published program can or should take the place of these other things—I suggest them only as supplements to the activities like reading aloud together, "writing," games, etc.

Some General Observations*

A striking fact about early readers is that they are often children who have been read aloud to a great deal. Not only are they read to often (daily or better) by parents, sitters, siblings, or someone else; presumably they also sit so that they can see the pictures and the words as the reading goes on. Other factors in the homes of most early readers are the presence

---

* To some extent this section repeats observations I have made in Part One. I run the risk of repetition to make certain that this information is available to people who begin with Part Two.

of lots of books, especially children's books, and people in the house who value reading and books. One more point about the early reader's environment: Since early readers are often also early scribblers, there usually are writing materials in abundance that the child can get at—paper, crayons, pencils, markers, chalkboard and chalk, maybe even a typewriter. Some early readers are also TV fans; it is interesting to speculate about the number of readers who have been inspired by "Sesame Street" and "The Electric Company."

It may help to say something here about the rate at which children progress in reading—especially when you begin with a very young child. Two- or three-year-olds often seem to learn by fits and starts, to be sponges one time and sieves the next. Don't worry. Take it as it comes. If you're interested in the letters, they'll be interested too, and sooner or later they'll learn them. Learning the letters takes the longest, sometimes a year or more, although it is not uncommon to read or hear about children who learned their letters in a day or two when they really got involved. About the best thing that can be said of the task is that children learn at their own speeds and in their own ways. It is usually folly to measure one child against another, so please don't try.

Once you have decided to teach your child about reading, it is especially important to go slowly in the beginning and recognize that the largest single step that your child will make in learning to read will be understanding some fundamental concepts:

1. What is spoken can be written (and vice versa).
2. Print stands for speech.
3. Reading is useful and pleasant.

In my view, if your child knows all these, you're well on the way. I consider these to be the essence of reading readiness.

Some Specific Suggestions

There are several standing suggestions which I believe will hold regardless of the teaching program you decide to follow.

1. Try to read to your child at least 20 minutes every day, in pleasant circumstances, and make sure that

she sits so she can see the words and pictures. The reading material should ordinarily be something your child wants. Ideally, the two of you will go to the library together and make a big occasion of selecting and comparing books.
2. Try to arrange for your child to watch "Sesame Street" and/or "The Electric Company" if possible. These TV programs, widely acclaimed, are grounded in the same research base and should make your task easier. I have reservations about a lot of TV watching in the life of any child—especially after age six or so—but before that a moderate amount can be helpful. (I consider up to an hour a day moderate.)
3. Encourage your child to draw, scribble, and write—have chalk and chalkboard, paper, markers, and pencils readily available in your child's room or someplace that they can be reached easily.
4. Play games involving basic reading skills—letter names, letter-sounds, words, and so forth. (See my kits on pages 113–161 for games.)
5. Get a set of magnetic plastic letters for the refrigerator door, and start to use them. (See Buyer's Guide, page 206.)
6. Try the Scholastic Press Record/Book sets, which have inexpensive paperback children's books matched with records of actors reading the same book. Your child can hear the book read and look at it at the same time. (If you've got a children's phonograph, your child can play the records and read the books unassisted. This is sometimes a nice solution for busy parents.)
7. Surround your child with books, newspapers, posters, and magazines. If you have a typewriter, let her use it if you dare.
8. Make written language important around your place—call attention to the times that you need to read and to what a great thing it is to be able to read.
9. Point out words and letters on signs, billboards, TV, labels, headlines, posters, etc.
10. Show your child how to write his or her name, your name, and the names of friends, pets, relatives, and others.
11. Go to the library or magazine rack or bookstore

together often—get some books and magazines for *both* of you. Your child should, by all means, see you reading, too, because your actions speak very loudly. If you can, make it clear that you value reading and get books for information and pleasure.

12. Relax—don't push. *Never work on reading unless your child wants to, and always quit when your child wants to quit* (preferably *before* the child wants to).
13. Keep the anxiety for your child to be "right" out of your voice. If you show him "X" and he says "Y" don't become tense or impatient. Children learn, but usually it takes time. Learn from mistakes—try to figure out why he confuses X and Y, and then try to clear up the confusion. That's teaching.
14. Follow my program outline in Chapter 6 (pages 111–112), or get one of the commercially available programs for teaching young children and use it. I recommend any of the following,* in no particular order (see Buyer's Guide, pages 203–204, for details).

    Children Discover Reading, by Stern and Gould
    Let's Read, by Bloomfield and Barnhart
    Listen and Learn with Phonics, by Watson

15. Do not use emotional pressure of any sort to get your child to learn to read. Never work on reading when your child does not want to work. Only work at those times your child wants to.

Remember to stop when your child wants to (preferably before he wants to) and *never push your child to read. Keep it a game.*

---

* Though it is quite difficult for inexperienced teachers because of its unusual format, one of the best teaching materials available is the Programmed Reading Series by Sullivan Associates, published by the Webster Division of McGraw-Hill. (Even the *Whole Earth Catalog* recommends it for teaching reading in the commune, or whatever.) Also useful is Dolores Durkin's text *Teaching Young Children to Read,* which gives many ideas and activities for kindergarten or primary teaching that can also be used in your home.

CHAPTER 6

Teaching Beginning Reading Skills: A Step-by-Step Program You Can Follow at Home

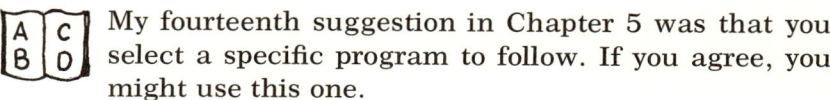 My fourteenth suggestion in Chapter 5 was that you select a specific program to follow. If you agree, you might use this one.

The program has been developed over the past eleven years, during which time I have been a parent, a preschool and elementary school teacher, a graduate student at Emory and Harvard, and now a reading specialist. The program is in the form of twenty-one "kits," lessons for parents or other tutors to use at home with young children individually.

I have attempted to distill what seems to me the best and most effective combination of all the methods and materials reviewed in Part One. In this program I will describe in some detail each of the games and homemade materials that are used.

I hope that it will work for you.

There are several things that this program is not meant to be. It is not:

1. Automatic—you'll have to work at it

2. Infallible—some kids don't learn to read easily with any method, including this one
3. A complete first-grade-to-high-school reading course —it leaves off about where the child can read children's books independently
4. Meant for high-pressure teaching. If you want to push your child, get another program—or, better yet, find some area less sensitive than reading to push, like table manners, toothbrushing, or cleaning up one's room

Teaching a child to read can be one of the most satisfying experiences you will ever have. There is only one major don't: *Don't get anxious and start to apply pressure.* Once you do that it isn't a game anymore for the child, so it's not fun any longer. It's working to please an adult, which is the antithesis of the kind of learning that this program seeks. Once you start to pressure the child—to teach because *you* want to teach today, or to fret over how much or how little progress is being made—then you've failed.

The Readiness Section of this program, Kits 1–4, is written in great detail. Directions are provided for such things as reading aloud, encouragement of writing, materials for parents and children to make together, use of media and mail, learning games to play, and selection of reading materials.

In the sections which follow Readiness, the basic instructions will not be repeated. Parents whose children already know letters and sounds, and who want to start with Level 5, are urged to read over Kits 1–4 anyway. Much of the teaching advice given in those kits is applicable throughout the program.

Troubleshooting

If at any time your child doesn't seem to be understanding the ideas you are trying to teach, back off and try to figure out why. Don't be anxious: After all, there's plenty of time.

The first question to ask yourself is, "Am I pushing too hard?" Another question is, "How did my child go about learning the previous material? Is there some special way she seems to learn?"

Then, if you're still not getting anywhere, take a week off. Don't even try to teach whatever it is that's not getting across for at least a week. Concentrate on reading aloud together, or writing stories, or something like that. Then, after you've been away from it for a while, see if you can come back for a fresh start and a fresh approach.

Some children, especially those with a learning disability, can have very serious difficulties in learning to read.

If your child gets to a point which he seems unable to go beyond, stop trying to teach him to read. Don't push, whatever you do, because that can cause a good many problems, emotional and otherwise.

Don't be afraid to depart from this program at any point to try your own ideas. Any game you can invent is likely to be better than mine because it comes from you, and your child will probably enjoy it for that reason. If you have any questions about what to do, or whether something might or might not be appropriate, please write to me at this address.

> Wood Smethurst
> Emory University Reading Center
> Fishburne Hall
> Atlanta, Georgia 30322

This is my project, and I like to talk about it. I'll also appreciate very much knowing what games you think up so I can tell other parents. Any ideas, changes, and additions you suggest will be more than welcome. Enjoy.

An Overview of the Program

Unit I: *Readiness*

> Kit 1: The capital letter names
> Kit 2: The lowercase letter names
> Kit 3: Introducing letter-sound associations
> Kit 4: Learning letter-sound associations
>
> Review Lesson I: At this point your child should be considered "ready" for reading.

Unit II: *Beginning to Read*

Kit 5: Rhymes, ending sounds, and some words to read
Kit 6: Some easy word families: *-ap, -at, -an, -ad*
Kit 7: Another middle sound and some new words: *-in, -it, -ill, -ig*
Kit 8: Beginning sounds of words; decoding selected pairs of words: *mat-pat,* etc.
Kit 9: Ending sounds of words; decoding selected pairs of words: *man-map,* etc.

Review Lesson II: By this point your child should be able to read some simple words, and should also understand several of the most basic concepts in reading.

Unit III: *Developing Reading Skill*

Kit 10: More ending sounds: *-and, -ack, -ip, -s, -ick, -ag*
Kit 11: Another middle sound: *-o, -ot, -ock, -op*
Kit 12: Still more middle sounds: *-en, -end, -eck, -et, -un, -up, -ud, -ut*
Kit 13: Blending letter-sounds; games
Kit 14: More consonant blends

Review Lesson III: By this point your child should have mastered many of the fundamental reading skills.

Unit IV: *Going Ahead with Reading*

Kit 15: Magic *e*
Kit 16: Learning: *ch, sh, th, wh, ph;* more vowel sounds
Kit 17: Two-syllable words and two-vowel combinations
Kit 18: More vowel combinations
Kit 19: Still more sounds: *-r* after vowels; soft *c* and *g*
Kit 20: Common sight words
Kit 21: Independent reading

Review Lesson IV: By now your child should be able to decode many words and read simple sentences. Your child should be reading easy children's books.

UNIT I: READINESS

Kits 1-4

This unit will help you develop your child's reading readiness. The unit concentrates on providing natural ways for you to help your child learn basic concepts, letter names, and certain letter-sound associations as well as recognize a few words on sight. Emphasis is placed on reading and writing for meaning.

Kit 1: The capital letter names

MATERIALS

> Capital letters poster (homemade—see page 115 for instructions)
> Capital letter cards (to be made of 3 × 5 inch index cards lettered by felt-tip marker)
> ABC books and other children's books from the library or bookstore
> Child's chalkboard and chalk

GOALS

The point of this kit is to help your child become interested in reading and in learning the names of the capital letters—just the names for right now. You needn't bother with their sounds, alphabetical order, or lowercase forms just yet. We'll get to those things in due time with later kits.

When your child can name all the capital letters, in any order that you point to them, you are ready for Kit 2.

Instructions

1. What to do

In this section I will try to summarize for you the things you will need to do in this kit. This summary is to give you the broad picture: Each aspect will be treated in more detail in following sections of this kit. Steps (*a*) and (*b*) will try to get your child interested in reading; steps (*c*) through (*h*) are to get her interested in letters.

a. First, I assume that you and your child are already reading together; if not, this is *the* place to start.

b. Now is also a good time to add to your child's book collection, with trips to the library or bookstore.

c. Make a poster or letter strip of the capital letters for your child's room, or make several posters and letter strips. Also make capital letter cards, using 3 × 5 inch index cards and felt-tip markers. Try to find plastic letters and a child's chalkboard in your local toy store, or order them by mail. Keep writing materials available and encourage your child to try to write for herself.

d. Print your child's name for him on a card, paper, or chalkboard using all caps, and print any other words he wants in the same way.

e. Play some of the letter learning games together.

f. Watch "Sesame Street" or "The Electric Company" together.

g. Write stories together—either stories you make up by yourself or with help from your child, or stories that she dictates for you to transcribe.

h. Use the written language all around you—signs, advertisements, labels, headlines, etc.—to call attention to different letters and words.

If you and your child are already accustomed to talking about letters, by all means keep it up; if you are not, this is a good time to start. In your reading together, or around the house, or on trips to the store, or whenever you think of it, point out a letter to your child as a matter of some interest. I recall saying things like the following to my own children:

"This is an S—see, it's got a wavy crooked shape like a snake. It's the letter S."

If this seems somewhat silly and undignified to you I can only admit that it is, a little. But then I believe that parents of small children are well advised to be a little silly and undignified sometimes.

As soon as your child knows the names of all the capital letters, start on Kit 2—even if you haven't done *all* the activities in Kit 1.

2. Things for you to make or buy

a. Capital letters poster. Make a capital letters poster for your child, using a favorite color* of felt-tip marker and a large sheet of paper (or several standard-size sheets of paper) or a large piece of poster board. Here are several possibilities (Figures 1 and 2).

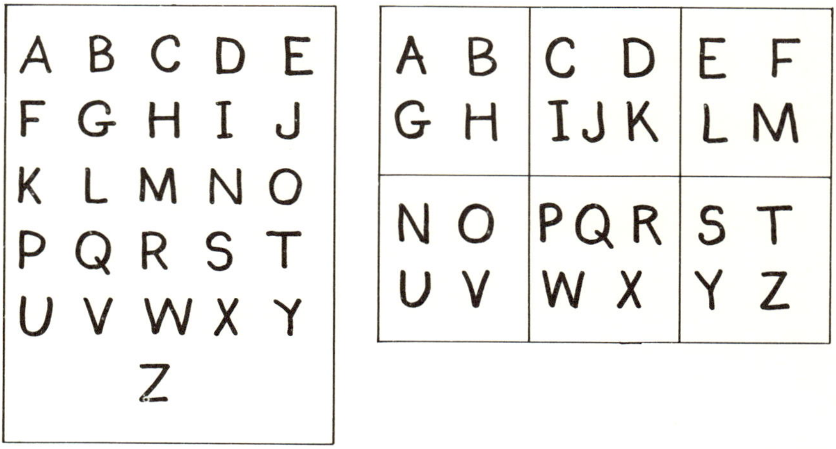

```
A B C D E          A B | C D | E F
F G H I J          G H | I J K | L M
K L M N O         ─────┼──────┼─────
P Q R S T          N O | P Q R | S T
U V W X Y          U V | W X | Y Z
    Z
```

Figure 1

```
A B C D E F G H I J K L M
N O P Q R S T U V W X Y Z
```

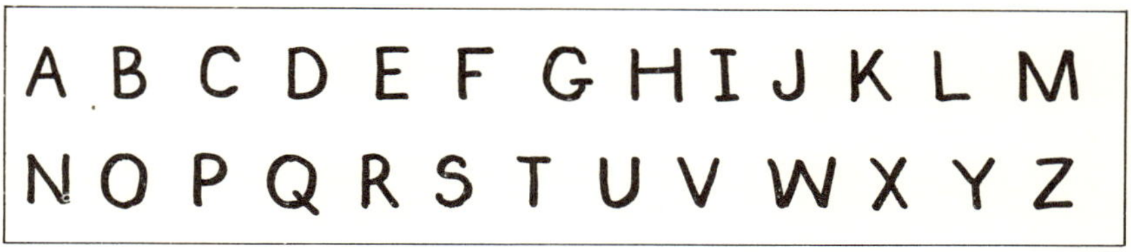

Figure 2

* If you and your child have no special color preference, blue is a good choice, I think, because it stands out and is attractive.

The poster can go on walls of your choosing, or the refrigerator, or a door, or what have you. I prefer the child's room for posters, but that's hardly necessary. I like the idea of a child being able to see the letters from her bed. But do what you like. You might even want to make a poster for the kitchen or another room and use a letter strip in the bedroom.

For those who might have forgotten, here is a chart of the capital letters and how to print them:

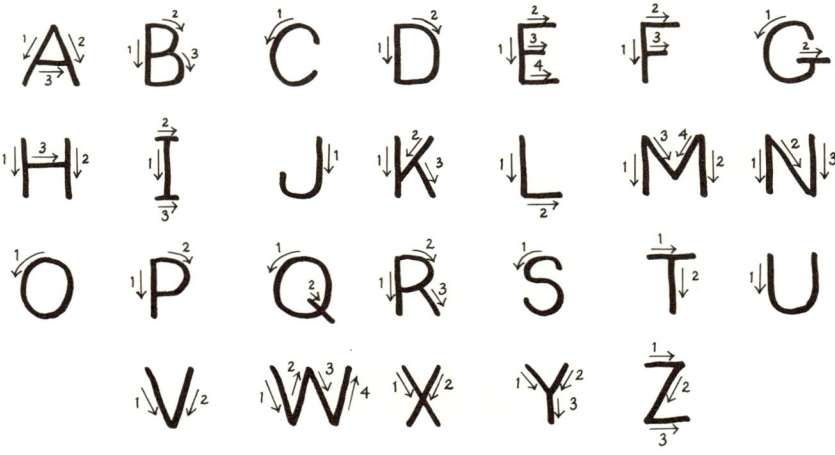

Figure 3

This program uses a simplified manuscript printing, similar to that found in most kindergarten and primary school language arts programs. You may find the numbers and arrows arbitrary, and to be unlike the way you print one or more letters. Feel free to stick to your method of writing letters, but carefully consider any variations in the actual *form* of a letter. This particular alphabet has been chosen to minimize confusions between letters and is closely similar to those used in most first grades and kindergartens. Directionality—up-and-down or left-and-right—is often difficult for youngsters, which is why I go to such lengths to minimize directional confusions between letters. M and W are made quite differently, as you can see, so that they are not so readily confused. The bars on the *I* are there to keep it from being mistaken for lowercase *l* or the numeral 1. There is no bar on the *J*, which helps to prevent *J*'s being mistaken for *I*. Okay?

Encourage your child to try to recognize her own name in capital letters and to write it in capital letters. Print it for her using large capital letters of the same form as on the poster. Another lively possibility is to get her to make her name with plastic letters or try to type it (hold your breath and set the typewriter on all caps). Once your child knows how to spell her name, learning to write it is largely a matter of time.

b. Capital letters wall strip. You might also want to make a letter strip for the top of your child's bedroom wall (or some other wall). This is especially useful if space is a problem. Any opaque white rolled paper will do—wide adding-machine paper, shelf paper, teletype roll paper, wrapping paper, and even used computer printout paper (folded twice or cut into about an 8-inch strip).

Using felt-tip marker, print the letters in some bright color (I prefer blue), as large as you can—2 to 4 inches is a reasonable size range, I think. In use, the strip might look like this:

Figure 4

I think a letter strip is best placed so that all the letters are easily visible from your child's bed. I know that this suggestion gets me perilously close to the Puritan ideal of "improving each moment" and all that, but a letter strip which your kid can see from the bed will get a lot of attention before and after naps and in the early morning. It is also one more thing that you two can talk about at bedtime.

c. Plastic letters. Sets of small (1½ × 1½ inch) plastic letters may be found in many toy and department stores, or by mail order (see Buyer's Guide, page 206, for purchasing information*).

If you choose to get the plastic letters, get the magnetized ones. These can go on the refrigerator, washer, or any other receptive metal surface, and are excellent for working with your child at odd moments.

d. Capital letter cards. You can make the letter cards for Kit 1 out of 3 × 5 inch index cards and black and blue felt-tip markers. Simply print the capital letter in black on the cards, one to a card. Draw a blue line across the bottom of each card to help your child remember which side is up (this is much more important with lowercase letters). Try to be reasonably consistent in size. Use the unlined side of the card.

An illustration:

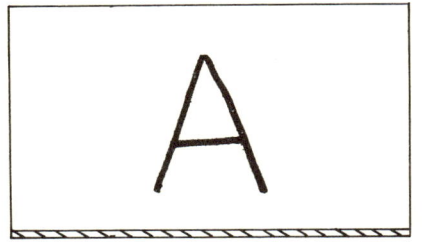
blue line

Figure 5

Follow the same simplified alphabet used on the poster.

e. Chalkboard and chalk. These should be easily found in stores near you. If not, they may be ordered by mail (see Buyer's Guide, page 205). A discussion of how your child's natural interest in writing can help him learn to read is found in Section 5 of this kit.

f. ABC blocks. You might also want to get toy store ABC blocks. These are usually not expensive and have been a standby for many years. In general, the more things you have around your child with the letters on them, the easier it will be for her to learn the letter names. (See Buyer's Guide, pages 205–210, for purchasing information on other items.)

---

* You will need the lowercase plastic letters for Kit 2, so if you want to save yourself trouble you might order capitals and lowercase at the same time.

3. Reading aloud

You should be reading to your child a total of at least 20 minutes daily—twice that, if possible. Be sure that you make reading together a warm, pleasant, relaxed time, easy and fun for both of you. Sit close together so your child can see the pages. Don't ever let it get to be a bore.

Only read to your child when he wants you to, and always stop before he gets bored. Keep it fun.

4. Books and magazines

This program is built mainly on reading and familiarity with books and written language. A good way to start out is by making a collection of children's books. Large, colorfully illustrated children's books are most likely to get your child's attention and approval. These books are available at libraries, and can be purchased inexpensively in paperback editions—see the Buyer's Guide, pages 207–208, for details.

I have no way of knowing what sort of books your child likes, or what sort you prefer. I have some difficulty with graded booklists, since children often seem to be able to understand and enjoy books of seemingly advanced phrasing and format. I recommend Nancy Larrick's excellent book *A Parent's Guide to Children's Reading* (1975), which provides good advice and background.

It is a good idea to go to the library with your child and make a considerable to-do over the selection of books to read together. It is, after all, an important matter, and deserves the careful consideration of both of you. With luck, you'll be able to find a librarian who knows children's books and is interested in helping you find the ultimate book. Be very sure to keep your child at the center of this book finding. (Many libraries have children's cards.) I think it is a good idea to have your child carry her books home, keep track of them (with some help, perhaps), and return them—underlining the point that she is an important part of this whole reading business.

Buying children's books can be expensive, though there are corners you can cut. Books—including this one—seem to be getting more expensive all the time. Paperback bookstores and publishers often have very attractive children's books in inexpensive paperback editions. I urge you to order the catalogue of the three major children's paperback publishers and take advantage of their low mail-order rates (Buyer's Guide, page 208). Another good source of inexpensive children's books is sometimes the supermarket or discount store.

A paragraph is in order here about the values exemplified in much literature for children. There is, truly, much to object to in many of the old standbys. In this area, as in any question of value, one parent may sharply disagree with another over what is or is not appropriate for children. Familiar works of children's literature have been attacked as violent, racist, sexist, militaristic, and on and on. (I was appalled recently when I re-read some of my *own* childhood books.) I urge you to look beyond the colorful pictures at what the book really says about values. I do not say (and I do not mean) that you should always shield your child from stories whose values you disagree with—I think it's sometimes better to go ahead and read the story but talk about the issue honestly.*

By reading ABC books with your child from time to time—and having them around for your child to read by herself—you'll find she'll learn many of the letters without your having to do much outright teaching.

5. Writing and scribbling

Your child should have ample writing material ready at hand that can be gotten at without his having to ask. I prefer to keep it in several places in the house—bedroom, kitchen, den, etc. Provide a chalkboard with plenty of chalk, as well as his own private supply of pencils (or washable felt-tip markers or crayons) and paper. Regular No. 2 pencils—not too sharp—are preferable, in my view, to the fat, clumsy "readi-

---

* Here is a way not to do it. My son Frank, a full-fledged railroad buff at ages three and four, thought the book *Tootle* was simply splendid. (I am convinced its values are dreadful.) After suffering in silence, on about the hundredth reading or so I just told him that I wasn't gonna read *Tootle* any more to him or to anyone else. *Ever.* I should have told him honestly the first or second time why *I* didn't like the book.

ness" pencils pushed by the schools. I've not made an all-out search, but I have never seen any persuasive evidence that these "readiness" pencils are easier to write with, or better for children, or anything else. Your child will probably find it simpler to write with an ordinary pencil, just as you do.

I think that the paper you buy should be unlined to begin with, though lined paper is acceptable. Once your child has begun to write in earnest—along about Kit 3, I think—you might begin encouraging the use of wide-lined paper. (Beginner paper is available in many drug stores, or you can buy by mail—see page 206 in the Buyer's Guide. Instructions are included in Kit 3 on the use of lines, etc.)

Whether she uses chalkboard or unlined paper, at this stage your child will probably be doing a great deal more scribbling than she does writing. Scribbling is a useful undertaking in and of itself; it is obviously good fun and may well be aesthetically pleasing to your child. Scribbling seems often to lead to writing, mapmaking, signs, and all sorts of great things. I believe that what some would regard as apparently aimless scribbling by your child is, in fact, an altogether worthwhile activity and that you would do well to encourage it.

One good way to encourage a child's interest in writing is to write little notes to him, on his blackboard or elsewhere. "Mommy loves Kevin" or "Susan has a dirty face" or "Today we go to the zoo" are messages with a high potential for audience response.

6. Writing together

Try writing stories together, or try getting your child to dictate stories to you that you print as they are dictated. Then the two of you read the stories together. These can be accounts of your trips together to the store, zoo, or wherever, or they can be more fanciful. This sort of shared work gives you many opportunities for talking about written language—letters, spelling, words, reading, etc. It also can be a great deal of fun, a thoroughly enjoyable joint endeavor. These stories are likely to become keepsakes for you—you won't believe the gems you'll come up with until you try it. It will pay you to

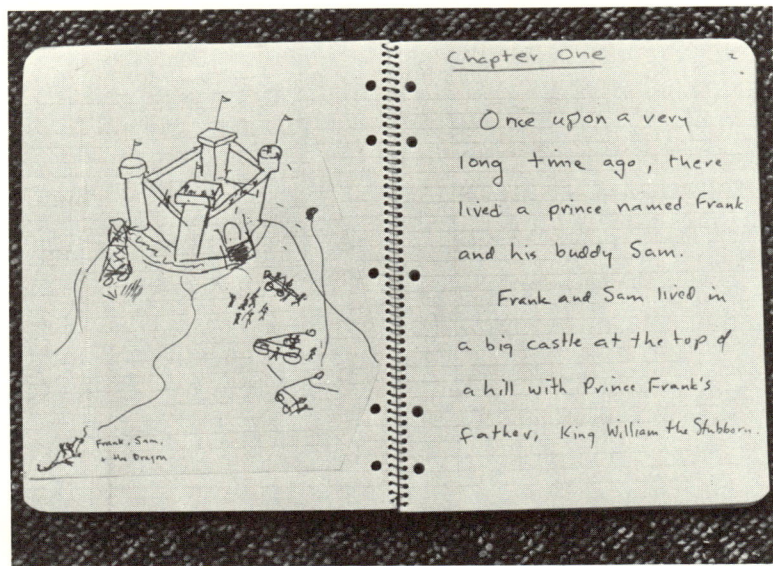

Figure 6

become adept at this, because writing together is a highly successful learning strategy for many children (Figure 6).

You may use lined or unlined paper, as you choose. (My stated preference for unlined paper applies to kids, not adults.) Use all capital letters to begin with, while your child is getting to know the capital letter names. When you finish Kit 1 you can go to capital and lowercase printing for your stories.

Label and/or write captions on her paintings or other art work.* Also you can write or have her write her own name on the paintings. Typical captions might be "Dragon eating an English muffin" or "It is raining and the house is on fire" or "This is a tree and a bird and an alligator." Let the kid sign it and date the painting—WENDY 7/75, CHARLES March 3, 1975, etc.

7. Things to make together

Parents and their children can make all sorts of things together which involve words and letters and reading. At this

---

* Ask "What is this painting?" or "What is this about?" and listen to the answer with respect.

stage, a letters scrapbook is not a bad idea. Together, you and your child go through old newspapers and magazines and cut out several examples of each capital letter. Then you sort and paste them in a scrapbook (Figure 7). (Take one or two pages per letter and leave some space—you'll want to add lowercase letters and pictures later.)

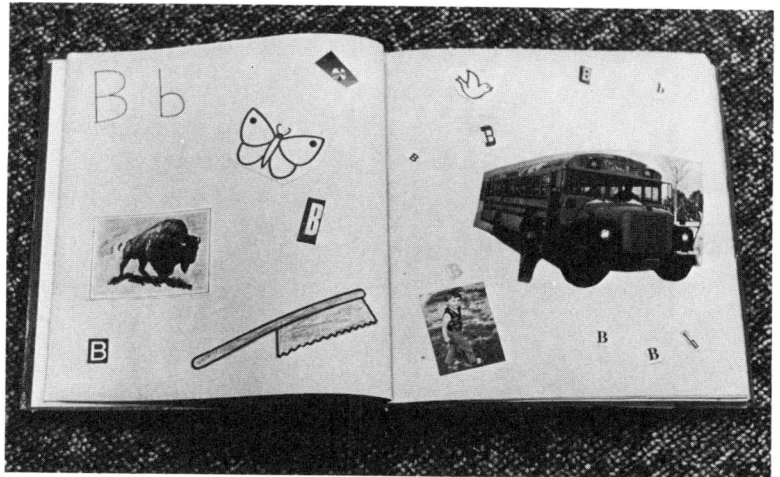

Figure 7

Another thing you can do is to cut large capital letters (10 inches high) out of construction paper and have him color or paint them or make a collage by pasting scraps of paper on them as in the illustration (Figure 8). Then you both can mount them on stiff paper and put them on the wall, or you can make a mural by mounting them on a long sheet of roll paper, butcher paper, or computer printout paper.

A salt tray (or sand tray, if you prefer) can be made of a shoebox top (or cookie tray or paper plate) covered with a loose layer of salt or dry sand. You and your child practice writing the letters in the salt with one or two fingers. This has great teaching advantages—the child gets tactile and kinesthetic feedback writing in the salt with her fingers. What is more, it's cheap, easy, and you can erase simply by shaking the tray a little from side to side.

Figure 8

Another activity which I enjoy (and which my wife regards with misgivings) is fingerpainting. Like fishing and watching sunrises, fingerpainting is clearly good for the soul. I admit that undertaking to fingerpaint with an active four-year-old requires solid preparation and effective supervision, but the result is well worth the trouble. Of course, finger-paintings change from one moment to the next, and, because fingerpainting is so plastic and imaginative, you don't want to load it down with some dull objectives like "We're gonna fingerpaint an *H* today." Better you should just fingerpaint together, and in the course of it you—and she—can make all the *H*'s you want to, but you should also make swirls and handprints and flowers and snakes and all the other nifty things that you can make fingerpainting. (Fingerpaints and paper are commercially available; see the Buyer's Guide, page

204; I have also included a recipe for homemade fingerpaint in the Buyer's Guide.)

A related activity is fingerpaint printing. You fingerpaint on a nonabsorbent plastic surface (a Formica countertop, for example, or a vinyl floor); then when you get something you want to keep (like the letter *H*, maybe, or an especially good flower), lay a sheet of newsprint down carefully over the fingerpaints, press gently, lift, and there you have a print. (This is great for flowers and for letters like *A*, *H*, *W*, etc., which do not face a special way—it will not work so well with *F*, *G*, *J*, *L*, *N*, *P*, *Q*, *R*, *S*, and *Z* because they come out backward.)

Still another activity you may enjoy doing together is making the capital letters out of Play-Doh or modeling clay. Roll the stuff out in "snakes," then twist it to form the letters. This is *most* helpful in teaching letters a child is having difficulty learning.

A final and related activity is to make cookies either shaped like the letters or decorated with the letters in colored frosting. Stiff cookie dough will roll and twist into letter shapes rather like Play-Doh—I prefer a dry cookie mix, incidentally. Upon baking, these letters have a tendency to spread, but they are eaten with gusto. The quick and easy way to get letter cookies is to make frosting letters on homemade or store-bought cookies using a tube of frosting to squirt the letters onto the cookies.

8. Own words

I have already discussed the usefulness of teaching your child to recognize and perhaps write her own name in capital letters. Your child may also want to learn other words—a pet's name, your name, etc. Where possible, print the word on an index card for your child, using all capital letters.

9. Sight words

These are common words which your child might learn to recognize "at sight," whenever you two encounter them in your reading. In later kits these words will include the many necessary but oddly spelled words like *here, said, come, were, their,* and so on. For right now, in Kit 1, the sight words that you can work on are the capital letter words *I* and *A*, as well as initial abbreviations—TV, EDT, PM, NFL, CBS, etc. Be alert for these in your reading together, and when you come to such a "word" point it out, let your kid read it, or read it together.

The purpose of all this is to show your child that there are things he can read, that there will be more and more of them, and that reading is not some exclusively grown-up activity, but, rather, is something that he can learn to do.

10. Games

Here are several games you can play to help your child learn the letters. These games are ordinarily played just for fun, so be careful not to add any pressure to them.

a. Win-my-cards game. Have a stack of letter cards and turn through them one at a time. As you place each card face up in a pile, the child has a chance to win your card by naming the letter. Those she names correctly she gets. Those she misses you keep (once you tell her the name of the letter she missed). At the end of the game count up her score in number of cards. It helps to ham it up, with exaggerated anguish or glee—especially as she gets more and more cards from your dwindling supply. You're both working toward the day when she wins all the cards.

Important: You should begin with a *limited* set of cards—just the ones your child knows and a few others that she might or might not know. The child should almost always get more cards than you do. Add cards as you go along.

b. "This is–show me–what is" game. This one is for learning new letters and borrows a Montessori technique of exposing children to new things. First show the child the letter card and say, "This is *A*. Say *A*." (The child repeats the letter name.) Then you talk about the distinctive features of *A* to him, calling attention to the sharp point and two legs and the bridge and anything else that seems remarkable about it and possibly interesting to him, mentioning the letter name often. Encourage him to trace it with his finger. Then say, "Show me *A*. Say *A*."

Once he has done this, express satisfaction and praise.

Then ask, "What is this?" Hopefully he will say "A," but it doesn't always work out that way. If it doesn't, don't worry or show disapproval. Just go back over the features again, and try to clear up any confusion. Then drop it and come back later. Don't run it into the ground.

c. Letter-of-the-day game. Each day you ask the child which letter she wants for her special letter today and show her the cards or the poster to pick from. After she picks one, having suitably deliberated, you make it your business to help her find the letter in signs, newspaper ads, labels, TV commercials, letterheads, book titles, magazines, etc. I suspect you will both find considerable pleasure and surprise at all the places you can find letters. (Be advised that Q and Z are tough—so pick some easy ones first like *E, A, O, S, R, T, M, N*.) When she has a particular letter for this day she keeps that card in a special spot—on her dresser, chalkboard, the refrigerator door, etc.

d. Letters-on-the-tree game. Once the child learns a letter, tack or tape that letter card on his wall or a bulletin board in a treelike array. It doesn't sound so good, but it seems to work. If you like, draw a tree with branches on a large sheet of paper or poster board. Then put the letters on the branches as they are learned (Figure 9).

e. Letters grab bag game. For this game you will need a No. 6 brown paper lunch bag (or small opaque plastic or cloth bag about 6 × 10 inches).

You'll also need a set of 52 white cardboard two-inch squares marked with two sets of uppercase letters (and numbered from one to five on the reverse), four red squares, and four green squares. You'll need a game board, laid out on a large sheet of paper poster board or tagboard (a legal-size folder spread open is perfect). Finally, you will need small markers, or pieces, to move around the board—bolts, thimbles, rocks, or small plastic toys will do fine (Figure 10).

To play the letters grab bag game you put the letter squares and the green and red squares into the bag, and each player draws to see who goes first. The player drawing the highest number starts—in case of ties, draw again.

Each player draws a square from the bag and *names the*

Figure 9

letter, then moves his or her piece the number of places indicated on the back of the square. (In hardnosed families if you can't name the letter you don't get to move.) If a player draws a red square he or she loses a turn; a green square gives an extra turn.

As each square is drawn, it is put aside and not returned to the bag. If you use all the squares before someone reaches *The End,* replace them in the bag and keep playing.

The game is over when a player reaches *The End.* (Make your own rules about whether you need the *exact* number to finish.)

This game is a great favorite.

A variation is to put alternating green or red dots every five places. Players landing on green get an extra turn, while players landing on red miss their next turn.

Don't be afraid to experiment with your own letter games.

Unit I: Readiness · 129

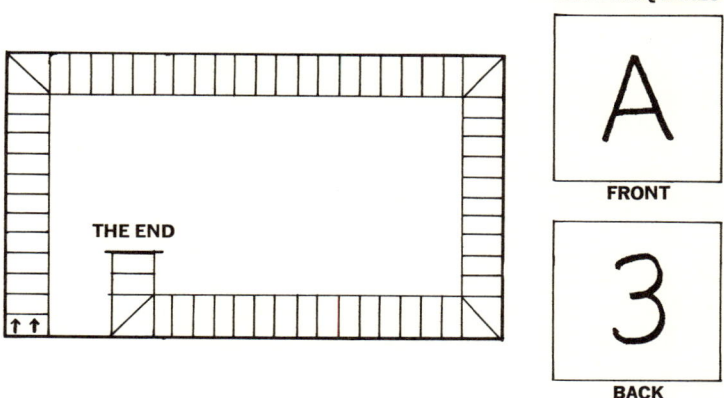

Figure 10

Any games you invent will probably fit your child better than my games will. (There are letter-learning games commercially available—see pages 209–211 of the Buyer's Guide for a listing.)

11. Mail

The postman can be a valuable ally in teaching your child to read. In later kits we will consider all sorts of activities involving your child in writing and receiving mail. For now, a solid first step might be to subscribe to one of the several good magazines for young children (see Buyer's Guide, page 208). These are usually not expensive, and they have interesting stories, games, and puzzles that you can do together.

Also of great interest to some children because of the beautiful pictures and the frequency of issue, the *National Geographic School Bulletin* is both inexpensive and attractive. This is a brief weekly, lavishly illustrated with color photographs of all sorts of things, with accompanying text. The text is very likely to be rather advanced for your kid, but the pictures might be just the thing.

12. Media

You may find television useful in helping your child learn the letters, too. I am distrustful of TV, especially in large doses and most especially for children over six. Carefully controlled and monitored, and in moderation (no more than one hour per day, certainly), television can enrich your child's world.

"Sesame Street," "The Electric Company," and "Captain Kangaroo" are my own favorites. These programs pay varying amounts of attention to letter learning, and are lively and usually fun to watch. "Sesame Street" is especially good, I think, and worth making a special effort to get your child to see.

13. If your child keeps on having trouble learning and remembering the letter names, take this as a warning to you to *go slow*. It often requires substantial periods of time for young children to learn their letters. Please don't rush things.

At our present state of knowledge about learning disabilities, it is hard for even the most expert clinician to diagnose reading disability in preschool children. Since the incidence of reading disability is estimated at between one in five and one in twenty boys, and perhaps one in fifty girls,* parents are well advised to be aware that their child *could* have such a reading disability.

I advise parents to seek a Learning Disabilities Evaluation if their child both (1) has difficulty learning beginning reading skills at home (such as letter names, letter-sound associations, and recognizing familiar words as wholes) *and* (2) then *continues* to have difficulty with reading after he or she starts school. This is especially true if there is a family history of reading problems (siblings, parents, uncles, grandparents), or if the child has a history of speech difficulties.

Kit 2: The lowercase letter names

MATERIALS

Lowercase letters poster
Lowercase letter cards
Plastic lowercase letters

---

* These figures are mine—you can find almost any figure you want in the literature. These are among the more conservative and seem about right to me. The fact of sex difference is of considerable interest, but is not understood.

Goal

The purpose of this kit is to help your child learn the names of the lowercase letters.

Go on to Kit 3 when your child can name all the lowercase letters in any order.

Instructions

1. What to do

In this section I will describe generally the activities of Kit 2; for more detail see the sections of this kit which follow.

First, introduce your child to the lowercase letters. Many authorities prefer that you call them *lowercase* instead of *little* or *small* because of the confusion that is caused children by the fact that some "little" letters are as tall as the capitals: f, b, l, etc.

(It can also be argued that the phrase *lowercase* has little meaning for a young child, while *small* or *little* or even *baby letters* may be easy for him to deal with. You are the best judge, I think, of whether it will confuse your child to call lowercase letters *small*. It is, of course, always possible to explain later that *lowercase* is another name for the little letters.)

It seems to me that the best place to start learning the lowercase letters is with the letters the child already knows—those which closely resemble their capital letter forms. The letters $c, f, k, j, o, p, s, t, u, v, w, x, y$, and z will probably be learned rather quickly—perhaps your child already knows them by now. To begin with, find out which letters he knows by simply asking him, or by playing the win-the-cards game, or by any other means you find appropriate.

Print the child's name for him, using capital and lowercase letters.

Make a poster of the lowercase letters with their capital letter forms, and make letter cards for the lowercase letters.

Continue to read aloud together, and go to the library and bookstore or book counter as often as you can manage.

Write stories together, and encourage your child's scribbling and attempts to write. Leave printed notes and messages for him and work together on your homemade ABC book of letters cut out of old magazines and papers and pasted in a scrapbook.

132 · *Teaching Young Children to Read at Home*

Talk about the lowercase letters when the chance presents itself, and play letter learning games together.

Teach your child to recognize his own name, as well as the word *a*.

Watch "Sesame Street" together, and talk about what you have seen.

Use the written language in your environment—signs, labels, headlines, books, magazines—to teach the letter names, and the idea that reading is useful and pleasant.

When your child knows the names of all the lowercase letters, go ahead to Kit 3, even if you haven't completed (or even started on) all the activities I suggest in Kit 2.

2. Things for you to make or buy

a. Lowercase letter posters and wall strip. Using felt-tip marker and following the general guidelines for poster making discussed in Kit 1 (page 115), make a wall poster of the lowercase letters to hang beside or near the capital letters poster from Kit 1.

For those who found the chart of capital letters on page 116 helpful, here is a similar chart of lowercase letters and how to print them:

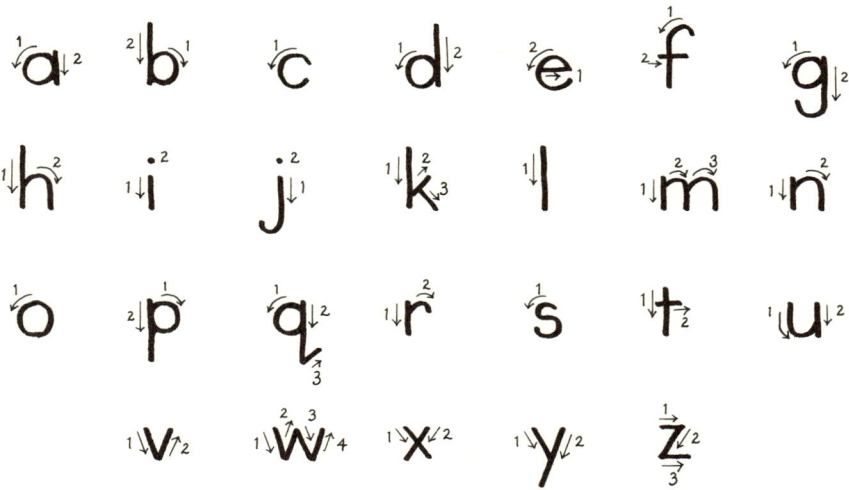

Figure 11

There are minor differences from publisher to publisher in handwriting systems, but none of these is so serious, in my judgment, as to be likely to cause problems for your child. Some authorities give the q a tail, for instance, while others prefer it tailless, like this q. I repeat: These differences are decidedly minor, and should be easily reconciled when and if your child encounters them. This manuscript alphabet was deliberately selected to be easy for young children to recognize and print, and for its close similarity to the writing systems most commonly used in American schools and kindergartens.

Here are two possibilities for lowercase letter posters and one model for a wall strip:

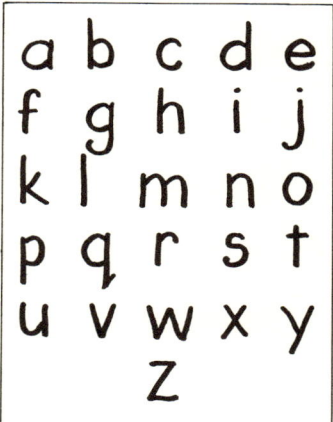

Wall strip

| a b c d e f g h i j k l m n o p q r s t u v w x y z |

Figure 12

A combination poster is shown in Figure 13.

b. Plastic lowercase letters. As I advised in Kit 1 (page 117), the magnetized plastic lowercase letters have many uses and are well worth their small cost. You may buy these at most toy stores or by mail. (See Buyer's Guide, page 206, for purchasing information.)

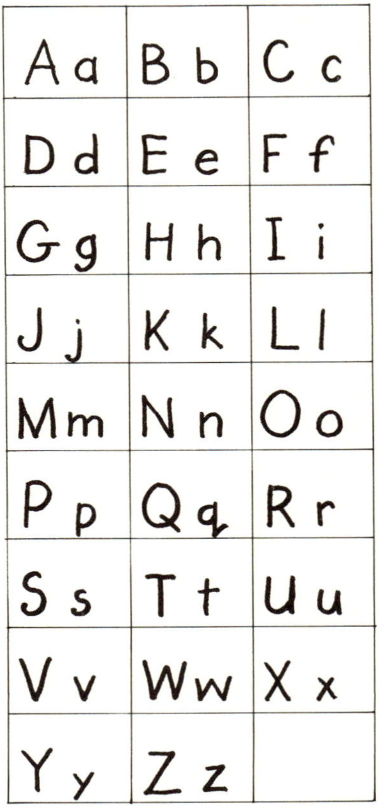

A a	B b	C c
D d	E e	F f
G g	H h	I i
J j	K k	L l
M m	N n	O o
P p	Q q	R r
S s	T t	U u
V v	W w	X x
Y y	Z z	

Figure 13

c. Lowercase letter cards. You can make lowercase letter cards for Kit 2 out of 3 × 5 inch index cards and felt-tip marker. Print the lowercase letters on the cards, one to a card. Try to be consistent in size and use the unlined side of the card. Follow the same simplified alphabet you used on the poster. Figure 14 is an example.

d. "Feelie" letters. These may be made in a number of ways and from a variety of materials. The basic point is to make a letter which your child may learn by touch as well as by sight.

One of the easiest ways to make feelie letters is to draw the letter on paper toweling, cloth, construction paper, or some other highly textured material. Then you cut it out and

Figure 14

paste it onto a smooth paper or cardboard surface, so that there is a sharp contrast of "feel" between the letter and its background. There, in essence, you have the feelie letter (Figure 15).

These feelie letters are especially useful in teaching chil-

Figure 15

dren the letters hardest for them to learn. Basically, what you do is have your child trace over the letter's shape with her fingers, really trying to get the feel of it. It sometimes helps to "follow the arrows"—have the child feel the letter as she might write it.

Blindfold and other guessing games may be played with these letters (see Games, page 140).

e. Magic slate. These old favorites are again commercially available (see Buyer's Guide, page 206). In the unlikely event that someone doesn't know what a magic slate is, I'll try to describe it. This slate has a dark waxed backing, covered by a grayish plastic sheet which is written on with a stylus. When the plastic sheet is lifted, the slate erases as if by magic. Presto!

These things have delighted many youngsters over the past 50 or so years they have been around. By all means get one if you can.

3. Reading aloud

A basic requirement of this program is that you read aloud to your child 20 minutes or more every day, in circumstances as pleasant as you can manage, from materials the child wants to hear. (Stock market quotations, Kant, or today's news from the Middle East ordinarily will not qualify.)

I'll suggest several books—most notably Nancy Larrick's *A Parent's Guide to Children's Reading*—but the ultimate judges are you and your child. Don't feel that you should enjoy a book just because it got an award or an authority recommended it.

I push 20 minutes per day of reading aloud as a minimum—more than that is fine, up to the point that it begins to become a drag to one or both of you, or threatens to swallow up all your time together, or all your child's playtime. (In my experience, what reading aloud mostly swallows up is naptime.)

4. Books and magazines

Continue your trips together to the library. If you haven't started yet, by all means do so. Taking your child on a special errand to get books for both of you speaks very clearly about the importance of books, libraries, and reading.

You might want to give some thought to subscribing to one of the magazines for children listed in the Buyer's Guide. While this is an expense, it is also a nice experience for your child to have his or her very own magazine come in the mail. A subscription makes a fine birthday or other gift that keeps on coming.

Parents who want to know more about children's literature are advised to get a copy of M. Arbuthnot, *Literature for Children;* and to look over current and back issues of *The Horn Book,* a magazine for children's librarians, and the *Children's Library Bulletin.* Also, the *New York Times Book Review* devotes one issue a year to children's books. *Ms.* magazine has a regular feature on nonsexist literature for children which is well worth looking into. Nancy Larrick's book entitled *A Parent's Guide to Children's Reading* (1975) is a classic in the field; it has been revised and is available in paperback. I regard this as a best buy.

5. Writing and scribbling

Check this section in Kit 1—make sure you have ample writing materials available to your child so that they can be used when the notion strikes. You will probably want to set some limits about these materials and their use, as well as a few "don'ts." (One wall of my son William's room still shows early felt-tip marker scribbling, and his brother Frank managed to make his mark indelibly on the door of our shared summer cottage.)

Don't be so concerned with the form of any letters your child should happen to make at this stage. I think you should be grateful for anything you can get.

Most young children have real difficulty in writing letters. Lowercase seems—and probably *is*—harder for them, though the Montessorians routinely teach four- and five-year-olds to write the lowercase letters. By all means show your child how to make the lowercase letters if he or she wants to learn—don't push it, though. Writing should be an entirely voluntary activity at this stage, I believe.

6. Writing together

As I discussed in Kit 1, there are many things you and your child can write together. Your writing can be factual: the story of your activities together, a journal, accounts of notable events (birthday parties, trips, ballgames, etc.). And, then again, you can write fiction, such as putting into writing some favorite bedtime story (I need not remind you that some of the very best children's literature was written that way). Mine have included the adventures of an imaginary friend or friends (a dragon who dotes on marshmallows, his new friend the bird, and a boy whose name was first Frank and is now William), as well as a fantasy story of a prince named Sam who refuses to slay—and thus befriends—a dragon. (Dragons have been very big around my place for a number of years now.)

Let me try to persuade you to keep a journal together—or maybe even a diary, where you write down the events of the day and any thoughts you may want to record. This will surely be a keepsake. All you have to do is try to write a few lines each day. It should make for fascinating reading at the time and also when you go back and see "what we did last month," etc. Another good thing about this sort of writing is that it helps your child to learn the relationships of written and spoken language naturally—by using them.

7. Things to make together

All those things which were suggested in Kit 1, Section 7, for you to make using capital letters can also be made with lowercase letters.

Add lowercase letters to the letters scrapbook described on page 123. Go through old magazines and newspapers together and cut out different examples of each lowercase letter, and paste them in the scrapbook. Be sure to leave room for pictures to be added in Kit 3.

You can cut lowercase letters out of construction paper, paint or color or paste things on them, and mount them on contrasting paper. Then you can put it all up on a wall or bulletin board, or on a mural, and it makes a fine display.

You can, if you really feel ambitious, make a letters bedspread or quilt or curtains, by cutting letter shapes out of scraps of cloth and sewing them on a contrasting fabric backing. This can be very attractive and can also be a delightful learning activity when done together. One Cambridge mother made such a bedspread with her son when he was sick, cutting the letters out with pinking shears and letting him help place them on the spread before she sewed them on the machine. As is true of the journal, you not only have a fine learning experience, but you also are making a keepsake.

By all means repeat the things you made for capital letters with the lowercase. For example, if capital letter cookies worked for you and your kid, make lowercase letter cookies too.

8. Own words

Show your child his name written in capitals *and* lowercase letters. (This is, in fact, a good place to start teaching the lowercase letters.)

Also show him the names of the family, pets, etc., written with both upper and lowercase. The easiest explanation of capitals that I know is, "Capital letters are used in a lot of ways, and one of the most important ways is to begin people's names." You need not go into a discussion of the rules for capitalization in English unless, of course, your child insists.

You might go so far as to print the names of members of the family on placecards for the dinner table, or on napkins or other things to be distributed. Your pupil might also be given the job of sorting the incoming mail into shoeboxes or similar bins marked with each family member's name.

I like the idea of word cards, 3 × 5 or 5 × 8 inch index cards or 3 × 11 inch construction paper cards with the child's own words printed on.*

9. Sight words

These are the common words that your child will need to know in order to read simple children's books. By learning to recognize a few of these at a time, she will eventually come to know most of them.

In Kit 1 your child learned to recognize the single capital letter words *I* and *A*, as well as caps used as abbreviations.

---

* If you have *not* read Sylvia Ashton-Warner's book *Teacher,* you probably should, not so much as pedagogical how-to but because you deserve a treat. *Teacher* is a fine book, and in it you get to know Sylvia Ashton-Warner, as talented and sensitive a person as you're ever likely to meet. One of the many ways she teaches is with "own words" on cards and elsewhere.

In this kit we will concentrate on your child's learning to recognize the words *a* and *the* (or *The*), when you both encounter them in your reading together or on signs, labels, newspapers, and so forth.

Don't try to push learning a lot of sight words just now—concentrate on getting the letters straight and learning to recognize the sight words *I, A, a, the, The*.

10. Games

You can use lowercase letters to play any of the games discussed in Kit 1, pages 126–129.

The *win-my-cards game* is a good one to use, adding a few lowercase letters at a time.

"*This is–show me–what is*" can be used to teach difficult letters effectively.

Letter-of-the-day game is, I think, an all-around winner, especially after your child has learned the capitals and is working on the lowercase letters. This game leads easily into the *letters-on-the-tree* routine, where today's letter selected at breakfast gets talked about and looked for all day and by bedtime is known well enough to "put on the tree."

The *grab bag game* is easily converted to lowercase. Add lowercase squares (with high number values) to the capitals until you have all 26 lowercase letters. You might want to take away some of the duplicate best-known capital letters as the number of lowercase squares grows—this is so the game will move quickly and so the lowercase letters will get a big play.

The matching game can be played solitaire or with you assisting. Probably you'll do better to start your child out playing the matching game with you there to help.

Spread the uppercase letter cards out, face up, on a rug on one side of the child and the lowercase letters face up on the other side. The child's task is to match the uppercase to lowercase letters, placing the lowercase cards with the uppercase ones.

Playing together, you take turns matching letters until all are done. When more than one child is playing you can, if you wish, keep score by counting the number of pairs matched by each player. This is rarely necessary, I find, and can be a negative experience for whoever "loses."

11. Mail

As I pointed out in the previous kit, the mailman can be a formidable ally in teaching your child about written language.

Let your child sort the incoming mail for various members of the family. I suggested in Kit 1 that you subscribe to some magazines for your child, so that there will be mail that's actually for her. You might also send her a note yourself now and then, and, if either parent travels or is out of town, picture postcards are most welcome. Relatives and friends can be enlisted in this effort, and you may thus find a pen pal with unsuspected talent. Cards and letters, of course, have to be answered, which provides a fine, natural reason for your child to combine written and spoken language in composing replies for you to write down.

With a little effort, you can develop a burgeoning correspondence involving your child, which should both increase her interest in writing and reading—and show her as well that these can be useful tools for *her*.

12. Media

In Kit 1, I suggested that you and your child watch television's "Sesame Street" or "The Electric Company" often.

I will suggest here that your child learn the alphabet song, if he doesn't already know it. You both can sing it together, pointing to the letters on the poster. This is a dandy bedtime or naptime activity, and I heartily recommend it.

The song is best learned, I believe, after your child knows the uppercase letter names, so that you avoid the confusion in so many kids' minds about *LMNOP* being one letter. I assume *you* know someone who will teach it to you, if necessary.

Another media thing you might do is get a record of the song (see the Buyer's Guide) and of any other letter songs you can find.

Still another—and this is a mindblower—is to make a Super 8 animated film of the letters, using plastic cutout letters, a movie camera that has a "single frame" switch, lights, tripod, and patience.

Basically, in making animated movies, what you do is take one frame at a time and move the letters slightly with each frame. Figure out your own pattern plan and background.

A splendid book about making animated films is *Teaching Film Animation to Children,* by Yvonne Anderson (1971).

Kit 3: Introducing letter-sound associations

MATERIALS

> Movable alphabet cards
> ABC books

GOAL

The goal of this kit is to get your child to associate sounds with most of the letters. It is *not* important that your child know *all* the letter-sounds just yet, but by the time you move to Kit 4 your child should be reasonably clear on these points:

1. Letters can stand for sounds.
2. Words have sounds in them.
3. Words have "beginning sounds."

INSTRUCTIONS

1. What to do

Since this kit is concerned with introducing letter-sound associations, all the activities of the kit will involve beginning sounds in words.

One of the best, traditional ways to make children aware of letter-sound associations is the ABC book. There are many of these commercially available, as well as in the libraries, and in this kit I will describe how to make your own from cut-up magazines and newspapers.

When your child is in the mood and you have time, sit down for a few minutes and read the ABC book together. Let him tell you what each letter is "for"—"*K* is for kangaroo," for example, or "what letter kangaroo begins with."* There are

---

* If your child in speaking substitutes one sound for another, or can't say certain speech sounds, prudence and common sense dictate that you *not*

inexpensive posters and wall strips for letter-sound associations available (see pages 209–210 in the Buyer's Guide). These are not difficult for you to make together, in fact. Also easy to make are the movable alphabet cards, which we begin using in this kit and continue using throughout the program.

While working in this kit and the next it will be useful if you can increase the amount of reading aloud that you and your child are doing to 15 to 20 minutes twice a day (or more), when possible. Try to hold the book so that your child can see it. You can begin talking about letter-sounds very naturally, going from your games of "What's that letter?" and "Can you find an S on this line?" to "Where's a letter that says 'ssss'?" or "Do you know what letter says 'ssss' in 'Sesame Street'?"

You can also play "beginning sounds" games with your child. There are several variations which might be fun. I like the "I'm thinking of something that begins with __" game, and both my sons still think the "I'm going to Boston" game is delightful. I list in Section 10 several such games which have been played successfully by parents and small children.

Continue to encourage your child's attempts at writing or "drawing the letters." Make sure writing materials are available.

Begin or continue writing stories to your child's dictation, and/or keeping a journal together. These can be excellent teaching devices (see pages 137–138).

Look for the sight word *and* in your reading together as well as on signs, labels, etc.

A *note of caution,* which applies to all the activities of this kit, is that the sounds to be associated with the letters vary in some cases. You might point out that letters like C, G, A, E, I, O, U, and Y sometimes represent other sounds, but

---

push on learning to speak "properly" the sounds in question.

For example, a child who says *th* for *s* should not be expected to say "S is for snake and soap and sugar" as you would say it. The reply "*Eth* ith for thnake" is entirely acceptable. A child can read and understand a sound without being able to say it. Most, though not all, speech difficulties are developmental and are resolved without therapy. Many speech problems *do* require professional diagnosis and treatment, though. If your child has a speech irregularity, my advice is to have him or her checked by age five by a qualified speech professional and if therapy is indicated to get on with it early, rather than putting it off.

that for now we'll concentrate on learning just one sound for each letter; we'll learn the others later. When ambiguity exists* explain it, but at this point in the program the speech sounds associated with the letters should be as follows:

A as in *alligator*
C as in *cat*
E as in *egg*
G as in *go*
I as in *if*
O as in *octopus*
U as in *uncle*
Y as in *yes*

Another caution is to be aware that, when you teach "C says *kuh*," you're including an *uh* sound in there that C doesn't actually say. This can lead to some problems later on—for instance, a child putting sounds together can encounter difficulty getting *cat* out of "kuh-a-tuh." This sort of blending *can* be taught, though, and the problem overcome, but you need to know beforehand that it exists. A way to minimize it is to cut the letter sound off as sharply as you can—practice saying P, T, G, B, K, H, J, and the others, trying to minimize the inclusion of other sounds.

When your child and you are fairly well into the business of learning the sounds, and when you are playing the games (or have tried them) described above, move gradually into Kit 4. Try to make certain your child understands the three concepts outlined on the first page of this kit:

1. Letters can stand for sounds.
2. Words have sounds in them.
3. Words have "beginning sounds."

2. Things for you to make or buy

a. Movable alphabet cards. A movable alphabet was devised by Maria Montessori for her Casa dei Bambini in

---

* You're going to encounter occasionally different sounds in some ABC books and elsewhere—G for *giraffe*, for instance, or E for *eagle*. The explanation given above is an honest statement of the facts, and usually is sufficient.

Italy. The letters, printed on small squares, are moved about to form words. Today, these materials are used widely in Montessori schools and also in commercial reading programs. Thus, in later kits, you and your child will be able to form several words in succession simply by changing letters around. Suppose he starts with the letters *M-A-N*, spelling *man*.

Then he	replaces the *M* with *P*,	*pan,*
then he	interchanges *N* with *P*,	*nap,*
then he	replaces *N* with *M*,	*map,*
and so on.		

Considerably more flexible than workbooks or other text materials, the movable alphabet seems especially suited to teaching young children. It lends itself well to games and informal learning situations. And it can be used by one child working alone, or by a child and tutor, or by small groups of children and adults.

This program utilizes a special homemade version of the movable alphabet, which the tutor prints on 3 × 5 inch index cards with red or black felt-tip markers. In Kits 3 and 4 we begin by associating speech sounds with the letters.

Preparing the Cards

MATERIALS:

Black and red felt-tip markers
Pencil
3 × 5 inch index cards

Finished cards should look like Figure 16.

You may make capital letters, but they are not absolutely necessary.

·Step 1: Drawing the "baseline"

The baseline is a light pencil line 3 inches from the top of each card. This line helps you to center the letters and to align the cards when you put them together (Figure 17).

Figure 16

A quick way to get the baseline drawn is to use another 3 × 5 inch card as a ruler. If you place the second card horizontally over the first card, held vertically, you can draw a line exactly 3 inches from the top of the first card.

·Step 2: Printing the letters

Use red marker for the vowels *A, E, I, O, U*, black marker for the other letters.

With a little practice, you can make reasonable approximations of the small letter forms. These should be about 1½ inches high for *m, n, c*, etc., and about 3 inches high for *p, t, g*, etc.

In printing the letters, remember to use the simplified letter forms.

    b. Letter-sound association poster or wall strip. You can make this yourself, either drawing the pictures (they don't have to be all *that* good) or cutting them out of magazines. (My strong preference, if cutout pictures are used, is to make the poster together with your child, letting him cut and paste wherever possible.)

I like the device of using a simple set of word associations for the letters, in which a single familiar noun is associated

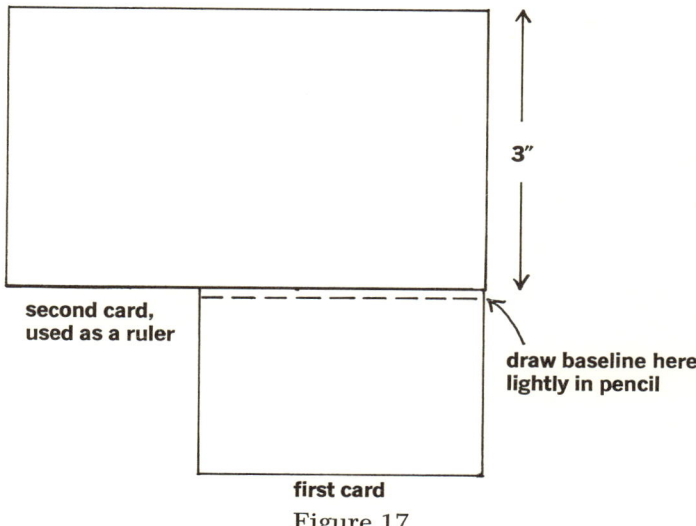

Figure 17

with each letter. The alphabet below is designed with young children in mind and features nouns selected for familiarity. If a word seems inappropriate for your child, feel free to substitute one of your own. (You might want to substitute *yolk,* say, for my *yoyo,* or *lion* for *ladder,* or "Sesame Street's" *Oscar* for my *octopus.* Fine; go ahead.)

A apple	J jar	S snake
B boy	K key	T table
C cat	L ladder	U umbrella
D dog	M man	V vase
E elephant	N nail	W woman
F fish	O octopus	X x-ray (exit?)
G girl	P penny	Y yo-yo
H hat	Q quarter	Z zipper
I Indian	R ring	

The layout of an ABC poster is important, I think. The objects need to be *very clearly* associated with the letters—about the last thing you need is confusion here. My preference is to divide the poster into 26 cells, or blocks, and put the letters (capital and lowercase) and one picture all well inside the block.

As I have said, I rather prefer magazine cutouts that your child has had a hand in, at least for some of the pictures. You can draw the ones that you can't find in magazines.

You can make a poster or a letter strip, or both, or neither, as you choose. These can make learning the letter-sound associations *so* much easier, though, and you can always buy one if you just can't make it.

3. Reading aloud

As I mentioned in the instructions, in this kit and the next you should try to have your child read to *more than* 20 minutes daily, if you can possibly manage it. I think that an average of 30 minutes or more per day of reading will be very helpful, especially if it is done in more than one sitting.

Don't let my urging you to spend more time reading make you read when your child really doesn't want to. Be careful to keep it pleasant, desirable. Don't let reading aloud get to be a chore, whatever you do—at least not for your child. (There may be occasions—a good many of them, perhaps—when there are things that you'd rather do than sit down and read *Peter Rabbit* for the thirty-fifth time to a child whose motivation, you suspect, has something to do with putting off bedtime.)

Keep it emotionally warm, too, and supportive. I think you should hold your kids when you read to them or at least sit next to them.*

4. Books and magazines

You will do well to get several ABC books from the library, bookstore, or the collections of friends whose children have outgrown them.

Please do not restrict your reading aloud time to ABC books—this can get dull for both of you. Leave ABC books

---

* With no evidence at all, I am still convinced that one of the main reasons I enjoy reading so much is that I long ago associated the love, warmth, and closeness of my parents' reading aloud to me with reading itself. Now when I read, I feel good, loved, safe, and okay, and the world backs off a little bit. This is escapist beyond question, but it does beat tranquilizers, booze, and all that.

with your child at naptime, say, or at odd moments during the day.

The "Sesame Street" books and magazine feature the letters prominently, and they are lively and colorful (see Buyer's Guide, page 209). There have also been a number of giveaway "Sesame Street" posters and the like in the past, but these may not be available any longer. Check on free materials with the ETV station in your area which carries the "Sesame Street" broadcasts.

Try occasionally reading aloud brief parts of newspaper articles or other things that you think might interest your child. Don't overdo it.

Mainly in your reading you should still read the things that your child wants to hear or that you feel fairly certain he will like.

5. Writing and scribbling

Keep writing your child notes, especially on her chalkboard, but also maybe tucked away in among her pajamas or under her pillow or beside her breakfast plate or in a regular place (like a family message center).

If you don't have a family message center try establishing one. All it takes is a chalkboard or bulletin board in some central place where each member of the family looks for messages, notes, calls, etc. (A note pad and magnets for the refrigerator door is what we use.) Having a place on the board and *actually getting messages* is a big deal for a four-year-old—most especially if there are older children who get messages too.

Lacking a family message center, you might do well to establish a regular place where your child can expect to find notes from you.

Encourage your child to write and scribble at any opportunity. Make quiet times when you are both writing or drawing at a table together. Also keep crayons and pencils and paper around the kitchen, for example, so that a child underfoot can be set to drawing at the kitchen table.

You should be getting somewhere by now in teaching your child to write her name. Concentrate on that for now. Even if it's scrawled, progress is progress.

Finally, encourage scribbling, drawing, and things in between. Keep steady in the faith that, someday, something legible will emerge.

6. Working together

a. Reading your writings. I have suggested that you and your child keep a journal together, or perhaps a scrapbook or photo album in which you mount snapshots or picture postcards and label them. Seize any occasion for writing something *directly related* to your child, and if possible do the writing in his presence and with his advice. Read what you write aloud as you are writing it, then read it again with your child after you've finished.

b. A scrapbook for your writings. It is a good idea to keep the stories that you write together in a scrapbook that your child can get to easily. Stories may be illustrated with artwork by your child in margins or on adjoining pages. This can become a favorite "book" of your child's; most children delight in reading about themselves.

7. Things to make together

a. Homemade ABC Book. Work on the letters scrapbook cutting out pictures from magazines and pasting them in the appropriate pages, where you have already pasted capital and lowercase letters.

Try to get several pictures of things beginning with each letter—apples, alligators, airplanes, etc.

This scrapbook can be an ongoing activity—you need not feel great urgency about "getting it finished." Finding a picture for the scrapbook might fit nicely into your letter-of-the-day game, if you're doing that. (It *is* possible to have a folder of pictures you have already torn out, which the child simply sorts through, rather than having her go through old magazines every day.)

b. In Section 6 of this kit I suggested that you and your child keep a family photo album together and that you consult on what to write beside each picture. Be sure to print the captions for maximum readability as your child grows in reading skill.

c. In Section 6 I also suggested that you collect your joint writings in a scrapbook. A portfolio or even a large envelope or folder will do, but I think you will be well advised to keep the stories in such a way that they are readily accessible for re-reading by your child at times you are not able to supervise closely.

8. Own words

Encourage your child to ask for words of her own to learn. As previously discussed, these should be important to her. If she can't think of any, you might suggest a few possible ones, but be careful not to oversell a word or the whole idea.

Print the word on an index card or tagboard, using a felt-tip marker. Or, alternatively, let her keep her words in a notebook of her own, in which you also write a story now and then.

9. Sight words

For Kit 3, the sight word to be learned is *and*.* Point it out in your reading, talk about it, spell it, show it to your child in one or two places on a page, and let him try to find other places where the word is used. Keep at it, as you read together, but *keep it a game,* and playful. Please don't make it a big deal whether or not your child can recognize the word *and,* and please, pretty please, don't let your eagerness to *teach* mess up your reading together. Point out *and* on labels, on signs, in newspapers, etc., whenever it seems appropriate to you. Remember to make it your child's word, not something you're just laying on him.

10. Games

a. I'm thinking of something that begins with __. This game is usually played with some restrictions on the things that the adult can be thinking of. You might limit it to things in the room, or on a shelf, in a drawer, seen from a window, or in a picture. All that's necessary is that your child know what the limits are. An example:

"I'm thinking of something on the kitchen table that begins with *S.*"

---

* The capitalized form, *And,* occurs only rarely, and can be learned later.

"Salt."

"Good for you! Okay, smarty, I'm thinking of something *else* on the kitchen table that begins with S."

"Spoon."

"Great! I'm still thinking of something on the kitchen table that begins with S."

"Sugar."

One tip: Don't overdo it. Be sure you demonstrate your surprise and pleasure when your child figures out what letter you were thinking of, but also be sure you don't show impatience with "wrong" or "foolish" answers. Try to see why your child answers as she does.

b. I'm going to Boston game. In this game the players take turns going through the alphabet, naming an object beginning with each letter in turn. For example, you might begin with "I'm going to Boston, and I'm taking an alligator." It would then be your child's turn to think of something beginning with B. "I'm going to Boston, and I'm taking a baby," she might say. "I'm going to Boston, and I'm taking a cat," you could respond.

And so the game goes. It requires some sophistication—and a lot of help from you on which letter comes next. Once kids understand it, however, they seem to like it. And so do I.

c. How many things can we find that begin with __? You and the child try to think of objects (or words) that begin with a particular sound. You have to be a bit watchful here, because of the pitfalls in our language and spelling. If you're doing S and the child says, "Ceiling," I think you ought to say, "Okay, fine, what else?" and not make an issue of it. In the fullness of time your child can learn how to spell *ceiling* correctly. Another related problem is with letters that children may *hear* in the word but that aren't in the spelling. For instance, some children might insist that *juice* begins with a *d*. If you'll listen to yourself say it, there *is* a hint of a *d* there, and many a child pronounces it "duce." So, be wary of thinking a kid's answer is stupid or wrong just because it isn't the one you expect. Amen.

d. Letter-sound-of-the-day game. This game is just a variation of the letter-of-the-day game in Kits 1 and 2. Each day you ask the child to pick which letter he wants for that day (possibly letters on a poster). Whenever he hears or sees a word having that first letter, you approve it heartily in some appropriate manner.

e. Win-my-cards game. This is also a variation on a game from Kits 1 and 2. Using the movable alphabet cards, you hold a few cards and turn through them one by one, and your child wins each card for which she can give an appropriate word association or a sound (either "snake" or "sss" would be okay for S, for example). You keep the ones she either misses or doesn't know. At the end of the game you count her cards with her. You can both exult about her winning so many. The great day comes finally when your child wins them all.

f. Letters grab bag game. You can modify this game to help you teach letter-sound associations in several ways. The easiest way is to change the rules. Instead of just naming the letter they draw, require players to name the letter *and* give a word beginning with it before they get to move.

Another modification is to add squares with simple drawings of the key words found on page 147, replacing the letters on the fronts of the squares (numbers remain on the backs). The child draws a square from the bag with a picture of, say, a *key* on it. She names the picture, "key," and gives the letter associated with it, "k," then gets to take her moves.

11. Mail

Keep an eye out for things you and your child can read about and send away for. My own experience with comic strip and cereal box offers has been mixed—a few outright winners offset by an equal number of losers. Nevertheless, I think there is useful experience to be had in your child's reading these offers as they come along and learning to fill out an occasional order blank. I'm not sure that the long period of waiting for the merchandise to arrive serves any useful purpose, but writing off for things *does* demonstrate, when they arrive, how useful writing can be.

Freebies, of course, are a whole lot more satisfactory to order, both in my philosophy and for my pocketbook. There exists a marvelous book called *1001 Valuable Things You*

Can Get Free, by Mort Weisenger (1974). This book includes all sorts of things like posters, pictures, films, samples, pamphlets, etc., that you and your child might enjoy. By all means get the book and send off for things together.

I am obviously trying to get you to interest your child in mail and correspondence, because this kind of activity gets the message across so clearly that writing and reading are useful and worthwhile and can lead to good things.

12. Media

In previous kits I have suggested that you watch television with your child, either "Sesame Street" or "The Electric Company" or "Captain Kangaroo"—which are my favorites. (I also expressed doubts and misgivings about children watching too much TV—I think more than an hour a day is too much. I prefer an average of 30 minutes of television a day, except for special occasions.*)

An important point here is that you actually watch the children's television show *with* your child, and talk about it with her. Invite her opinions, and listen carefully to what she says.

Kit 4: Learning letter-sound associations

MATERIALS

>Movable alphabet cards
>Books, magazines
>ABC books
>Poster or wall strip

GOAL

The goal of this kit is to help your child associate speech sounds with each of the letters. Your child will not need to know *all* the sounds each letter represents. Move to Kit 5 when he is regularly able to give one sound for each letter.

---

* Fanatics like me who have been known by their families to watch televised football for 12 hours a day around New Year's may expect some credibility problems when limiting television exposure is discussed.

Your child should have some understanding of the following seven ideas or concepts in order to learn to read. The first three were discussed in Kit 3:

1. Letters stand for sounds.
2. Spoken words have sounds in them.
3. Words have "beginning sounds."

The remaining four concepts are these:

4. Words are written with letters—you put letters together to make written words.
5. Words are spoken by saying sounds—you put sounds together to make spoken words.
6. Words can be spoken or written: You can write any word you can speak; you write words with letters and say them with sounds.
7. Words have "beginning" sounds, and often have "middle" and "ending" sounds as well.

INSTRUCTIONS

1. What to do

Keep reading aloud to your child, and venture into poetry and nursery rhymes if you haven't already done so. (Kit 5 will take up and use rhyme and rhyming games, so that reading poetry occasionally at this stage may prove helpful as well as pleasant.)

Work on learning the letter-sounds and associating key words with each letter. Suggestions are given in this kit for a clothesline mobile, as well as for games to play. Remember to keep the learning a game, and play only when your child wants to.

Add to—and perhaps finish—your homemade ABC scrapbook, and keep it where your child can look at it and show it to his friends.

Write things with your child—to dictation or collaboratively—and encourage his attempts at writing.

Use some of your odd moments to teach the sight word *you*, following my suggestions from previous kits or devising a strategy of your own.

Finally, in all the activities of this kit, try to make sure your child understands the seven concepts or basic ideas listed earlier. (However, these concepts do *not* have to be mastered before you move on to Kit 5.)

1. Letters stand for sounds.
2. Spoken words have sounds in them.
3. Words have "beginning sounds."
4. Words are written with letters—you put letters together to make written words.
5. Words are spoken by saying sounds—you put sounds together to make spoken words.
6. Words can be spoken or written: You can write any word you can speak; you write words with letters and say them with sounds.
7. Words have "beginning" sounds, and often have "middle" and "ending" sounds as well.

How can you tell whether your child understands these concepts? One way is to ask her, of course. Another is to discuss the way people talk, using larynx, lips, tongue, teeth, and so on, to make the various sounds. Still another way is to teach the concepts by saying them to her from time to time, then watching to see if she understands. If your child doesn't seem to understand or care about the last four concepts, be sure you're not pushing her.

Your child *will* need to understand these concepts in order to read in the fullest sense of the word, but she would get them sooner or later. *Don't push* or show impatience, whatever you do. Many young children find it quite difficult to think of words as divisible, and these children may also have trouble putting sounds together to form words. If your child encounters difficulty at this point, ease up on teaching these concepts. Some children learn the concepts after they have begun reading words.

When your child can give a speech sound, or a word, for each letter, move on to Kit 5. In fact, it is perfectly all right to move into Kit 5 even though there may be several letter-sounds that still give your child trouble.

2. Things for you to make or buy

a. Homemade alphabet scrapbook. Keep on with activities of cutting out (or drawing) pictures to go with each letter. You should have several words to associate with most letters by now—please remember the notes on which letter-sounds to use for letters which have several pronunciations (page 144).

As a help, I list some common words which can be used to associate with letters.

- A—apple, alligator, astronaut, actor, actress, andiron, ant (aunt)
- B—boy, baby, bed, ball, bag, baloney, bubblegum, balloon, bank
- C—cat, cap, cape, can, candy, car, cook, cookie, cup
- D—dog, dandelion, dirty, dirt, dust, daisy, dig
- E—elephant, egg, echo, exit, end, elevator, escalator
- F—flag, fox, friend, foot, fender, frame, fix, fig, flag, food
- G—girl, grass, goat, garbage, green, grow, glass, go, goofy
- H—hat, horn, hook, hop, hope, hanger, hockey, hustle, hiccup, hoof, hand
- I—Indian, igloo, itch, icky, ink, in, into, inch
- J—jar, jet, jump, jumprope, junk, jiggle, jungle, jog, jingle
- K—key, kangaroo, kite, king, kick, kiss
- L—ladder, lamp, lion, lasso, loop, letter, lip, leg
- M—man, money, monkey, mixer, matches, muffin, mop, mat
- N—nail, nickel, needle, no, never, nasty
- O—octopus, ox, Oscar, olive
- P—penny, patch, pitch, pin, pan, pot, potato, pansy, petunia, pinch, pet, pig
- Q—quarter, queen, quick, quit, quilt
- R—ring, rocket, rip, roof, run, rag, red, rub
- S—sock, smoke, sandwich, sand, sing, song, stop, snake, slip, sled, sugar
- T—table, top, tiger, toes, tiptoe, train
- U—umbrella, ugly, up
- V—vase, violin, violet, very, victory
- W—woman, wax, win, wick, witch, wet, wash, watch
- X—x-ray (box, exit, ax, ox, fox, Max, fix, etc.)*

---

* I use X in these words because it is rare as an initial letter, and usually takes a /Z/ sound. I have never seen a child confused by this.

Y—yoyo, yellow, yolk, you, yes, yummy
Z—zipper, zombie, zoom, zoo, zigzag, zebra

  b. Clothesline mobile. You might do well to collect objects or small pictures representing each of the letters and the associated word (Figure 18).
  A small plastic (or real) apple, pictures (or small figurines) of a boy, cat, dog, elephant, girl, etc., can be hung up along a clothesline along with the letters. Or possibly

Figure 18

these objects could be displayed along a shelf or in a corner somewhere. I have seen the clothesline mobile used to good effect, however, and recommend it to anyone who wants to spend the time. It keeps the objects both *in* view and *out* of harm's way. In ordinary circumstances, they don't get broken or mixed up or separated from their letters. In short, a fine idea and well worth the trouble.

   3. Reading aloud
   Keep on reading aloud with your child an average of 30 minutes each day. Try to make the time that you spend reading together as close and pleasant as you can: Minimize distractions, and read only when your child really wants you to. (This raises an obvious exception to the rule of 30 minutes reading per day—if your child really does not want reading at a particular time, don't force it. Find another time.) It seems

highly unlikely to me that your child will not ever want to be read aloud to *at all, ever.* Occasionally your child might decide that the way to get to you is to refuse to cooperate in something you want to do, like reading. If this happens, don't read. Either stop where you are until the behavior or attitude improves, or don't start at all until you're guaranteed a cooperative, attentive audience. "My reading aloud is for listening to," is a Ginott-like argument I've found to be honest and logically persuasive to a variety of two- to five-year-olds—I know it's lacking grammatically, but then you can't have everything. Anyhow, I think it is worth taking some pains to assure your child's attention.

I believe that the usual cause of inattention is disinterest in the material being read. I have no compunction about editing as I read, shortening here or adding emphasis there. If you are careful to read things your child *wants* to hear, and only to read when your child wants to be read to, then you should find little difficulty with attention. Finally, I try to make it a rule always to quit before my child is ready to quit.

4. Things to read

Now is a splendid time for you to get into poetry, if you and your child are not already there. The main reason to read poetry aloud with him is that it is fun, but the idea of rhyme can also be quite helpful in teaching your child to read. Certainly your librarian will be able to suggest several collections of poetry for you and your child.

5. Writing and scribbling

Continue to encourage your child's efforts with pencil and paper. Keep writing materials in supply at strategic points around the house, and urge your child to use them.

6. Writing together

Keep on writing your journal, or begin one if you haven't already done so.

Also use the ordinary occasions of list making, labeling, etc., to get your child involved. Having him help you with a grocery list or a note to the babysitter is a useful way to proceed.

7. Things to make together

Poetry and quotes scrapbook. I wish I had kept a book of poems and short quotes that my children and I have enjoyed. I didn't, but such a project might be fun for you to do.

8. Own words

These are words from your child's experience that she wants to learn. Her "own words" can be names of friends, family, pets, or almost anything, for that matter, that interests her. These words aren't restricted to nouns, necessarily, either, though I suspect you will find that more nouns are requested than other words.

As I suggested earlier, it's a good idea to print these words for your child on index or other cards so they can be kept together and/or displayed when she wants to.

9. Sight words

The sight word for Kit 4 is *you.*

Point it out in your reading together, talk about it, and spell it, "*Y-O-U* spells [pointing to each other] 'you.'"

10. Games

a. "What letter [or sound] does ___ begin with?" In this game the child is asked to produce the name of a letter associated with a sound or vice versa. This is self-explanatory and is an apparently simpleminded game. Yet it is enjoyed by children, especially as being rather more difficult than the games of Kit 3, where the letter-sound was suggested.

b. People's initials. Children are often fascinated by their own and other people's initials. You might make a scrapbook—or a collection of snapshots—using people's initials. Or, you can play guessing games like, "Who is J. W.?"

c. The letter-word challenge game. This game is played by two (or more) players alternately naming a letter and the next player having to name an object or word (or words) beginning with that letter. If one object only is required, the player who names it gets to challenge with another letter, which the other players have to find a word for.

Another way of playing this game is to name things beginning with the suggested letter (by turns) until you run out of names. The last person who can name something wins and gets to suggest the next letter.

d. Win-the-cards game. Turn through the deck of movable alphabet cards one at a time. For each letter your child tries to name a word or thing beginning with that letter. He keeps each card for which he is able to give a word.

An alternate way is to take turns with the cards, trying to name things beginning with each letter. You can make it tougher, if and when you want to, by limiting the things named to animals or toys or household items or whatever.

11. Mail

If your child enjoys it, by all means continue to encourage and develop her correspondence with friends, relatives, politicians, and the world in general. Although you will undoubtedly be doing most of the writing for a while yet, this can prove well worth the effort.

12. Media

Use television as a tool, as entertainment, as an extension of experience, and be careful not to overdo it.

Review Lesson I (Kits 1-4)

The first four kits have brought your child to what can be regarded as readiness for reading. If your child has mastered the skills of the first four kits, he or she should have all the basic skills necessary to learn to read.

REVIEW EXERCISES

1. Go over all the letters and see if your child can still name them and give a sound for each.
2. Review the concepts covered in Kits 3 and 4. Try to make sure your child understands these.
3. Review your teaching by asking yourself these questions:
    a. Am I (or is somebody) reading to him daily for at least 20–30 minutes?

  b. Am I taking her on trips to the library or bookstore?

  c. Are there lots of children's books around the house?

  d. Am I avoiding pressure situations?

  e. Does my child seem to enjoy the program?

  f. Do I *always* make the instruction a game?

If you answer *any one* of these questions "no," you'll need to fix it. If (*d*) is "no," either shape up or quit the program.

UNIT II: BEGINNING TO READ

Kits 5-9

This unit helps your child get started in learning to decode simple words. Concepts of rhyme and "word family" are taught, and various words are decoded.

Reading aloud with your child continues, and several sight words are learned.

Kit 5: Rhymes, ending sounds, and some words to read

MATERIALS

> Movable alphabet cards
> Some books of children's poetry and nursery rhymes
> Marker pen and paper

GOAL

The purpose of this kit is to help your child become aware of the endings of words. A great deal is made of rhymes—it will prove helpful if you read poetry and nursery rhymes together. Also, a few rhyming words are offered for your child to read in the context of a game.

Specific goals for this kit are as follows:

1. Learning the concept of rhyme
2. Recognizing when one word rhymes with another
3. Identifying "ending sounds" in words
4. Beginning to look at written letters in words as standing for sounds

Go on to Kit 6 when your child can do (2) and (3) regularly with the words on page 166. If your child can do (2) and (3), it is a fair bet that he understands something of (1) and (4).

INSTRUCTIONS

1. Read some poetry aloud to your child. Find poems that you both like, if possible, and call attention now and then to rhymes in the poems. Another good place to find rhymes is in songs—*stream* and *dream* in "Row, Row, Row Your Boat," for instance.

One of the beauties of reading poetry to children is that you can keep going back to favorite poems. This is, of course, a made-to-order invitation to look for rhymes.

2. It is easy to teach a child to identify rhymes when she understands what rhyme means. I like to begin explaining rhyme by saying that "the ends of the words sound alike," and illustrate with examples—fun-sun, silly-Billy, happy-pappy, fat-rat, etc. I try to avoid getting into spelling patterns at the beginning. The easiest way to teach rhyme is to rhyme some words, aloud, and try playing some rhyming games. I should add that most children will understand this without difficulty. If your child has trouble with the concept of rhyme, she probably hasn't been exposed to enough poetry, nursery rhymes, and songs. If that's the case, spend more time together on these things.

Here are some rhyming games you can play:

a. "I'm thinking of a word that rhymes with *up*," or "I'm thinking of something you drink out of that rhymes with *up*." This game is easy and pleasant for child and adult.

b. "How many words can you think of that rhyme with *hat*?" You can do this one as a cooperative effort or take turns asking and answering, whichever suits your child and your mood.

c. Rhyming pairs. You give the child two words which rhyme or do not rhyme. His task is to tell you whether they rhyme or not. "Fat-cat." "They rhyme." "Fat-man." "They don't rhyme."

3. *Making some rhyming words.* Use the movable alphabet cards to make the rhyming words, and *make it a game*, remember.

Try these rhyming words. "See how many rhymes you can make with the word *cat*." You form *cat* with the movable letters. As your child suggests each new word, you make it with the letters—quickly getting your child to make the words, if possible. This is a dandy game, and the more you play it using a variety of word families, the more insight your child should have into reading.

A good variation is to take turns making rhymes with the cards—you start, let her make one, then you make one, etc.

Another variation is to print the words with a pencil or (preferably) a felt-tip pen and let your child try to write if she wants to.

Still another is to make the words with movable plastic letters—the magnetized ones are excellent, whether used on a metal surface or not. There is an open invitation in these letters to make words with them.

4. *A note on writing.* As we have discussed, many—perhaps most—children who read early also write (or *try* to write) early. You should do whatever you can now to encourage any efforts at writing. Some children seem to "take" naturally to a chalkboard; others prefer pencil and paper. The felt-tip pen holds a great fascination for many youngsters. Your task is to encourage your child to write in whatever way you're able.

Although the warning will be rather premature where children are just beginning to write, it is important for parents of such children not to be uptight about spelling. The research of Charles Read, Carol Chomsky, and others indicates that early-writing children follow their own spelling systems, which for them are very effective. You'll just confuse the issue by trying to get your beginning scribbler to spell according to adult conventions or to write from left to right consistently. Before he reaches school age he'll probably have most of this straightened out.

5. The final step in this kit is to play a game with rhyming words where *you* produce the words in sequence and let her figure out what they are. Either the movable alphabet cards or a felt-tip pen are useful in this: Take your pick.

Begin by making the base word—for example, *man*. Read it aloud for your child and say you're going to make words that rhyme with it. Then, one at a time, make words like *pan, fan, can, tan, van,* and so on. Let her see if she can figure out what a word is, and, if she can't, tell her and go on. Don't make a big production of this—it's a game, a logical extension of the rhyming game you have played earlier. Have fun with this; and, if it isn't fun, then quit and play a game that *is* fun.

Some words to play with:*

bat	can	cap	bad
cat	fan	lap	dad
fat	man	tap	had
hat	pan	map	mad
mat	ran	nap	pad
pat	tan	zap	sad
rat	van		
sat			

These are just my words. You or your child may think of others.

6. *An important reminder:* Please remember to play reading games *only* when your child wants to. Try to quit before he gets tired, while he still wants to play. Don't wear out his interest—at the first sign of disinterest or innattention you know you've already played too long. Quit right then and there.

* Explain or omit any unfamiliar words.

Kit 6: Some easy word families:
-ap, -at, -an, -ad

MATERIALS

> Movable alphabet cards
> Felt-tip pen and paper
> Children's books

GOAL

By the end of this kit your child should be able to read some words in isolation and to recognize a few words when they are encountered in print.

These goals may seem modest, but I remind you that there is plenty of time, and much is gained by starting off slow and easy.

Go on to Kit 7 when your child can recognize words on page 168 when they are written *in families*—that is, on seeing (and being told, if necessary) *bad, dad,* and *had,* your child should be able to read *sad.*

INSTRUCTIONS

1. Reading aloud to your child is crucially important at this stage. Expeditions together to the library or to the bookstore should be made regularly, certainly once every two weeks. You should also talk to your child about the books you're reading together and involve other members of the family in the reading as well. It seems important to me (but I can't prove it makes any difference) that both parents read to the child and get involved in the learning-to-read games. Certainly grandparents, visitors, siblings, and babysitters are excellent candidates to do a bit of reading to your child. I believe that the more your child is read to, and the more interesting books and reading are in her life and in the lives of people around her, the more likely she will be to learn to read well and easily.

2. As you read to your child, be on the lookout for any of the words in this lesson that he might be able to recognize. Some of them are quite common—*and, sat, man, can, ran, had*—and you should come across a few of them in any reading session. Begin by pointing out to him one of *his* words on the page—most kids find this delightful. If he wants, invite him to find more. As you read along, from time to time (as your judgment, the story, and your pupil permit) call attention to a word he can read.

3. Using the words introduced in Kit 5, continue to play the rhyming games from pages 164 and 165, in which you both try to make rhyming words with a "base" word, or in which you write the rhymes and your child tries to say what they are. When you are able to write all the *families* of words below, starting with any word, and have your child get them all, or nearly all, then you're ready to move on.

The words are, as in Kit 5:*

bat	can	cap	bad
cat	fan	lap	dad
fat	man	tap	had
hat	pan	map	mad
mat	ran	nap	sad
pat	tan	zap	pad
rat	van		
sat			

4. No matter how proud you may be, restrain the urge to show off your kid's reading at this stage. *Never, never, never,* have your child perform in reading for grandparents, neighbors, etc. If you do, you change the easy, relaxed emotional interaction you've built up for your reading together with something else entirely. Playing unthreatening games with you is *very* different from performing for grandmother or anyone else. Performers are tense, anxious to be right. Both these qualities are absolute death to the learning process that your child and you are using!

5. Keep on trying to get your child to write. Be sure that you have an abundance and variety of writing materials and that they are accessible. Displaying them attractively is a good way to increase their use in a preschool classroom, and I suspect this is true at home as well.

* Explain or omit any unfamiliar words.

Kit 7: Another middle sound and some new Words: *-in, -it, -ill, -ig*

MATERIALS

Movable alphabet cards
Marker pen and paper
Reading books

Goal

The goal of this kit is for your child to learn:

1. That there are often "middle sounds" in words
2. That he or she knows words whose middle sound is *a*
3. That there are other words with other middle sounds
4. That he or she can read some more words whose middle sound is *i*

Go on to Review Lesson I when your child can read all the words in Instruction (3).

Instructions

1. Your child probably has favorite books and passages in his books. When you read to him, remember to be sure that you sit so that he can see the print. At favorite spots, you will probably be asked to show "where it says that." You should encourage this. Point out here and there the names of characters and memorable words or phrases like "Zzap!" or "Bump, bump, bump," or whatever.

2. As I have urged repeatedly in previous kits, you should encourage your child's writing, of any and all sorts. Again, if any words come out, don't worry about the spelling.

3. In your word and rhyming games (see pages 164–166), begin to introduce the following word families:*

it	bill	big	in
bit	fill	dig	pin
fit	hill	fig	fin
hit	mill	pig	
lit	pill		
sit			

When you start a rhyming game, go ahead and read the first word to your child, if need be.

These words should be played with until she knows them fairly well before you go on to the next kit.

4. A new game to play is the "mystery word" game. Each day—or several times a day, if you like—a new mystery word

---
* Explain or omit any unfamiliar words.

is spelled out on the refrigerator door in plastic magnetic letters or printed on a card. Deciphering this word is worth an apple, perhaps, or a cookie, at the going rate.

5. Another warning is in order against the temptation to pressure your child. A quick summary of don'ts.

a. Never, never, never insist on playing any reading game—or reading aloud—when your child does not want to.

b. Don't keep on playing a game after your child's attention begins to wander.

c. Never continue playing a reading game when your child wants to quit.

d. Don't let games or reading go on so long that your child becomes bored—always try to quit while he's still interested.

e. Don't show off your child's reading, at least not yet.

Kit 8: Beginning sounds of words; decoding selected pairs of words: *mat-pat,* etc.

Materials

> Movable alphabet cards
> Movable plastic letters
> Marker pen and paper
> Children's books and magazines

Goal

By the time she leaves this kit, your child should be able to discriminate between two words which differ only in their first sounds. Don't expect infallibility—she'll probably make mistakes—but you should stick with it until she understands the differences between these words.

Go on to Kit 9 when your child can discriminate between the words in the pairs on page 171.

INSTRUCTIONS

1. A new game begins here, involving the decoding of pairs of words. This game is meant to lead your child into fairly confident word discrimination skills.

"Which of these is _____ ?" or "Show me _____ ." Present two words at the same time, either written or spelled out with the movable alphabet or plastic letters. For example: "Here we have two words, *pat* and *fat* [point each one out, and talk about the differences—*pat* begins with *p* and *fat* begins with *f*, etc.]. Show me *pat*." If the child points to *pat*, you say, "Okay, great! Which one says *fat*?" (or, "Very good—the other one says *fat*").

Or, if he points to the wrong one, just say, "That one says *fat*—see the *f* at the beginning. Which one says *pat*?" "Fine!" or "Good for you!" (Or, "That one says *fat*—the first letter is *f* for *fff*. Which one says *pat*?")

2. At this stage of the program small reinforcers sometimes are helpful, especially for the paired-word discrimination games. This adds an element of "winning" that can powerfully aid motivation at a time when you may be glad to have the help. As reward, you can give a raisin or a token or a penny or a small candy for each correct word.

3. Paired words to give are as follows, concentrating on discriminating between the sounds at the beginning of words.*

hand-land	cat-bat	fat-pat
band-hand	sat-pat	fan-pan
sand-hand	can-pan	cap-lap
lamp-damp	in-pin	cat-rat
tap-lap	big-dig	hat-fat
tan-man	pig-big	fat-sat
man-pan	fig-dig	bat-hat
tap-cap	bit-sit	bad-dad
ran-van	fit-hit	had-bad
pad-bad	bill-mill	dad-had
mad-sad	pill-fill	dad-pad
can-ran	sit-fit	fan-tan

* Explain or omit any unfamiliar words.

4. You may try other combinations as well—these words are given only as a guide. However, the pairs you make up in this kit should differ *only* in their first letter. That is, the combination *pan-fan* is okay for this stage of the game: *pan-pat* and *pan-pin* are too hard—they come in later kits. Please don't rush it. Just concentrate now on doing well the easy stuff, having fun, and getting the difference between *pan* and *fan* really understood.

Kit 9: Ending sounds of words; decoding selected pairs of words: *man-map*, etc.

MATERIALS

>Movable alphabet cards
>Movable plastic letters
>Felt-tip pen and paper
>Children's books
>Typewriter, if available

GOAL

By the time your child finishes this kit he should be able to discriminate between two familiar words whose only difference is in their last letter.

Go on to Kit 10 when your child can discriminate between the words in pairs on page 173.

INSTRUCTIONS

1. In your reading, look for examples of familiar words and point them out to your child.

2. Encourage writing and other forms of production of words, using the plastic letters, movable alphabet, or any other means available.

If you have a typewriter, now is a good time to introduce your child to it, if you have not already done so. You have to explain the differences in type (the forms of *a*, *t*, and *g* to which she's accustomed differ from those on the typewriter), but after that your child should be able to do a great deal alone. Don't expect great things at first. A certain amount of "messing around" is a useful beginning, so try not to be impatient. For now it's sufficient for your child just to have the exposure to one more way of producing written language. (In my own experience with two rather heavy-handed boys, it has been helpful to lay down some rules at the beginning about how the typewriter can and cannot be used—I discourage banging, key jamming, ribbon pulling, etc. You do what you like, however.)

3. Following the general format of Kit 8, play the pair decoding game (page 171) presenting sets of paired words to your child. These words differ only in their last letter, so you're concentrating on "ending sounds."

4. Present the following pairs of words, all of which differ only in one letter at the end of the word:*

fat-fan	bad-bat	map-mat
man-map	cap-cat	cat-can
pan-pat	pad-pat	pin-pig
tap-tan	dad-dam	big-bit
sat-sad	can-cap	fit-fin
rat-ran	pad-pan	fig-fin

*Explain or omit any unfamiliar words.

Review Lesson II (Kits 5–9)

MATERIALS

Movable alphabet cards
Movable plastic letters
Felt-tip pen and paper
Children's books
Typewriter, if available

REVIEW

Your child by now has begun reading. The words and concepts of Kits 5–9 include useful and necessary skills for any beginning reader. Go over the words and concepts of Kits 5–9. Play rhyming games from page 164. Review word families from Kits 5, 6, and 7. Play pair-decoding games, using word pairs from Kits 8 and 9. Read and write together.

UNIT III: DEVELOPING READING SKILLS

Kits 10–14

This unit will help your child become adept at some basic reading skills. The unit concentrates on teaching decoding of short vowel words. The requirement of being read aloud to for a minimum of 20 minutes daily becomes more of a shared experience as your child grows in reading ability.

Kit 10: More ending sounds:
-and, -ack, -ip, -s, -ick, -ag

MATERIALS

    Movable alphabet cards
    Movable plastic letters
    Felt-tip pen and paper
    Typewriter, if available

GOAL
    This kit should help your child learn several new "families" of words with new ending sounds. This should considerably expand the number of words she can read.
    Go on to Kit 11 when your child can read all the words listed in Instruction 3, page 175, and can also read them with *-s* added.

INSTRUCTIONS
    1. Be sure you continue to read to your child 20 minutes a day.
    2. Get your child to try to write his or her whole name. Get your child writing other things too, if you can; be sure writing

materials are accessible and in working order (pencils sharp enough, crayons unbroken, chalk fresh, markers not dried out, etc.). By all means try a chalkboard if you haven't already.

3. Play the rhyming games used in previous kits (pages 164–166), with the following "families" of rhyming words:*

Dick	sip	back	bag
kick	tip	Jack	rag
lick	lip	pack	tag
pick	dip	rack	wag
sick	nip	sack	
tick	rip	tack	
wick	hip		

4. Another step to take is to add -*s* to any word covered so far. To do this, present the original word, for example *hat,* using the movable alphabet or plastic letters. You can say something like this: "I'm going to add an *s* to *hat,* like this, and make it *hats.*" Then play around with making plurals of other words covered (or third-person singular forms of verbs, such as *hits,* or possessives, such as *cat's*). The usual pronunciation of -*s* at the ends of words is *s* (as in *ants*), but sometimes (as after *g*, for instance) it is pronounced *z* (as in *eggs*). Most children learning to read accept this—they see *bags* and read *bagz* without comment. Others read *bagss . . . bagz.* Still others need it explained that *s* at the end of a word says either *s* or *z* depending on which one fits the way you say it.

5. Sight words for Kit 10 are *to* and *do.*

Follow the teaching procedure for sight words outlined on page 151. Review the sight words taught in previous kits.

* Explain or omit any unfamiliar words.

Kit 11: Another middle sound:
-o, -ot, -ock, -op

MATERIALS

    Movable alphabet cards
    Movable plastic letters
    Felt-tip pen and paper
    Children's books

GOAL

By the end of this kit, your child should be able to recognize several words which have *o* as the middle vowel.

Go on to Kit 12 when your child can recognize the words in Instruction 2.

INSTRUCTIONS

1. Continue to read aloud to your child and to encourage his writing efforts. Besides his own name, encourage him to write names of family, playmates, pets, places, things, etc.

2. Play the rhyming games (pages 164–166) with the following new words.*

hot	hop	sock
cot	cop	dock
dot	pop	lock
lot	mop	rock
pot	sop	cock
tot	top	clock
		tick-tock

3. Play the word-pair games (page 171), using pairs (or threesomes) of words whose middle vowel is different. Here are some examples:*

hip-hop	sand-send
fun-fin	band-bend
put-pat	land-lend
cap-cop	lick-lock
map-mop	had-hid
sit-sat	pan-pin
cat-cot	fan-fin
bat-bit	sap-sip-sop
hit-hat-hot	tap-tip-top
sack-sick-sock	pat-pit-pot
bump-jump-lump	mit-mat-met
fill-fell-fall	cab-cob-cub

* Explain or omit any unfamiliar words.

Kit 12: Still more middle sounds:
-en, -end, -eck, -et, -un, -up, -ud, -ut

MATERIALS

>Movable alphabet cards
>Movable plastic letters
>Felt-tip pen and paper
>Children's books

GOAL

This kit will introduce your child to words spelled with *e* and *u*. By the end of this kit your child should be able to read a wide range of words.

Go on to Kit 13 when your child can read the new words in Instructions 2 and 3.

INSTRUCTIONS

1. By now your child may be able to read some simple books, with your help. As you read aloud with her, encourage her to read words and sentences for herself.

2. Introduce the following rhyming families using *e* and *u*, playing the rhyming games of previous kits.*

jet	end	fun	duck	neck
met	bend	bun	buck	deck
get	lend	sun	luck	peck
let	mend	run	suck	
net	send	gun	tuck	
pet	tend	nun		
set				
vet				

hen	up	mud	cut
den	cup	bud	nut
men	pup		
pen			
ten			

* Explain or omit any unfamiliar words.

3. As in the preceding kits, try presenting words in groups which differ only in their middle vowels. For example:*

ran-run
luck-lack-lick-lock
pet-pot-pat-pit (*put* is not pronounced as you'd expect it
    to be, so it is omitted)
but-bit-bat-bet
net-nut-not
pan-pin-pen
suck-sack-sick-sock
rock-rack
sit-sat-set
hat-hot-hit-hut
top-tip-tap

4. Perhaps your child can be persuaded to write something—and he should be praised and taken seriously when something has been written. Even if it looks like hieroglyphics, take the time and trouble to figure out what it is supposed to say and why your kid wrote it like that. Once you've done this, *both* of you have really learned something. Please don't worry about reversals and bizarre spellings (many of them are quite logical if you think about it). Encourage your child to write, if you can, without becoming a nag about it.

* Explain or omit any unfamiliar words.

Kit 13: Blending letter-sounds; games

MATERIALS

Movable alphabet cards
Movable plastic letters
Felt-tip pen and paper
Children's books

GOAL
By the time your child is finished with this kit, she should be able to blend several consonants in reading.

Go on to Kit 14 when your child can read the new words listed in Instruction 3.

INSTRUCTIONS

1. Continue the reading, as well as the trips to the library and bookstore. Show your child what you are reading, and let him look for some of *his* words in it from time to time.

2. Continue to encourage writing. If you have not already done so, see if you can get a correspondence going between your kid and a distant aunt, uncle, cousin, or friend. As I have suggested earlier, mail just for your child can be a powerful inducement to read and write—it is a great joy to many children, including my own. Certainly it's worth a try.

3. Introduce your child to the idea of putting several letters together to make a blend. Say the words slowly and then repeat them at normal speed: ":a-a-n-n-d, *and*," "b-a-a-n-n-d, *band*," "f-f-l-l-a-a-p, *flap*." Go over these rhyming blends, then play the rhyming game with them. Don't be surprised if blending proves difficult for your child to learn in the beginning. Point out blends in your reading (*and* is a fine one, and so is *stop*).

Say blends slowly (like f-l-a-t or s-l-a-p) and have your child try to guess what word you're saying. This builds awareness of the blending process.

Keep playing the word games of previous kits using an occasional blend from this list.* After a while your child should begin to get the idea.

lip	lick	top	bump
slip	stick	stop	dump
flip	trick	drop	pump
clip	slick	flop	mumps
trip	flick		stump
		best	grump
end	and	nest	slump
spend	stand	pest	stump
	brand	rest	
pot	grand	test	
spot		vest	
		crest	

* Explain or omit any unfamiliar words.

belt	tap	ring
felt	trap	bring
melt	flap	sting
	slap	sing
bang	clap	sling
hang		
fang	ant	song
gang	pant	long
rang	pants	
sang		

Kit 14: More consonant blends

MATERIALS

Movable alphabet cards
Movable plastic letters
Felt-tip pen and paper
Children's books

GOAL

By the time your child finishes this kit, she should be reasonably comfortable with consonant blends.

Go on to Review Lesson III when your child can read the words listed in Instruction 2.

INSTRUCTIONS

1. Be sure you are reading to your child *at least* 20 minutes a day—preferably twice that much. In your reading, give some attention to the books that have won the Newbury and Caldecott awards. These are usually first-rate and are much enjoyed by children. Your librarian can be a valuable resource; be sure to ask for advice on what to read.

2. Present these groups of words, many of which involve consonant blends. Feel free to go ahead and make up other groups besides these.*

---

* Explain or omit any unfamiliar words.

slip-trip
flip-flap-flop
trap-slap
flat-rat
bell-belt-bent
flop-flap-flip
best-belt-bent
sent-tent-went
ant-tan
damp-dump
lamp-limp-lump
lamb-limb
skip-slip-snip-snap-slap
best-rest-crest

send-spend
sent-spent
lend-send-bend-mend
belt-felt
bang-gang
gang-gong
song-sang-sing
bring-ring-sing
ring-rang-rung
ding-dong
sing-sting-string
trap-strap-strip
song-strong

Review Lesson III (Kits 10-14)

MATERIALS

Movable alphabet cards
Movable plastic letters
Felt-tip pen and paper
Children's books

OVERVIEW

Your child by now has been doing most of the things a reader does. Mastery of the words and concepts of Kits 11-14 means that your child is reading—not well, perhaps, but she is certainly able to read.

REVIEW

1. Using movable alphabet cards or marker pen, make words at random from the preceding kits and see if your child can read them. Make a note of those words which give her trouble. Remember that young children sometimes forget things they knew quite well a few days or weeks before, so don't be too surprised to find your child has forgotten a letter name or a speech sound or the like.

When you have time, analyze the words that gave your child difficulty. Was there anything that the words had in common? What similar words could you give her to practice with?

Play the game again, giving attention to the areas where your child needs help. *Don't hurry—there's plenty of time.*

2. As you read with your child, look for words and passages he can read. The book you practice on need not be a familiar one, necessarily, but I think it will be more interesting for both of you if it is.

UNIT IV: GOING AHEAD WITH READING

Kits 15–21

In this unit we try to help your child move toward independent reading. No attempt is made to teach every phonics rule used in English spelling, but we do try to show the most important principles.

The goal, however, is reading comprehension, which you have been building since the beginning with your reading aloud together, discussions, story writing, journal keeping, and so forth.

Kit 15: Magic *e*

MATERIALS

> Magic *e* movable alphabet card—letter a *very* different color (gold, baby blue, etc.)
> Movable alphabet cards
> Plastic letters
> Felt-tip pen and paper
> Children's books

GOAL

This kit is meant to introduce your child to the silent *e* added at the end of a word which makes the middle vowel become long or "say its name." For example, when you add the magic *e* to *tap,* it becomes *tape;* the *a* "says its name," or takes the long sound. It works for other vowels besides *a*. For instance:

hop-hope   pet-Pete
cut-cute   kit-kite

Go on to Kit 16 when your child can read all the new words listed in Instructions 2 and 3.

INSTRUCTIONS

1. Continue to read aloud to your child. Try some new field of interest—dinosaurs or mythology or *Winnie-the-Pooh* or something you haven't been reading about. Children will frequently listen to and enjoy books considerably advanced for their years, if they are sufficiently interested in the subjects.

2. Introduce the idea of magic *e* by explaining it and giving some examples. A sample explanation might be, "The magic *e* doesn't make a sound, but it makes the middle vowel 'say its name'—that's why we call it 'magic *e*.' It changes the way we pronounce the middle letter, but it's silent itself." Show the new "magic *e*" card, and explain that it is a different color "just to remind you that it isn't an ordinary *e*." Demonstrate the way magic *e* works, using word pairs:*

tap-tape	pet-Pete	kit-kite
hop-hope	van-vane	pin-pine
mad-made	man-mane	pop-pope
cut-cute	hid-hide	rod-rode
kit-kite	rid-ride	not-note
pet-Pete	bit-bite	tot-tote
tap-tape	spit-spite	cod-code
mat-mate	win-wine	bed-Bede
rat-rate	twin-twine	tub-tube
hat-hate	shin-shine	dud-dude
cap-cape	fin-fine	hop-hope
dam-dame	spin-spine	cut-cute

3. Here are some word families that use magic *e*. You should play the rhyming games from pages 164–166 with these.*

* Explain or omit any unfamiliar words.

late	bake	ride	tale
date	cake	side	sale
gate	fake	hide	gale
hate	lake	tide	male
grate	make	wide	pale
plate	rake	slide	Yale
slate	sake	glide	
	take	bride	bike
bite	wake		like
kite	snake	dude	dike
lite	stake	Jude	Mike
nite	brake	nude	trike
		rude	
hope	cute		bone
dope	lute	cube	cone
nope	mute	lube	lone
pope		tube	stone
rope	dune		
	tune		
	prune		

4. With parental help, your child might be able to write fairly sophisticated prose by now—be sure to provide plenty of opportunity. Thank-you letters are always in order, as are letters of inquiry about subjects in which you're both interested. As I have said, I believe keeping a diary or journal is a splendid idea. At least *try* keeping one together about the things you do together and share the writing and "reading back." This could be part scrapbook, too, with photographs or clippings in it as well. Write to dictation any chance you get, and let your child read this back to you also.

Kit 16: Learning *ch, sh, th, wh, ph;* more vowel sounds

MATERIALS

    Movable alphabet cards, including magic *e* card
    Plastic letters
    Felt-tip pen and paper
    Children's books, newspapers, magazines

GOAL

This kit is intended to help your child learn to associate sounds with various combinations of letters. These are:

> *ch, sh, th, wh, ph,*
> *oo* as in *book*
> *oo* as in *tool*
> *-o* as in *so*
> *-o* as in *do*
> *-e* as in *me*
> *-ee* as in *bee*

Go on to Kit 17 when your child can read the new words listed in Instructions 3 through 7, pages 187 and 188.

INSTRUCTIONS

1. Keep up your reading aloud together. Where the text is easy, take turns reading words. You read a few words, then stop at a word your child should be able to read, and let him read it.

2. Explain the idea that there are several sounds that two letters stand for together, which are not like the sounds they make separately. These "speech consonants" are *not* blends. They are separate sounds. (By this time you may find that your child already knows some or all of these.)

> *sh* as in *ship*
> *ch* as in *chop*
> *th* as in *that*
> *th* as in *with*
> *wh* as in *when*

3. Present words, using felt-tip pens, movable alphabet cards, or plastic letters.*

---

* Explain or omit any unfamiliar words.

sh:

ship	cash
shut	mash
wish	mush
fish	slush
shack	shush
shave	sh!
shame	

ch (also *tch*):

chop	witch
chip	ditch
chap	much
chub	Dutch
chum	patch

These can be lumped together or taught separately, whichever you prefer.

th:
(voiced and unvoiced, as in *this* and *bath*, respectively)

voiced *th*:	unvoiced *th*:	*wh*:
this	bath	when
that	path	whip
these	with	which
them	Beth	while
those	thick	white
the	thin	whap!
	thump	whack!
	thud	

ph:
(This really doesn't quite belong with the rest, because in these words *ph* simply takes the sound of *f*.)

phone
telephone
elephant

4. Introduce the long *e* sound associated with *-e* and *-ee*, as in *she* and *bee*. Try these words:*

---

* Explain or omit any unfamiliar words.

be	bee	see	glee	sleet
me	beet	meet	fee	greet
the	feet	feel	sleep	gleem
he	sheep	three	whee	thee
we				
she				

5. Introduce *oo* sound, as in *too:**

too	toot	pool
zoo	tool	zoom
boo	cool	room
		loop

There are also two words spelled with just one -*o* that sound like -*oo*. These are *do* and *to* and were learned in Kit 10 as sight words. Ask your child just to remember that *to* and *do* are different.

6. Introduce the words: *no; so; go; ho, ho, ho.*

In the long process of learning written English, your child will learn to deal with endless exceptions and special cases. Treat these as a matter of course, and go on.

7. The letter -*oo* can be pronounced either as in *too* or as in *book*. Tell this to your child and then show him the words:*

look	But spook
book	and kook.
cook	
hook	
rook	
shook	
took	

Certain words can go either way, depending on your pronunciation, as *hoop* and *coop*. It is reasonably safe to say that, when it comes before *k*, -*oo* is pronounced as in *book*. Otherwise it's usually pronounced as in *too*, though not always. The best approach in teaching this is for the child to *try* the most common pronunciation first, then, if that doesn't produce a recognizable word, go to less common pronunciation.

* Explain or omit any unfamiliar words.

8. Try helping your child write a list of every word she knows how to read. You might even set up an index file of 3 × 5 inch word cards, if you are *very* ambitious. This is an unsurpassed way to show your child how much she is learning. But put whole word families on a card, unless you want an *enormous* file—by now your child can probably read hundreds of words.

Kit 17: Two-syllable words and two-vowel combinations

MATERIALS

    Movable alphabet cards
    Movable plastic letters
    Felt-tip pen and paper
    Children's books, newspapers, magazines

GOAL

This kit will introduce:

1. Certain two-syllable words made by adding suffixes to words already familiar, or to one-syllable roots.

| handy | bigger | batting | britches |
| candy | biggest | bending | dishes |

2. Two-vowel combinations which represent a variation on their sounds, such as *law, oil, our, out*.

INSTRUCTIONS

1. Introducing the ending *-ing*.*

win-winning	run-running	go-going	ring-ringing
slip-slipping	drip-dripping	do-doing	sing-singing
hop-hopping	shut-shutting	fix-fixing	
shop-shopping	cut-cutting		
pat-patting	hit-hitting		
zip-zipping	spin-spinning		

* Explain or omit any unfamiliar words.

Notice that final consonants often double when adding *-ing*. Point this out to your child.

2. Introduce the *-y* ending. Explain that at the end of a word *-y* is not pronounced as in *you* at all. It acts like *i* at the end of words—at the end of two-syllable words, it is pronounced as in *candy*.* Consonants also double before *-y* sometimes.

candy	Terry	plenty
handy	Timmy	twenty
puppy	Jimmy	dandy
guppy	Billy	fancy
penny	Kenny	silly
happy	Cathy	bully
jelly	Tony	
belly	Henry	
Kelly	Tommy	

Naturally, there are exceptions. In one syllable words, *-y* at the end is pronounced as long *i*.

by	fly	cry	fry	sky
my	spy	dry	sly	try

Also, when there's a magic *e* after it, *y* sounds like $\bar{i}$, as in *good-bye*.

bye	good-bye	lye	aye	eye

3. Introduce the comparative endings *-er* and *-est,* using words from the following list:*

big-bigger-biggest	hot-hotter-hottest
fat-fatter-fattest	slick-slicker-slickest
thin-thinner-thinnest	sad-sadder-saddest
dumb-dumber-dumbest	mad-madder-maddest
fast-faster-fastest	dim-dimmer-dimmest
wet-wetter-wettest	red-redder-reddest
still-stiller-stillest	thick-thicker-thickest

4. Introduce the *-ez* sound of *-es*, as in *dishes*—this sound follows some words ending in *-s*, *-sh*, *-x*, and *-ch*.*

* Explain or omit any unfamiliar words.

box-boxes
miss-misses
kiss-kisses
ax-axes
moss-mosses
wish-wishes
crunch-crunches
punch-punches
fuss-fusses
fox-foxes
bus-buses

mess-messes
pass-passes
witch-witches
sash-sashes
boss-bosses
muss-musses
mass-masses
hatch-hatches
catch-catches
match-matches
flash-flashes

5. Keep on reading and encouraging your child to write. Try to provide your child some time alone with his books. Don't make reading alone an exile, but see if you can work it out—usually it works out by itself. Don't push it, though.

6. There are vowel combinations, though, which don't make the sound of just one of the vowels, but instead represent a blend of the sounds. Examples of these are *oi*, as in *oil*, *ou*, as in *out*, *ow*, as in *now*, *aw*, as in *law*, and *au*, as in *haul*.

Here are some examples. Introduce these as you think best, but without making a big deal of them. Explain or omit unfamiliar words.

oi:
oil
boil
coil
soil
toil

ow (as in *bow-wow*; also can be *ow* as in *low*):
bow-wow
now
cow
town

brown
how
pow!
gown

ou (also can be *ou* as in *soul*):
out
pout
sour
couch
ouch
pouch
clout
shout

aw:
slaw
law
draw
flaw
craw
lawn
dawn

au:
haunt
taunt
flaunt
taut
laud
gaudy

ow:
low
bow (as in *tie a bow*)
snow
slow
mow
glow
grow
show
throw
blow

ou as in:
soul
pour

7. Writing is of increasing importance. Pen pals, notes, letters, even junk mail are helpful at this stage. Seize any pretext to write off for things, thank public officials, write letters to distant relatives and friends—there are plenty of reasons to write and plenty of people to write to, if you give the matter enough thought.

Kit 18: More vowel combinations

MATERIALS

Movable alphabet cards
Plastic letters
Felt-tip pen and paper
Children's books

GOAL

This kit will introduce your child to ways of combining vowels in words.

INSTRUCTIONS

1. Keep on reading aloud, the more the better. Also, remember that your trips together to the library are more important now than ever.

2. Writing remains important, too. Using felt-tip pen and paper or the plastic letters, try leaving messages for your child to answer. If you haven't done this yet, you might start with short questions which can be answered simply—say with "yes" or "no," or some other easy words. Then, as the game is established, you can move on to more elaborate communications. Remember *not* to worry about spelling! If you can't read what your child writes, have him read it to you.

3. Introduce the following vowel combinations.*

ai:
jail	rain	paid
pail	pain	maid
fail	lain	laid
nail	main	raid
hail	vain	
mail		
rail		
sail		
tail		
wail		

ea:
beat	deal	freak	bean
neat	meal	leak	mean
heat	real	peak	lean
seat	seal	streak	Jean
meat	heal	beak	

team	cheap	sea	*but also:*
beam	heap	tea	steak
seam	leap		break
cream			
			and:
			head
			lead
			dead

oa:
oat	oak	groan
boat	soak	
moat		
coat		
goat		

4. Introduce the spelling *qu-*, which is the way *q* almost always appears in English. It is only used alone, I believe, in

---
* Explain or omit any unfamiliar words.

words taken directly from the Arabic (such as *Iraqi* and *qaf*) which, in the ordinary course of preschool reading, your child should not encounter often. As a general rule, we can expect *q* and *u* to be found together in English.

The sound that *qu* makes is like *kw*. Introduce these words:*

quit	quick	queen	squint
quite	quote	quints	squeeze
quilt			

    * Explain or omit any unfamiliar words.

Kit 19: Still more sounds:
-*r* after vowels; soft *c* and *g*

MATERIALS

    Movable alphabet cards
    Plastic letters
    Felt-tip pen and paper
    Children's books

GOAL

The goal of this kit is to help your child become familiar with several more letter-sound combinations.

INSTRUCTIONS

1. Continue to read aloud to your child and keep the book-choosing and library-going fun. If it gets to be a chore, try to figure what makes it that way and stop that.

2. Continue to encourage your child to produce written material.

3. Introduce the sound of -*er*, as in *her*.*

her	thinner
dinner	cutter
bigger	err
fatter	

    * Explain or omit any unfamiliar words.

In many words, *-ir, -ur, -urr,* and *-or* stand for the same sound.*

sir	fur	word
fir	cur	sailor
third	burr	tailor
bird	purr	
chirp	slur	

4. In many words, *r* changes the sound of the *o* or *a* before it in a different way.*

a:			*o:*
art	far	farm	or
chart	car	harm	for
part	par	charm	corn
cart	jar	card	morning
tart	bar	hard	born
dart	tar		horn
mart			

5. Before *l* or *ll, a* sometimes represents a slightly different sound as in *all,* and *o* usually becomes long, as in *old.**

all	old
fall	gold
ball	roll
gall	poll
hall	mold
call	colt
mall	fold
pall	hold
tall	bold
wall	folk
Walt	
malt	
halt	

* Explain or omit any unfamiliar words.

6. Introduce "soft" c and "soft" g. The soft sound of c, pronounced like s, is found when c is followed by e, i, or y.* Examples:

c:
ice	dice	Cindy
cedar	cider	Tracy
cellar	cinders	pounce
decide	Cy	cent
civil	mercy	certain
cyst	twice	cigarette
emergency	mice	cirrus
cell	once	Nancy
ace	cigar	

The "soft" sound of g, pronounced like j, is found sometimes (but not always) when g is followed by e or y. When soft g occurs in the middle or at the end of a word, it is sometimes accompanied by a d. Here are some examples of soft g:*

g:
edge	page	gadget	digest
lodge	gauge	widget	suggest
pledge	gouge	budget	
sludge	cage	fidget	
grudge	rage		
Madge	sage		
dodge			
budge			
fudge			
judge			

Here are some examples of soft g at the beginning of the words:*

gentleman	Gemini	geology
gelatine	Georgia	gem
gentle	gerbil	geography
German	gyp	germ
geranium	gym	gesture
George	edgy	gel
gee	geometry	general
genuine		

* Explain or omit any unfamiliar words.

7. Before *-nd*, *i* sometimes takes the long sound, as in *find*.*

>   find
>   wind (as in *wind a watch*)
>   mind
>   bind
>   hind
>   kind
>   rind

* Explain or omit any unfamiliar words.

Kit 20: Common sight words

MATERIALS

Word cards, to be made with felt-tip pen on 3 × 5 inch index cards

GOAL

This kit will attempt to get your child into learning to recognize certain of the most common words as wholes, quickly and accurately.

INSTRUCTIONS

1. Using felt-tip pen and index cards, make a set of word cards for those words from the sight word list in Instruction 2 which your child doesn't know yet. It will be helpful in printing the words on the cards if you first draw a guideline in pencil, but this is not absolutely necessary. Or, if you like, you may print the words on the lined side of the card. Print the words, using the same simplified letter forms as in previous kits. Letters should be about ¼ inch to ½ inch high.

* Explain or omit any unfamiliar words.

A sample card might look like this:

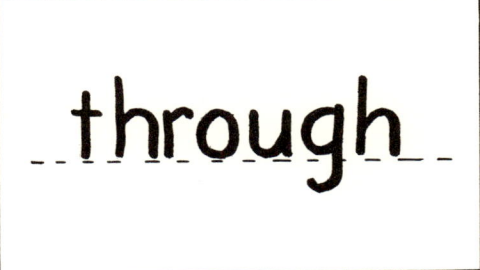

Figure 19

2. A master list of common sight words:

a	girl	now	three
about	give	nowhere	through
again	go	of	to
all	good	often	too
also	good-bye	old	took
although	has	one	toy
another	have	only	two
any	her	onto	under
anyone	here	open	underneath
are	house	ought	until
as	how	out	us
away	I	over	walk
baby	in	party	want
be	into	play	was
been	is	put	water
beneath	knot	said	way
blue	know	say	we
boat	laugh	saw	were
boy	little	see	what
come	look	seen	whatever
could	may	should	when
cough	maybe	so	whenever
cow	me	some	where
day	mother	something	wherever
do	many	that	which
dog	Miss	the	who

done	Mr.	them	why
down	Mrs.	their	will
eat	Ms.	then	with
ever	my	there	would
every	never	they	yellow
find	nevertheless	this	you
for	night	thorough	your
from	no	though	

3. Most of the letter games described in Kits 1 and 2 can be adapted for sight words. One of the most effective is the "word tree," in which the child puts the word cards he can read onto an array on the wall, on a door, etc. The more words he can read, the more leaves on his tree.

4. Another game consists of taping cards with the names of household objects onto the objects—lamp, chair, sofa, table, light, door, etc. Once the child can identify the words *on* the objects, you then take all the cards off the objects and have the child restore them to their proper places.

5. Another game is "today's word." Each morning the child gets to choose a word, any word, that she wants for that day. You ceremoniously make up the card and give it to her, or put it up in a conspicuous place. That word is hers. When she finds it in print, uses it, or hears it, you make a big deal about it.

6. Still another game, especially useful for very common words, is "find the word." You show the child a page on which the word can be found, and challenge him to find it. This game is particularly appropriate for most of the word list given in this kit.

7. As you read aloud to the child, remember to stop now and then to let her read words you know she recognizes. Often this can be carried to the point where you "take turns" reading to one another.

8. When your child can recognize most of the words on the first cards you have made, begin to add a few more easy words from the sight word list. Point these words out when you encounter them in your reading. *Go slow.* These words are "spelled funny," in my son William's phrase.

Kit 21: Independent reading

MATERIALS

> Word cards
> Movable alphabet cards
> Children's books

GOAL

This kit will attempt to get your child to read independently.

INSTRUCTIONS

1. Continue your reading together. Increasingly, have your child read parts of the story to you.

2. Keep the house full of reading materials that interest you and your child. Discuss the things you read with one another. Encourage your child to talk about her reading with you and with anyone else who will listen.

3. Continue to encourage your child to write.

4. Have your child read aloud to (and instruct?) another child who is a less expert reader. This "each one teach one" approach can work wonders.

Review Lesson IV (Kits 15-21)

These kits were designed to help your child get to the point where he could read some things by himself. Though the kits seemed to concentrate on small details, it is mastery of these details that will build your child's reading confidence.

REVIEW EXERCISES

1. Review the words covered in Kits 15-21, forming them at random with the cards or plastic letters, or writing them with felt-tip pen. Note those words which give your child difficulty; provide more practice with similar words.

2. Read alternately together—you read a few words and stop, let your child read a few words, and then you read again.

Note where your child has difficulty and work on it at a later time, or right then if the situation permits.

3. There's not much need to review your teaching here. If you've reached this point, you're bound to have been effective.

Make yourself a Master Teacher certificate. You've earned it.

A Buyer's Guide to Teaching and Learning Materials for Home Instruction

This buyer's guide was prepared for your convenience. I have listed a great variety of materials that some parents might possibly want—certainly nobody would want all of them.

Most of these materials are available locally in school-supply and office-supply stores. I have listed mail-order sources in case you cannot find an item—usually it's cheaper to buy locally. I have *not* attempted to give price information because of the difficulties involved in keeping up with fluctuating prices.

For my own convenience, I have used only a few major sources of mail-order supply. Several are headquartered in Atlanta, where I can talk to their management and pass on observations and complaints. Neither I nor McGraw-Hill has any connection with these suppliers.

Addresses of suppliers are given under the items listed, except for the major suppliers for whom I use symbols (MB, A+, B&T, etc.). Stock numbers are the same for all suppliers.

Major Suppliers

A+ School Supply, Inc. (A+)
3879 Covington Highway
Decatur, Georgia 30032
Telephone (404) 288-6140

Atlanta Milton Bradley, Inc. (MB)
384 Forrest Avenue, NE
Atlanta, Georgia 30312

Ideal School Supply Company (I)
11000 South Lavergne Avenue
Oak Lawn, Illinois 60453
Telephone (312) 425-0800

The Stevens Company (S)
1021 Columbia Avenue, NE
Atlanta, Georgia 30309

Baker and Taylor School Supplies
(B&T)
824 West 8th at Izard
Little Rock, Arkansas 72203

1391 Chattahoochee Avenue, NW
Atlanta, Georgia 30318
Telephone (404) 351-0127

R. B. Walter, Inc. (W)
2718 Piedmont Road, NE
Atlanta, Georgia 30305

St. Regis Consumer Products
Division (SR)
3300 Pinson Valley Parkway
Birmingham, Alabama 35217

P. O. Box 94029
3851 Yale Street
Houston, Texas 77018

Kenworthy Educational Services, Inc. (K)
P. O. Box 3031
Buffalo, New York 14205

I. COMPLETE PROGRAMS

Children Discover Reading series, by Catherine Stern and Toni S. Gould. The best materials I know for teaching reading to preschoolers one-to-one. Colorful and attractive: five workbooks. (You will want the teacher's edition which has complete instructions included.) About $15.00. Order through your bookstore or direct from L. W. Singer Publishing Company, 249–259 West Erie Boulevard, Syracuse, New York 13202.

Let's Read: A Linguistic Approach, by L. Bloomfield and C. L. Barnhart. The classic parent-taught reading program, beginning with letter names and going to a point at which the child can read fluently. No illustrations. Order through your bookstore or direct from Wayne State University Press, 5980 Cass Ave., Detroit, Michigan 48202.

Listen and Learn with Phonics, by Dorothy T. Watson. A set of books and records for home teaching. Contains three books, three records. "Turn-a-word wheel" and a word chart, letter strips, and instructions. About $25.00. (W., B&T, A+) Americana Interstate, Mundelein, Illinois 60060.

MCP Kindergarten Reading Program. A beginning reading program—or a readiness program that teaches beginning reading skills. Program consists of workbooks, lesson plans, and pre-primary readers, which are quite well done. Attractive and colorful. About $30.00. Order direct from Modern Curriculum Press, 13900 Prospect Road, Cleveland, Ohio 44136.

Ball-Stick-Bird. The brilliant, innovative approach to teaching beginning reading devised by psychologist Renee Fuller. Uses all capital letters. About $35.00 for five books and teacher's guide. Order from P. O. Box 195, Ourings Mills, Maryland 21117.

Your Child Can Learn to Read: A Guide for Parents and Teachers, by Margaret McEathron, 1952. A simple and inexpensive phonics program for home use. Step-by-step lessons, drills, games. Two inexpensive workbooks, *I Learn to Read,* Books 1 and 2, must be ordered separately. Less than $5.00. Dated, and not as colorful or elaborate as the others, but passable. (K)

Programmed Reading, Sullivan Associates, Cynthia Dee Buchanan, senior author. Twenty-one books, plus a primer, storybooks, and three teacher's guides. This program may be difficult to teach unless you have some teaching experience. You do not need all the books to begin with, however. The primers and Book 1, plus the teacher's guides, should get you started. Order through your bookstore or direct from Webster Division, McGraw-Hill, Avenue of the Americas, New York, New York 10020.

II. BASIC MATERIALS FOR TEACHING

A. ART SUPPLIES AND FINGER PAINTS

Newsprint Sheets. Drawing and scribbling paper, unlined. Sizes 9 by 12 inches, 12 by 18 inches, 18 by 24 inches, and 24 by 36 inches. My own preference is for the large sizes. (A+, SR)

Roll of Newsprint. Single roll, 262 inches long, 28 inches wide. Nice for murals, full-length self-portraits, etc. One roll should last you a pretty good while. #9660: SR

Sargent Fingerpaint. Eight-ounce jars in any of the following colors: black, blue, brown, green, orange, red, yellow, white, violet. #22-73xx: B&T

Sargent Fingerpaint Set. Box of four two-ounce jars of fingerpaint in blue, black, yellow and red. Also six sheets of fingerpaint paper, mixer, and instructions. #66-7012: B&T

St. Regis Nifty Fingerpainting Pad. Fingerpaint paper, 40 sheets per pad, 22 by 16 inches. #8808: SR

Uncle Wood's Homemade Fingerpaint Recipe.
Take 1 cup Ivory Flakes, 2 tbs. cold cream, ⅓ cup water. Put in a bowl and stir vigorously, or blend, with powdered tempera paint or food color to make whatever color you like.

Uncle Wood's Instant Fingerpaint Recipe.
Take an aerosol can of shaving cream, a plastic countertop (beside the sink, preferably because this is really messy), and vegetable coloring. Spray and spread the foam, adding a few drops of coloring as you go.

Rapid Mix Vivitone Powdered Tempera Paint. If you prefer to mix your own tempera paints (you can make it *much* thicker than suppliers do), try powdered tempera. Each jar makes two quarts. #838: B&T, MB

Colorbrite Watercolor Marker Assortment. Twelve watercolor markers in a box. Reasonably washable. Non-toxic. #60-A12: B&T

B. CHALKBOARDS, CHALK, AND ERASERS

Beginners Chalkboard. Oak-framed standing chalkboard designed for children from prekindergarten to grade 3. Full-size chalk trough. Five feet high, two feet, four inches wide. Available in green or black surface. #700-328: B&T

Child's Chalkboard Room Divider. Large 48 by 48 inch school-green chalkboard. Tubular steel legs with nonskid plastic tips. Unit is 4 feet wide and 4 feet high overall. No chalk tray. #240-226: A+, B&T

Tabletop Metal Chalkboards.
  18 inch by 24 inch, green metal trim. #M310: B&T
  24 by 36 inch, green metal trim. #M311: B&T
  24 by 36 inch combination flannelboard and metal chalkboard (green chalkboard on one side, flannel on other side). #FN320: B&T

Crayola white chalk. Writes easily, erases well. Can be dusty. #320: B&T

An-Du-Septic Dustless Chalk. Not as easy to erase, but is less dusty. If allergy is a factor, go with this one. #1403: B&T, A+

E-Z-Syte Polychromatic Chalk. A special chalk, yellow-gold in color. Visible, relatively dustless, and easy to write with. #1420: B&T, A+

Chalkmaster Custodial Eraser. Really gets the job done. Six inches long. #807-628: B&T

C. FLANNELBOARDS

Flan-O-Graph. Table model black flannelboard, 18 by 24 inches. Has storage compartment for felt pieces. #7800: B&T, MB, A+

Flannelboard. Functional wood framed, 28 by 40 inches. Inexpensive. ID 9771: I

D. LETTERS AND NUMERALS

Playskool Magnetized Plastic Letters. Multicolored plastic letters with magnets on back. Thirty-six pieces in each set. Lowercase #25; capital #28: B&T

Cutout letters and numbers. Cardboard 2¾ inches in red, blue, yellow, black, and white. Specify color. Capital letters and numbers 1-10, #401; lowercase letters, #402: B&T

Cardboard letters. Heavy cardboard letters; uppercase letters 2 inches high. Lowercase cardboard letters, #7508; uppercase cardboard letters, #7901: MB, B&T

Instructo Flannelboard Letters. Capital and lowercase letters for flannelboards. Set also includes punctuation marks. Letters are three inches high. #40: B&T

Flannelboard Letters. Red letters, goes with *Flan-O-Graph*. Lowercase, #7804; capitals, #7801: B&T, MB

Alphabet Desk Cards. Complete alphabet in cursive on one side, manuscript on the other. Useful for a child just beginning to write. #ID2284: I

Ruled Letter Cards. Like the movable alphabet cards, only smaller. Box contains 500 letters, capitals and lowercase. #1590: K

Playskool Alphabet Blocks. The classic wooden alphabet blocks. Inexpensive. Thirty embossed wooden letter blocks in a can. #214: MB

Nifty Play Blocks. Giant 9-inch cube, reinforced cardboard blocks. Sturdy and colorful—each block will support over 200 pounds. Capital and lowercase letters, with illustrations. About $12.00. #9920: SR

E. WRITING MATERIALS

Aero Magic Writing-Erasing Slate. Heavy construction, mylar film, unlined. Designed for steady use, guaranteed for one year of heavy duty use. (S)

Manuscript Writing Practice Slate. A Magic Slate writing portfolio. Heavy cardboard folder with lined magic slate on one side, manuscript alphabet chart on the other. Highly recommended. (S)

Learning to Print and Write Pencil Tablet. Choice paper for beginners, designed especially to suit preschoolers. 48 pages per pad, 9 by 12 inches. #48-2138; also available in reams, #50-7020: B&T

Writing Is Fun Workbook. A workbook your child can use in learning to print. Capitals, lowercase, and numerals are included. #205-286: B&T

Super Pencil. The absolutely last word in space-age technology brought to the readiness pencil! Specially shaped and molded of high-impact plastic to fit a child's hand. Available in colors, for right or left hand. Zaner Bloser, 612 North Park Street, Columbus, Ohio.

III. READING READINESS

Kid's Stuff: Reading and Writing Readiness, by Cherrie Farnette, Imogene Forte, and Barbara Loss, 1975. For parents concerned with reading readiness, this book provides more than 300 pages of ideas, exercises, and intensely practical how-to—both suggestions and material. Expensive—around $10.00—but worth it. Incentive Publications, Inc., P.O. Box 12522, Nashville, Tennessee 37212.

IV. ABC BOOKS AND RECORDS

Golden Animal Alphabet Record. LP record with alphabet songs. #LP244: B&T
The First Golden ABC Record. Alphabet song and others on LP record. #LP196: B&T
The Golden ABC Book. Popular, well illustrated, and colorful. Order through your bookstore.
Space Alphabet, by Irene Zacks, pictures by Peter R. Plasencia, New York, Prentice-Hall. Order through your bookstore.
Whitman ABC Coloring Book. Drawings by Vincent Fago and Dorothy Fago. Order through your bookstore. Western Publishing Company, Racine, Wisconsin.
Sesame Street ABC Book. Order through your bookstore. Golden Press, New York.

V. STORYBOOKS AND RECORDS

LP Golden Record and Book Sets. Each set includes an LP record and book. #GST1-14: B&T
Super Books, Jo Anne Nelson. Forty extremely easy books for beginning readers to read by themselves (or with very little help). Colorful and well designed—even interesting. Order from your bookstore or direct from J. B. Lippincott Company, Educational Publishing Division, East Washington Square, Philadelphia, Pennsylvania 19105.
MCP Preprimary Readers. Ten colorful eight-page storybooks for beginners. Sold only as a set, including teacher's guide. Order from Modern Curriculum Press, 13900 Prospect Road, Cleveland, Ohio 44136.
The Electric Company Easy Reader Golden Books. Colorful and fun to read as well as inexpensive. Order through your bookstore. Published by Western Publishing Company, Racine, Wisconsin.
The Electric Company Guide Activity Book and Newsletter. Over 200 pages of games, puzzles, minimovies, songs, crosswords, stories, and things to do. Periodic newsletters keep you informed about each program's goals and contents before air time.

Order from *The Electric Company Guide Activity Book*, North Road, Poughkeepsie, New York 12601.

Children's Books in Paperback. High quality children's books are available from several publishers in inexpensive paper editions. Write for a catalogue.

    Scholastic Press
    Englewood Cliffs, New Jersey 07632

    Dell Publishing Co.
    1 Dag Hammerskjold Plaza
    245 East 47 Street
    New York, New York 11017

    Reader's Digest Services, Inc.
    Educational Division
    Pleasantville, New York 10570

    Viking Paperbound Books
    625 Madison Avenue
    New York, New York 10022

VI. CHILDREN'S MAGAZINES

Child Life. Published 10 times a year; contains fiction, poems, arts and crafts, activities, and games. For children from preschool through grade 6. 1110 Waterway Blvd., Indianapolis, Indiana 46206.

Ebony, Jr. A magazine primarily for black children, *Ebony, Jr.*, concentrates on the black experience. Each issue includes a teacher's guide. Ten issues per year. 1320 South Michigan Avenue, Chicago, Illinois 60616.

Electric Company Magazine. If your child watches "The Electric Company," by all means subscribe to this magazine. Lively, well illustrated. Monthly. Dept. S-11, North Road, Poughkeepsie, New York 12601.

Highlights for Children. Directed toward children from ages two to twelve. Articles, games, arts and crafts, and activities. No advertising. Eleven issues per year. 2300 West Fifth Avenue, Columbus, Ohio 43216.

Humpty Dumpty's Magazine for Little Children. Stories for beginning readers. Large type. Published 10 times per year. For children ages three to seven. Bergenfield, New Jersey 07621.

Jack and Jill. Stories, games, and activities for children ages five to twelve. Published 10 times per year. 1110 Waterway Blvd., Indianapolis, Indiana 46206.

Kids Magazine. This magazine is written and illustrated by children (though it is edited, printed, and mailed to you by some exceptionally talented adults). For and by children five to fifteen, though I have seen four-year-olds who liked it also. 747 Third Avenue, New York, New York 10017.

Mister Roger's Letter. A real bargain, if your child likes Misteroger's TV show. Inexpensive, monthly, and supplements the television program. Family Communications, Inc., 4801 Fifth Avenue, Pittsburgh, Pennsylvania 15213.

National Geographic School Bulletin. Thirty issues, published weekly during the school year. Colorful, interesting, although it may be somewhat old for your child. My own experience with reading this magazine to preschool children has been good, however, and the pictures are nearly always interesting. 17th Street and M Street, NW, Washington, D.C. 20036.

Ranger Rick's Nature Magazine. This may be a little old for your child, but if he or she likes nature, it may be a favorite. Basically for elementary school children. Features stories, pictures, and activities, all centered on nature study. I really like this one. National Wildlife Federation, 1412 16th Street, NW, Washington, D.C. 20036.

Sesame Street Magazine. This colorful magazine is aimed at children who watch the television program. Both you and your child should enjoy this one. Monthly, for preschoolers. Dept. S-13, North Road, Poughkeepsie, New York 12601.

VII. POSTERS AND LETTERSTRIPS

Alphabet Wall Cards. Thirteen alphabet and two numeral cards; white on mustard or red background. #50-2616: B&T

Alphabet Parade Letterstrip. Twenty-six colored circus wagons with letters (capital and lowercase) in each wagon. Illustrations on wheels of associated words (alligator, bear, carrot, etc.). #T471: B&T

Manuscript Animal Wall Chart (letterstrip). Eight cards 8 by 22 inches each, with pictures of animal associated with each letter. Capitals, lowercase, and numerals. Study guide included. B50-2622: B&T

Alphabet Posters. From Harvard Coop, Cambridge, Mass. 02138: "A Is for Animals," 24 × 34; "*Sesame Street* Cooky Monster ABC," 24 × 36; "Here We Go from A to Z," 21 × 28. From Botolph Gallery, 44 Brattle Street, Cambridge, Mass. 02138: "Eleanor Lander's Alphabet Print," 41 × 31, a handsome six-color original silk screen. About $15.

Alphabet Express (letterstrip). Colorful engine, caboose, and 26 cars, each car carrying a capital and lowercase letter, plus pictures of associated objects. #770: B&T, A+

VIII. LETTER LEARNING GAMES AND PUZZLES

The ABC Game. This is a card-matching game, easy to play and fun. Inexpensive. #2162: W

Alphabet Bingo. Letter learning game using both capital and lowercase letters. #T103: B&T

Canned Alphabet (learning game). Cardboard capital letters in color with a vinyl letterstrip. Letters are colorcoded in accordance with a planned learning sequence. Instructions. A Best Buy. #1800: A+, B&T

ABC Lotto. Contains lowercase letters, numbers, and associated objects. Six playing boards and thirty-six covering cards. Two to six people can play. #100: B&T

Alphabet Punch-a-Shape Letter Learning Game. Padded tray and uppercase and lowercase templates for punching out letters. Expensive. #T301: B&T

IX. LETTER-SOUND ASSOCIATION AND LEARNING MATERIAL

Alphabet Cards. Upper- and lowercase letters, associated pictures, 31 cards 10⅛ by 13½ inches in two colors, two for each vowel, illustrating long and short sounds. #T225: A+, B&T, MB

Playskool Picture Alphabet. Twenty-four full-color 2⅞ by 4⅝ inch interlocking picture puzzles mounted on woodboard. Self-correcting letters cannot be mismatched. Expensive. #7005: B&T

Alphabet Picture Flash Cards. Letters (both capital and lowercase forms) on a card with a symbol in color (apple, banana, etc.). Useful for teaching letter-sound association. Card 8 by 4 inches. Kit includes instructions for learning games and teaching exercises. #9502: MB, B&T

The Giant Alphabet Box. Big flashcards. Capital and lowercase letters on one side, picture on the reverse. Cards 9 by 13 inches, color on white stock. #285: B&T

Fun Box Letter Recognition Game. Shaped cut-out letters are matched to corresponding cards which contain associated pictures. (For example, H fits into a card with a picture of a horse, in color—and nowhere else.) A useful learning game. #601: B&T

Initial Consonant Bingo. Two hundred eighty-eight different matching pictures and beginning consonants. Materials for up to 36 players. #T104: B&T

X. TEACHING RHYMES

Objects that Rhyme. Twenty toy models of things that rhyme—cork and fork, mouse and house, star and car, for example. #2692: B&T, I

Rhyming Pictures. A boxed set of cards with pictures of objects that rhyme. #2694: B&T, I

XI. PHONICS GAMES

The Doghouse Game. An inexpensive teaching game for students who are learning short vowel sounds. Fits into my program at about Kit 10. #2155: W, K, B&T

Turn-a-Word™ Three five-sided hardwood blocks on an axle that turns to form three-letter words (hat, fat, rat, etc.). #J0682: MB

Reading Games Book, by Guy Wagner and Max Hoiser #95802.
  Listening Games, #95801
  Math Games, #95826
  Language Games, #95803
  (B&T)

Junior Phonics Rummy. A matching game teaching short-vowel easy words. Inexpensive. #2154: K, B&T

XII. GAMES FOR ADVANCING READERS

Picture-Word Matching Game. Child matches picture to words by drawing a crayon line on plasticized cards that wipe clean with damp cloth. #9824: SR

UNO—A Phonics Game. The ultimate phonics game, goes from beginnings to high levels. #2192: MB

Combination Form-a-Word Kit. Teaches word blends, prefixes, suffixes, and syllables. #1200: K

XIII. TEACHING ADVICE AND "HOW TO"

Teaching Young Children to Read. Dolores Durkin, Boston, Allyn and Bacon, 1972.
  The best, most complete how-to text for young children. Order through your bookstore.

The Great Reading Turn-on. Joan Beck and Marjorie Hopper, Racine, Wis., Golden Press, 1972.
  Full of practical and imaginative suggestions, games, and activities. Order through your bookstore.

Reading: How To. Herb Kohl. New York, Dutton, 1973.
  A simple, easy-to-read book about teaching reading. Order through your bookstore.

Basic Phonics Manual. A summary of phonics for amateurs. Uses word families to illustrate concepts. #5325: B&T

Phonics in Proper Perspective. A. W. Heilman. Columbus, Ohio, Merrill, 1968.
  A thorough discussion of phonics for the tutor. Understandable and useful. Order through your bookstore.

XIV. SCHOOL AT HOME

The Calvert School. A complete kindergarten-through-high school curriculum, for teaching your child at home. Can also be used to supplement your child's regular school. Calvert is a nationally known, nonprofit independent school. Their school-at-home program is described in more detail on pp. 23–24 above. Write The Calvert School, Tuscany Road, Baltimore, Maryland 21210.

A Reading List for Parent-Teachers

I have tried to select, from the enormous literature on reading instruction, a few books which I believe would be helpful and interesting to parents. I take the liberty of listing them in some sort of shaggy precedence that accords with *my* notion of their likely usefulness to the parent-teacher. As in most other things, however, parents are generally better judges of their needs than experts are. If you want to start in the middle or at the bottom of the list, by all means go ahead.

Any of these books will be informative, I think. I hope you enjoy them and find them helpful.

Teaching Young Children to Read. Dolores Durkin. Boston, Allyn and Bacon, 1972.
>This is the basic text for teaching reading in preschools. Contains thorough treatment of the question of reading readiness. Detailed information on teaching methods and materials. Carefully written.

A Parent's Guide to Children's Reading. 4th ed. Nancy Larrick. New York, Bantam Books.
>This book provides a clear and insightful review of the books available. It also includes useful essays on various aspects of reading to, by, and with children.

Learning to Read: The Great Debate. Jeanne S. Chall. New York, McGraw-Hill, 1967.
>A balanced, scholarly, and eminently readable inquiry into the phonics/look-say debate and into the broader questions of beginning reading instruction.

The Great Reading Turn-on. Joan Beck and Marjorie Hopper. Racine, Wis., Golden Press, 1972.
>A worthwhile book, full of low-pressure suggestions and ideas for ways to teach your child about reading. Beck's essential idea is to get your child interested, excited about reading. Well worth your investment.

Revolution in Learning: The Years from Birth to Six. Maya Pines. New York, Harper & Row, 1967.

> A clear, easy-to-read account of the explosive changes that took place in early childhood education in the sixties. Somewhat dated now, but well worth reading. Contains the best and least-biased summary of Montessori that I know.

Teacher. Sylvia Ashton-Warner. New York, Bantam Books, 1971.

> One of the best books ever about teaching young children. Ashton-Warner's way of teaching is not always as successful for other people as it was for her, but the chance to observe a master teacher at work is priceless.

Children Who Read Early. Dolores Durkin. New York, Teachers College Press, 1966.

> This is the report of Durkin's landmark studies on early reading. A *must* if you're seriously interested in the question.

Children and Television: Lessons from Sesame Street. Gerald Lesser. New York, Random House, 1974.

> A lucidly written (and delightfully illustrated) account of the "Sesame Street" experience, written by the Harvard psychologist who served as chairman of the Board of Educational Advisors. If your child watches "Sesame Street," you should read this book.

Teaching Them to Read. Dolores Durkin. Boston, Allyn and Bacon, 2d ed., 1974.

> A textbook on reading instruction for elementary teachers. Gives background and detail on the essentials of reading instruction.

Teaching to Read, Historically Considered. M. M. Mathews. Chicago, University of Chicago Press, 1966.

> A solid, thoughtfully written and readable history of reading instruction. Anyone with a taste for the nooks and crannies of history will likely find this book absorbing. One of my favorites.

Reading: How To. Herb Kohl. New York, Dutton, 1973.

> A book about reading, with the avowed intent to demythologize it. Kohl concentrates on the affective, meaning-related concerns of children learning to read.

Preschool Reading Instruction: A Literature Search, Evaluation, and Interpretation. Final Report. W. E. Blanton. ERIC, 1973 (ED 069 345. ED 069 346, and ED 069 347).

> Published by ERIC (Education Research Information Clearinghouse). Available on microfiche and Xerox copies. May be ordered through your library, using the numbers cited. Of particular interest as a reference work.

Understanding Reading: A Psycholinguistic Analysis of Reading and Learning to Read. Frank Smith. New York, Holt, 1971.

> If you're *really* interested in knowing about what goes on when

people read, Smith can help. Easy to read, and as clear as this sort of thing is ever likely to be.

Why Johnny Can't Read—and What You Can Do about It. Rudolf Flesch. New York, Harper & Row, 1955.

An irreverent and one-sided polemic about phonics and the American reading establishment. Fun to read, but consistently calls a spade a bloody shovel.

Approaches to Beginning Reading. R. C. Aukerman. New York, Wiley, 1971.

This book outlines the several different approaches to reading instruction and reviews over 100 published programs.

References

Adamson, J. W. 1946. *"The illiterate Anglo-Saxon" and other essays on education, medieval and modern.* New York: Cambridge University Press.
Alcott, W. A. 1836. *The young mother.* Boston: Light and Stearns.
———. 1843. "There is no school like the family school." The mother's assistant. Vol. 3, no. 2, January 1843.
Almy, M. C. 1949. *Children's experiences prior to first grade and success in beginning reading.* New York: Bureau of Publications, Teachers College, Columbia University.
Anderson, Irving, and Walter Dearborn. 1952. *The psychology of teaching reading.* New York: Ronald.
Anderson, R. H. 1969. *Teaching in a world of change.* New York: Harcourt, Brace & World.
Anderson, Yvonne. 1971. *Teaching film animation to children.* New York: Van Nostrand.
Anonymous (Terman Introduction). 1918. See Terman, L. M., 1918.
Appleton, Elizabeth. 1815. *Private education; or a practical plan for the study of young ladies. with an address to parents, private governesses, and young ladies.* London: H. Colburn.
———. 1821. *Early education: Or the management of children considered with a view to future character.* London: Cox and Baylis.
Arbuthnot, May, and Zena Sutherland. 1972. *Children and books.* 4th ed. Glenview, Ill.: Scott, Foresman.
Ariès, Philippe. 1962. *Centuries of childhood.* New York: Vintage Books.
Aristotle. *Politics.* Book 7.
Ashton-Warner, Sylvia. 1971. *Teacher.* New York: Bantam Books.
Aukerman, R. C. 1971. *Approaches to beginning reading.* New York: Wiley.
Austin, M. C., et al. 1962. *The torchlighters: Tomorrow's teachers of reading.* Cambridge, Mass.: Harvard University Press.
Bakewell, Mrs. J. 1843. *The mother's practical guide in the early training of her children: Containing directions for their physical, intellectual, and moral education.* From the 2d London ed. New York: Lane and Sandford, for the Methodist Episcopal Church.
Ball, Samuel, and G. A. Bogatz. 1970. *The first year of "Sesame Street,"* Princeton, N.J.: Educational Testing Service.
———, and ———. 1973. *Reading with television: An evaluation of "The Electric Company."* Princeton, N.J.: Educational Testing Service.
———, et al. 1974. *Reading with television: A follow-up evaluation of "The Electric Company."* Princeton, N.J.: Educational Testing Service.

Barbe, W. B. (ed.). 1965. *Teaching reading.* New York: Oxford University Press.
Baron, S. W. 1942. *A social and religious history of the Jews.* Vol. 2. *The Jewish community.* New York: Columbia University Press.
Beck, F. A. 1964. *Greek education.* New York: Barnes & Noble.
Beck, Joan. 1964. *Short cuts to reading you can teach your child.* Chicago: The Chicago Tribune. (Adapted from D. T. Watson's *Listen and Learn with Phonics* [1961] by Joan Beck and Becky.)
———. 1967. *How to raise a brighter child: The case for early learning.* New York: Trident Press.
———. 1969. Personal communication, May 2.
———, and Marjorie Hopper. 1972. *The great reading turn-on.* Racine, Wis.: Golden Press.
Beck-Watson. 1964. See Beck, Joan, 1964.
Berle, A. A. 1915. *The school in the home.* New York: Moffat, Yard and Co.
Bestor, A. E. 1953. *Educational wastelands: The retreat from learning in our public schools.* Urbana, Ill.: The University of Illinois Press.
Bettelheim, Bruno. 1966. The danger of teaching your baby to read. *Ladies Home Journal.* Vol. 83, pp. 38–40, September.
Bevan, F. L. 1857. *Reading without tears: A pleasant mode of learning to read.* London: Longmans.
Beyer, Evelyn, 1968. *Teaching young children.* New York: Pegasus.
Blanton, W. E. 1972. Preschool reading instruction: A literature search, evaluation, and interpretation. Final report. ERIC: ED 069 345, ED 069 346, and ED 069 347.
Bloomfield, Leonard. 1942. "Linguistics and reading." *The Elementary English Review.* Vol. 19, no. 4, pp. 125–130, April, and no. 5, pp. 183–186, May.
———, and C. L. Barnhart, 1961. *Let's read: A linguistic approach.* Detroit: Wayne State University Press.
Bogatz, G. A., and Samuel Ball. 1971. *The second year of "Sesame Street": A continuing evaluation.* Princeton, N.J.: Educational Testing Service.
Boone, R. G. 1889. *Education in the United States, its history from the earliest settlements.* New York: Appleton.
Brown, M. W. 1924. *A study of reading ability in pre-school children.* Unpublished master's thesis. Stanford, Calif.: Stanford University.
Bruner, J. S. 1960. *The process of education.* Cambridge, Mass.: Harvard University Press.
Brzienski, J. E., and J. L. Hayman, Jr. 1962. *The effectiveness of parents in helping their preschool children to begin reading.* Denver, Colo.: Denver Public Schools.
Carroll, John. 1964. *Language and thought.* Englewood Cliffs, N.J.: Prentice-Hall.
———. 1966. Some neglected relationships in reading and language learning. *Elementary English.* Vol. 43, pp. 577–582, October.
Cazden, Courtney. 1972. *Child language and education.* New York: Holt.
———. 1973. Progress report on in-classroom research on "The Electric Company." New York: Children's Television Workshop, February.
Chall, J. S. 1967. *Learning to read: The great debate.* New York: McGraw-Hill.

Cheira, Edward. 1938. *They wrote on clay.* Edited by G. C. Gameron. Chicago: University of Chicago Press.
Child, Lydia. 1835. *On the management and education of children, being Mrs. Child's "mother's book."* London: John W. Parker.
Chomsky, Carol. 1971a. *On language learning from 5 to 10: The acquisition of syntax in children.* Cambridge: M.I.T. Press.
———. 1971b. Write first, read later. *Childhood Education.* Vol. 47, no. 6, pp. 296–299, March.
Churchill, W. S. 1930. *My early life.* New York: Charles Scribner's Sons.
Cipolla, C. M. 1969. *Literacy and development in the West.* Baltimore: Penguin.
Claiborne, Robert. 1974. *The birth of writing.* New York: Time-Life Books, The Emergence of Man Series, Time, Inc.
Cohan, Mayme. 1961. Two and a half and reading. *Elementary English.* Vol. 38, pp. 506–508ff, November.
Conant, J. B. (ed.). 1962. *Learning to read—A report of a conference of reading experts.* Princeton, N.J.: Educational Testing Service.
———. 1967. *Learning to read: A report of a conference of reading experts.* Princeton, N.J.: Educational Testing Service.
Coote, Edmund. 1596. *The English Schoole-Maister (The English Schoolmaster).*
Cox, C. M. 1926. *Genetic studies of genius.* Vol. 2. *The early mental traits of three hundred geniuses.* Stanford, Calif.: Stanford University Press.
Crampton, Gertrude, and Tibor Gergely. 1946. *Tootle.* New York: Golden Press.
Cremin, A. L. 1970. *American education: The colonial experience 1607–1783.* New York: Harper & Row.
CTW '72. *A Special report from the Children's Television Workshop.* 1972. Office of Public Affairs, Children's Television Workshop, 1 Lincoln Plaza, New York.
Cubberley, E. P. 1919. *Public education in the United States.* Boston: Houghton Mifflin.
Dallmann, Martha, et al. 1974. *The teaching of reading.* 4th ed. New York: Holt.
Davidson, H. P. 1931. An experimental study of bright, average and dull children at the four-year mental level. *Genetic Psychology Monographs.* Vol. 9, pp. 119–287.
Dechant, E. V. 1964. *Improving the teaching of reading.* Englewood Cliffs, N.J.: Prentice-Hall.
———. 1970. *Improving the teaching of reading.* 2d ed. Englewood Cliffs, N.J.: Prentice-Hall.
Dewey, John. 1898. The primary education fetich. *Forum.* Vol. 25, pp. 315–328.
Diack, Hunter. 1965. *The teaching of reading.* New York: Philosophical Library.
Disney, Walt, Productions, Inc. 1973. *Wonderful world of reading.* Danbury, Conn.: Grolier.
Dissertation abstracts. 1969. "The humanities and social sciences." Microfilm. Vol. 29, no. 7, June. Ann Arbor, Mich.: The University of Michigan.
Dolbear, Katherine E. 1912. Precocious children. *Pedagogical Seminary.* Vol. 19, pp. 461–491.

Doman, G. 1964. *How to teach your baby to read.* New York: Random House.
———. 1968. German translation. *How to teach your baby to read.* Freiberg, Germany: Hyperion.
———, G. L. Stevens, and R. C. Orem. 1963. You can teach your baby to read. *Ladies Home Journal.* Vol. 80, pp. 62ff, May.
Durkin, Dolores. 1961. Children who read before grade one. *Reading Teacher.* Vol. 14, pp. 163–166, January.
———. 1963. Children who read before grade 1: A second study. *Elementary School Journal.* Vol. 64, pp. 142–148, November.
———. 1966. *Children who read early.* New York: Teachers College Press.
———. 1968. When should children begin to read? In *Innovation and Change in Reading Instruction.* Sixty-seventh Yearbook of the National Society for the Study of Education. Chicago: University of Chicago Press.
———. 1969a. *Reading and the kindergarten: An annotated bibliography.* Newark, Del.: International Reading Association.
———. 1969b. A two-year language arts program for pre-first grade children: First year report. Paper delivered at American Educational Research Association meeting in Los Angeles, California, Feb. 7.
———. 1970. Reading readiness. *The Reading Teacher.* March, pp. 528–534.
———. 1972. *Teaching young children to read.* Boston: Allyn and Bacon.
———, et al. 1973. Day care and reading. *The Reading Teacher.* February.
———. 1974. *Teaching them to read.* 2d ed. Boston: Allyn and Bacon.
Durrell, D. D. 1956. *Improving reading instruction.* New York: Harcourt, Brace & World.
Edey, M. A. 1974. *The sea traders.* New York: Time-Life Books.
Englemann, Siegfried, and Therese Engelmann. 1966. *Give your child a superior mind.* New York: Simon & Schuster.
Evans, J. L. 1965. Teaching reading by machine: A case history in early reading behavior. *A V Communication Review.* Vol. 13, pp. 303–308.
Flesch, Rudolf. 1955. *Why Johnny can't read—and what you can do about it.* New York: Perennial Library, Harper & Row.
Forester, C. S. 1967. *Long before forty.* London: Joseph.
Fowler, William. 1962a. Cognitive learning in infancy and early childhood. *Psychological Bulletin.* Vol. 59, no. 2, pp. 112–152.
———. 1962b. Teaching a two-year old to read: An experiment in early childhood. *Genetic Psychology Monographs.* Vol. 66, pp. 181–283.
———. 1965. A study of process and method in three-year-old twins and triplets learning to read. *Genetic Psychology Monographs.* Vol. 72, pp. 3–89.
———. 1966. Longitudinal study of early stimulation in the emergence of cognitive processes. Paper presented to the Society for Research in Child Development. Chicago, Ill., Feb. 7.
Gates, A. I. 1936. "Reading readiness: A study of factors determining success and failure in beginning reading." *Teachers College Record.* Vol. 37, pp. 679–685.
———. 1937. The necessary mental age for beginning reading. *Elementary School Journal.* Vol. 37, pp. 497–508.
———, and G. L. Bond. 1936. A study of factors determining success and failure in beginning reading. *Teachers College Record.* Vol. 37, pp. 679–685.
———, G. L. Bond, and'D. H. Russell. 1939. *Methods of determining reading*

readiness. New York: Bureau of Publications, Teachers College, Columbia University.

Gattegno, Caleb. 1970. The problem of reading is solved. *Harvard Educational Review*. Vol. 40, no. 2, pp. 283-286.

Gedike, Friedrich. 1791. *Children's book for the practice in reading without the ABC's and spelling*. Berlin.

Glynn, D. M. 1964. *Teach your child to read*. London: Pearson.

Goertzel, Victor, and M. C. Goertzel, 1962. *Cradles of eminence*. Boston: Little, Brown.

Goodrich, S. G. 1838. *Fireside education . . . by the author of Peter Parle's tales*. New York: F. J. Huntington.

Gwynn, Aubrey. 1926. *Roman education from Cicero to Quintilian*. Reprinted ed., 1966. New York: Teachers College.

Hainstock, E. G. 1968. *Teaching Montessori in the home: The preschool years*. New York: Random House.

―――. 1971. *Teaching Montessori in the home: The preschool years*. New York: Random House.

Harman, David. 1970. Illiteracy: An overview. *Harvard Educational Review*. Vol. 40, no. 2, pp. 226-243.

Harris, A. J., C. Morrison, B. L. Serwer, and L. Gold. 1968. A continuation of the CRAFT PROJECT comparing reading approaches with disadvantaged urban Negro children in primary grades. New York: Division of Teachers Educators, City University of New York. Selected Academic Readings, Rockefeller Center, 630 Fifth Avenue, New York 10020.

Hart, Archibald. 1947. *Calvert and Hillyer: 1947*. Baltimore: The Calvert School.

―――. 1972. *Calvert and Brown: 1947-1972*. Baltimore: The Calvert School.

Hart, John. 1570. *A methode or comfortable beginning for all vnlearned, whereby they may bee taught to read Englishe, in a very short time, with pleasure: So profitable as straunge, put in light*. London: Henrie Denham.

Heffernan, Helen. 1960. Significance of kindergarten education. *Childhood Education*. Vol. 36, pp. 313-319.

Hildreth, Gertrude. 1958. *Teaching reading*. New York: Holt.

Hillman, Rosemary. 1963. In defense of the five-year-old. *Saturday Review*. Vol. 46, pp. 77ff, Nov. 16.

Hollingworth, Leta. 1942. *Children above 180 IQ*. New York: World.

Holmes, Jack. 1962. When should and could Johnny learn to read? In *Challenge and experiment in reading*, J. A. Figurel (ed.). Newark, Del.: International Reading Association.

Holt, John. 1969. *The underachieving school*. New York: Pitman.

―――. 1971. Big Bird, meet Dick and Jane. *Atlantic Monthly*, May.

Huey, E. B. 1908. *The psychology and pedagogy of reading*. New York: Macmillan. Republished in 1968 by Massachusetts Institute of Technology Press, Cambridge.

Hughes, Felicity. 1971. *Reading and writing before school*. New York: St. Martin's.

Hunt, J. McV. 1961. *Intelligence and experience*. New York: Ronald.

Hurd, G. M., and E. L. Rimmel. 1961. *Preparing your child for reading*. Boston: Houghton Mifflin.

Hymes, J. L. 1963a. More pressure for early reading. *Childhood Education*. Vol. 39, pp. 34-35, September.

―――. 1963b. When should reading instruction begin? In *Reading as an intel-*

lectual activity, J. A. Figurel (ed.). Conference proceedings, vol. VIII. New York: International Reading Association.

———. 1970. Teaching reading to the under-six age: A child development point of view. From the *34th Claremont Reading Conference Yearbook*, Malcolm P. Douglas (ed.), pp. 79–83. Claremont, Calif.: Claremont Reading Conference.

———. 1973. Teaching reading to the under-six age: A child development point of view. In *Perspectives on elementary reading*, Karlin (ed.). New York: Harcourt Brace Jovanovich, pp. 131–135.

Ilg, F. L., and L. B. Ames. 1964. *School readiness*. New York: Harper & Row.

———, and ———. 1972. *School readiness: Behavior tests used at the Gesell Institute*. New York: Harper & Row.

Iredell, Harriet. 1898. Eleanor learns to read. *Education*. December, pp. 233–238.

Johnson, Clifton. 1904. *Old-time schools and school books*. New York: Macmillan. Republished in 1963 by Dover, New York.

Karger, Gertrude. 1969. *A review of compensatory education programs*. Cambridge, Mass.: Harvard Graduate School of Education.

Karlin, Robert (ed.). 1973. *Perspectives on elementary reading*. New York: Harcourt Brace Jovanovich.

Kasdon, L. M. 1958. Early reading background of some superior readers among college freshmen. *Journal of Educational Research*. Vol. 52, pp. 151–153, December.

Keay, F. E. 1918. *Ancient Indian education: An inquiry into its origin, development, and ideals*. London: Oxford.

Keele, R. L., and G. V. Harrison. 1971. The effect of parents using structured tutoring techniques in teaching their children to read. Paper presented at a meeting of the American Educational Research Association, New York, Feb. 4–7. Eric RE 003 448.

Kramer, S. N. 1961. *Sumerian mythology*. New York: Harper.

———. 1967. *Cradle of civilization*. New York: Time-Life Books, Great Ages of Man series, Time, Inc.

Kuhn, A. L. 1947. *The mother's role in childhood education: New England concepts, 1830–1860*. New Haven: Yale University Press.

Larrick, Nancy. 1975. *A parent's guide to children's reading*. 4th ed. New York: Bantam Books.

Lee, Harper. 1960. *To kill a mockingbird*. New York: Bantam Books.

LeShan, Eda. 1967. *The conspiracy against childhood*. New York: Atheneum.

Lesser, Gerald. 1972. Learning, teaching, and TV production for children: The Sesame Street experience. Cambridge, Mass.: *Harvard Educational Review*. Vol. 42, May.

———. 1974. *Children and television: Lessons from Sesame Street*. New York: Random House.

Levin, Harry, and Joanna Williams (eds.). 1970. *Basic studies on reading*. New York: Harper & Row.

Luckert-Doman. 1968. *You can teach your baby to read*. German translation.

Lynch, E. F. 1914. *Educating the child at home: Personal training and the work habit*. New York: Harper.

———. 1931. *Bookless lessons for the teacher-mother*. Minerva. N.Y.: The National League of Teacher-Mothers.

McCracken, Glenn. 1959. *The right to learn*. Chicago: Regnery.

McEathron, Margaret. 1952. *Your child can learn to read.* New York: Grosset & Dunlap.

McKee, Paul, J. E. Brzienski, and M. L. Harrison. 1966. *The effectiveness of teaching reading in kindergarten.* Denver, Colo.: The Denver Public Schools.

Martineau, Harriet. 1837. *Society in America.* 3 vols. London: Saunders and Otley.

Martinez, Armando. 1970. Literacy through democratization of education. *Harvard Educational Review.* Vol. 40, no. 2, pp. 280–282.

Mason, C. M. 1886. *Home education.* London: Kegan Paul.

Mathews, M. M. 1966. *Teaching to read, historically considered.* Chicago: University of Chicago Press.

Mead, Margaret. 1961. Questions that need asking. New York: *Teachers College Record.* Vol. 63, pp. 89–93. (Frontispiece quote, p. 92.)

Mill, J. S. 1873. *Autobiography (1806–1873).* Reprinted ed., 1975. New York: Henry Holt.

Miller, Merle. 1974. *Plain speaking: An oral biography of Harry S Truman.* New York: Putnam.

Minton, Judith. 1972. *The influence of "Sesame Street" on reading readiness scores of selected kindergarten children.* Unpublished doctoral dissertation. New York: Fordham University.

Moore, O. K., and A. R. Anderson. 1967. The responsive environments project. In *Early education: Current theory, research and practice,* R. D. Hess and R. M. Bear (eds.). Chicago: Aldine.

Morphett, Mabel, and Carleton Washburne. 1931. "When should children begin to read?" *Elementary School Journal.* Vol. 31, pp. 496–503, March.

Morris, Ronald. 1963. *Success and failure in learning to read.* London: Oldbourne.

Morrison, Coleman, A. J. Harris, and I. T. Auerbach. 1969. *A comparison of the reading performance of early and non-early readers from grade one through grade three.* ERIC: ED 028 041.

The New York Times Book Review, Mar. 10, 1974. Review of *The Electric Company Easy Readers.* By John Culhane, pp. 8, 9.

Olilla, Lloyd. 1971. Pros and cons of teaching reading to four- and five-year-olds. A paper presented to the 1971 conference of the International Reading Association. In R. C. Aukerman, *Some Persistent Questions on Beginning Reading,* IRA, Newark, Delaware, 1972.

Palmer, E. L. 1972. Formative research in educational television production: The experience of the Children's Television Workshop. In *Quality in instructional television,* W. Schramm (ed.). Honolulu: University of Hawaii Press.

Parke, M. B. 1957. Reprinted 1969. *You can teach your child to read.* New York: Grosset & Dunlap.

Patrick, G. T. W. 1899. Should children under ten learn to read and write? *Popular Science Monthly.* January, pp. 382–391.

Perkinson, H. J. 1968. *The imperfect panacea: American faith in education 1865–1965.* New York: Random House.

Perlish, H. N. 1968. *An investigation of the effectiveness of a TV reading program along with parental home assistance in helping three-year-old children learn to read.* Unpublished doctoral dissertation. Philadelphia: University of Pennsylvania.

Pilch, Judah, and Meir Ben Horin. 1966. *Judaism or the Jewish school.* New York: Bloch Publishing Co.
Pines, Maya. 1967. *Revolution in learning: The years from birth to six.* New York: Harper & Row.
Pirenne, Henri. 1973. *Economic and social history of medieval Europe.* New York: Harcourt, Brace.
Prior, Matthew. 1717. *Alma: or, the progress of the mind.* London.
Quintilian (Marcus Fabius Quintilianus). ca. A.D. 91 *Institutio Oratoria.* Vol. I, with English translation by H. E. Butler. Loeb Classical Library. New York: Putnam, 1920.
Read, Charles. 1971. Preschool children's knowledge of English phonology. *Harvard Educational Review.* Vol. 41, no. 1, pp. 1–34.
Rickover, H. G. 1959. *Education and freedom.* New York: Dutton.
———. 1962. *Swiss schools and ours: Why theirs are better.* Boston: Little, Brown.
———. 1963. *American education, a national failure: The problem of our schools and what we can learn from England.* New York: Dutton.
Rodgers, Norma. 1971. What is reading readiness? International Reading Association, Micromonograph, Newark, Delaware.
Sartre, J. P. 1964. *The words.* Greenwich, Conn.: Fawcett, Crest Books.
Scripture, E. W. 1897. In the Japanese way. *Outlook.* Vol. 60, pp. 556–557.
Segal, Marilyn. 1966. *Run away, little girl.* New York: Random House.
Sheldon, W. D. 1963. Should the very young be taught to read? *NEA Journal.* Vol. 52, pp. 20–22.
Smethurst, Wood. 1970. *The nonprofessional teaching of beginning reading skills to young children outside schools.* Unpublished Ed.D. dissertation. Cambridge, Mass.: Harvard University, Graduate School of Education.
Smith, Mortimer. 1949. *And madly teach: A layman looks at public school education.* Chicago: Regnery.
——— (ed.). 1956. *The public schools in crisis: Some critical essays.* Chicago: Regnery.
———. 1965. *A citizen's manual for public schools.* Boston: Little, Brown.
Smith, N. B. 1963. *Reading instruction for today's children.* Englewood Cliffs, N.J.: Prentice-Hall.
———. 1965. *American reading instruction.* New York: Teachers College Press.
Smith, W. A. 1955. *Ancient Education.* New York: Philosophical Library.
———. 1969. *Ancient Education.* New York: Greenwood Press.
Steinberg, Danny, and Miho Steinberg. 1970. Reading in the crib. Unpublished manuscript. Champaign-Urbana: University of Illinois.
Stevens, G. L., and R. C. Orem. 1968. *The case for early reading.* St. Louis: Warren H. Green. (Introduction by Buckminster Fuller.)
Stoner, W. S. 1914. *Natural education.* Indianapolis: Bobbs-Merrill.
———. 1916. *Manual of natural education.* Indianapolis: Bobbs-Merrill.
Stoner, W. S., Jr. 1915. *Facts in jingles.* Indianapolis: Bobbs-Merrill.
Strang, Ruth. 1954. Reading development for gifted children. *Elementary English.* Vol. 31, pp. 35–40.
———. 1963. Should parents teach reading? *PTA Magazine.* March, pp. 7–9.
Strickland, Charles. 1973. A transcendentalist father: The child-rearing practices of Bronson Alcott. *History of Childhood Quarterly.* Vol. 1, no. 1, pp. 2–51.

Sutton, M. H. 1969. Children who learned to read in kindergarten: A longitudinal study. *The Reading Teacher.* Vol. 22, 595–602ff.
Swift, T. H. 1919. *Education in ancient Israel to 70 A.D.* Chicago: London Open Court Publishing Co.
Terman, L. M. 1918. Introduction, An experiment in infant education (anonymous). *Journal of Applied Psychology.* Vol. 2, pp. 219–228, September.
———. 1925. *Genetic studies of genius.* Vol. 1. *Mental and physical traits of a thousand gifted children.* Stanford, Calif.: Stanford University Press.
Terman, Sybil, and C. C. Walcutt. 1958. *Reading: Chaos and cure.* New York: McGraw-Hill.
Thompson, J. W. 1960. *The literacy of the laity in the middle ages.* New York: Burt Franklin.
Tinker, M. A., and C. M. McCullough, 1968. *Teaching elementary reading.* New York: Appleton-Century-Crofts.
Tomlinson, E. 1956. Language arts skills needed by lower class children. *Elementary English.* Vol. 33, pp. 279–283.
Torrey, J. W. 1968. Learning to read without a teacher: A case study. *Elementary English.* Vol. 46, pp. 550–556ff.
Trace, Arther, Jr. 1962. *What Ivan knows that Johnny doesn't.* New York: McGraw-Hill.
———. 1965. *Reading without Dick and Jane.* Chicago: Regnery.
Tyack, D. B. (ed.). 1967. *Turning points in American educational history.* Waltham, Mass.: Blaisdell, Ginn.
von Däniken, Erich. 1972. *Gods from outer space?* New York: Bantam.
Walcutt, C. C. (ed.). 1961. *Tomorrow's illiterates: The state of reading instruction today.* Introduction by Jacques Barzun. Boston: Little, Brown.
———, Joan Lamport, and Glenn McCracken. 1974. *Teaching reading: A phonic/linguistic approach to developmental reading.* New York: Macmillan.
Warner, W. L., M. Maker, and K. Eells. 1949. *Social class in America.* Chicago: Science Research Associates.
Watson, D. T. 1961. *Listen and learn with phonics.* Mundelein, Ill.: Americana Interstate.
Webster, Noah. 1798. *The American spelling book.* Boston: Isaiah Thomas and Ebenezer Andrews. Also titled *The first part of a grammatical institute of the English language* and *The elementary spelling-book,* and published by a variety of printers.
Weisinger, Mort. 1974. *1001 valuable things you can get free.* New York: Bantam Books.
Who Watched the Electric Company? 1972. "The Electric Company in-school utilization study: The 1971–72 school and teacher surveys." A summary of the major findings of a study conducted for the Children's Television Workshop. Center for the Study of Education, Institute for Social Research, Florida State University, in conjunction with Statistics Research Division, Research Triangle Institute.
Wiener, Norbert. 1953. *Ex-prodigy: My childhood and youth.* New York: Simon & Schuster.
Witte, Karl. 1914. *The education of Karl Witte.* Translated by L. Wiener. New York: Thomas Y. Crowell.
Zborowsky, Mark, and Elizabeth Herzog. 1952. *Life is with people.* New York: Schocken Books.

INDEX

ABC blocks, 118
ABC books, 4
  homemade, 150
ABC posters, 147–148
ABC's, 46
Adamson, J. W., 17
Alcott, Bronson, 30
Alcott, Anna, 30
Alcott, William, 30
Alphabet cards, movable, 144–146
Alphabet scrapbooks, 157–158
American Spelling Book, The (Webster), 22
Americana Publishing Co., 37
Ames, L. B., 40, 48
Ancient societies, tutorial tradition in, 11–12
Anderson, A. R., 49n., 53–54
Anderson, Yvonne, 142
Appleton, Elizabeth, 19
Arbuthnot, M., 137
Ariès, Philippe, 20
Aristocratic tutorial tradition, 19–20
Aristotle, 14
Armed Forces Network, 37
Ashton-Warner, Sylvia, 139n.
Auerbach, I., 66, 71–73

"Back to phonics" movement of 1950s and 1960s, 32
Ball, Samuel, 35, 51, 77, 78, 85, 86
Barnhart, Clarence, 33, 91, 108
Baron, S. W., 13
Beck, F. A., 14
Beck, Joan, 36, 37, 82, 91, 98, 101
Beginning sounds of words, decoding pairs of words and, 170–172

Beginning to read, 163–173
  beginning sounds of words and decoding pairs of words in, 170–172
  ending sounds of words and decoding pairs of words in, 172–173
  materials for, 163, 166, 168, 170, 172, 173
  middle sounds, 168–170
  rhymes, ending sounds, and words to read, 163–166
  word families, 166–168
  (*See also* Reading)
Bestor, A. E., 47
Bettelheim, Bruno, 40, 100–101
Bevan, F. L., 19
Birth of Writing, The (Claiborne), 45–46
Blanton, William E., 50–52, 85
Blending words, list of, 179–181
Blends, vowel, word list of, 191–192
Blocks, ABC, 118
Bloomfield, Leonard, 33, 47, 90–91, 108
Bloomfield–Barnhart materials, 90
Bloomfield-Barnhart program, 33
Bloomfield primer, 47
"Blueback Speller" (Webster), 22, 47
Bogatz, G. A., 35, 51, 77, 78, 85, 86
Books and magazines, 119–120, 136–137, 148–149
Boone, R. G., 18
Brown, M. W., 49n.
Brzienski, J. E., 34, 50, 66, 70–71, 85, 96

Calvert and Brown (Hart), 46
Calvert and Hillyer (Hart), 46

227

Index

Calvert School of Baltimore, 23–24, 46
Capital letter cards, 118
Capital letter names, 113–130
Capital letter poster, 115–117
Capital letter wall strip, 117
"Captain Kangaroo," 74, 130, 154
Cards:
    capital letter, 118
    lowercase letter, 134
    movable alphabet, 144–146
Carroll, John, 83
Casa dei Bambini, 49n., 144
Catechisms, 46
Cavour, Count de, 65
Cazden, Courtney, 35, 82
Chalkboards and chalk, 118
Chall, Jeanne, 32, 90
Chan, Julie, 37
Cheira, Edward, 11
Chicago, University of, 59
Chicago Tribune, The, 36, 98
Children:
    those who read with little or no instruction, 26–30
    young: defined, 6
        home reading instruction for, 3–9
        history of, 10–48
    (*See also* Early readers)
Children and Television (Lesser), 47
Children Who Read Early (Durkin), 66, 95n., 99
Children's Language and Education (Cazden), 82
Children's Library Bulletin, 137
Children's Television Workshop (CTW), 35, 36, 75, 79, 86
Chomsky, Carol, 58, 83, 95, 165
Churchill, Winston, 19–20
Cipolla, C. M., 14, 16
Claiborne, Robert, 11, 13, 45
Code emphasis approach in teaching reading, 90, 91

Cohan, Mayme, 54, 84
Coleman, Ed, 82–83
Comics strips, 36–37
Communications media (*see* Media)
Conant, J. B., 47
Consonant blends, 179–181
Consonant combinations and vowel sounds, 185–189
Cooney, Joan Ganz, 35
Coote, Edmund, 20, 46
Cotton, John, 22
Cotton, Josiah, 22
Council for Basic Education, 32
Cox, Catherine, 62, 63, 99
CRAFT Project, 66, 71, 73
Cremin, A. L., 21, 22, 46
CTW (*see* Children's Television Workshop)
Cubberley, E. P., 21, 23
Culhane, John, 9

Dallmann, Martha, 8
David (Old Testament king), 13
Davidson, H. P., 49n., 64
Davis, Evelyn, 79
"Day Care and Reading" (Durkin), 9
Dearborn, Walter, 53–54
Denver Public Schools, 34, 70
Denver Television Project, 66
Detroit Word Recognition Test, 71
Developing reading skills, 174–182
    blending letter-sounds, 178–181
    ending sounds, 174–175
    materials for, 174, 176, 177, 180, 181
    middle sounds, 175–178
    (*See also* Reading)
Dewey, John, 40
Dickens, Charles, 65
Disney, Walt, 4
Dolbear, Katherine E., 86, 100
Doman, Glenn, 18, 36, 91–93
Dumas, Alexander, 64–65

Durkin, Dolores, 8, 9, 43, 47–48, 49*n*., 50, 52, 58, 61, 66–70, 84, 85, 87, 95–99, 108*n*.
Durrell, D. D., 72

Early Education (Appleton), 19
Early readers:
  characteristics and background of, 96–97
  IQ of, 97
  and parent teachers, teaching and learning evaluated by, 98–99
  physical and psychological aftereffects, 59–60, 100–101
  problems and achievements of, after completion of school, 99–100
  social difficulties of, 100
  socioeconomic status (SES) of, 68, 69
  subsequent school and reading experiences of, 98
  (*See also* Research on home reading teaching, case histories)
Early reading:
  inappropriate manner of instruction in, 39–42
  inappropriateness of reading to the lives of young children, 42–43
  opponents of, 38–43
  possible interference with child's schoolwork, 39
  possible physical or psychological harm from, 38–39
  (*See also* Home reading; Home reading instruction)
Edey, M. A., 12
Educating the Child at Home (Lynch), 32
Education Research Information Clearinghouse (ERIC), 52
Educational movements involving home reading instruction, 30–34
Educational Testing Service (ETS), 75, 78
"Eleanor Learns to Read" (Iredell), 83
"Electric Company, The," 4, 6, 35, 84, 87, 106, 107, 114, 130, 141, 154
Easy Readers, 9, 35
Elementary English Review, 47
Emerson, Ralph Waldo, 65
Ending sounds of words, 163–166, 174–175
  and decoding pairs of words, 172–173
Engelmann, Siegfried, 64, 100
Engelmann, Theresa, 64, 100
English Schoole-Maister, The (Coote), 20, 46
Environment, learning, and home reading, 97
Eratosthenes, 16
ERIC (Education Research Information Clearinghouse), 52
ETS (Educational Testing Service), 75, 78
Europe in the Middle Ages and later, reading and writing in, 17–18
Evans, James L., 55–56

Feelie letters, 134–136
Fingerpainting, 124–125
Fireside Education (Goodrich), 47
Fireside Education Movement, 30–31
Flesch, Rudolf, 33, 47, 90, 91
Fordham University, 83
Forester, C. S., 26–27
Formal instruction, defined, 6–7
Formative research, defined, 75*n*.

Fowler, William, 49n., 56, 59–60, 84–86, 94, 97, 100

Games, 126–129, 140, 151–153, 160–161, 199
Gates, A. I., 43, 82
Gates-MacGintie tests, 57
Gattegno, Caleb, 36
Gedike, Friedrich, 40
Gedike primer, 18
Genetic Psychology Monograph (Fowler), 59
Genetic Studies of Genius (Terman), 62, 63
"Getting Your Child Off to a Good Start in Reading" (Chan), 37
Gingerbread method of reading instruction, 17
Goertzel, M. C., 86, 100
Goertzel, Victor, 86, 100
Going ahead with reading, 183–201
  common sight words, 197–199
  games in, 199
  independent reading, 200
  letter-sound combinations, 194–197
  materials for, 183, 185, 189, 192, 194, 197, 200
  two-syllable words and two-vowel combinations, 189–192
  vowel combinations, 192–194
  vowel sounds and consonant combinations, 185–189
  (*See also* Reading)
Goodrich, S. G., 47
Gould, T., 108
Great Reading Turn On, The (Beck), 37
Greece, ancient, reading and writing in, 13–15
Gwynn, Aulrey, 15

Hainstock, E. G., 91
Harris, A. J., 66, 71–73

Harrison, G. V., 52, 83, 85
Harrison, M. L., 85
Hart, Archibald, 24, 46
Hart, John, 17, 46
Hayman, J. L., Jr., 34, 50, 66, 70–71, 85, 96
Hebrews:
  reading and writing instruction among, 12–13
  tutorial tradition among, 13
Herzog, Elizabeth, 13
Hildreth, Gertrude, 8, 65–66
Hillman, Rosemary, 40
Hobbes, Thomas, 65
Hollingworth, Leta, 62–64, 86, 99, 100
Holmes, Jack, 44–45
Holt, John, 35
Home reading:
  analysis of process, 94–101
  learning environment and, 97
  material for (*see* Materials, home reading)
  specific program for, 109–201
  (*See also* Beginning to read; Developing reading skills; Going ahead with reading; Readiness)
  troubleshooting, 110–111
  (*See also* Early readers; Early reading; Reading)
Home reading instruction, 3–9
  branches of, 18–38
  via communications media, 34–38
  educational movements involving, 30–34
  gingerbread method of, 17
  history of, 10–48
  procedures for, 97–98
  suggested, 105–108
  research on, 49–83
    case histories, 52–62
    empirical studies, 66–75
    retrospective studies, 62–66
    reviews on, 51–52

Home reading instruction (*Cont.*):
"Sesame Street" studies, 50–51, 75–83
(*See also* Instruction; Teaching reading)
Home reading teachers:
characteristics and background of, 96–97
defined, 6
and pupils, teaching and learning evaluated by, 98–99
Home teaching, defined, 6
(*See also* Tutorial tradition)
Home-teaching movements, 30–34
Hopper, Majorie, 37
Horace (Roman poet), 75
Horn Book, The, 137
Hornbooks, 46
How to Teach Your Baby to Read (Doman), 18, 36, 91
Huey, E. B., 40, 95
Hughes, Felicity, 93
Hurd, G. M., 70, 91
Hymes, J. L., 41–43

Ickelsamer primer, 17
Ilg, F. L., 41, 48
Illinois, University of, Champaign-Urbana Reading Center at, 57
Indiana, University of, 51
Indus Valley civilization, reading and writing in, 12
Infant schools (*dardeki kheyder*) for Jewish children, 13
Informal instruction, defined, 6–7
Informal path to reading, 87–90
Instruction:
children who read with little or none, 26–30
formal, defined, 6–7
informal, defined, 6–7
(*See also* Home reading instruction)
International Reading Association, 4, 9, 52

IQ, relationship to early reading, 97
IQ tests, Stanford-Binet, 54, 67
Iredell, Harriet, 83
Israel, teaching of Hebrew in, 13
Israel abn al-Nakov, Rabbi, 13

Johnson, Clifton, 21, 22
Journal of Applied Psychology, 53
Journal of Educational Research, 66

Kasdon, L. M., 8, 42, 66
Keay, F. E., 12
Keele, R. L., 52, 83, 85
Kramer, Samuel Noah, 45
Kuhn, A. L., 30–31, 47

Ladies Home Journal, 36
Larrick, Nancy, 119, 136, 137
League of Mother-Teachers, 32
Learning:
"osmosis," 83
and teaching, evaluated by teachers and pupils, 98–99
"Learning, Teaching, and Television Production for Children" (Lesser), 47
Learning environment and home reading, 97
Learning to Read: The Great Debate (Chall), 32
Lee, Harper, 28
LeShan, Eda, 40–42
Lesser, Gerald, 35, 47, 51, 75, 76, 79, 85
Let's Read (Bloomfield and Barnhart), 33, 108
Letter cards:
capital, 118
lowercase, 134
Letter combinations, word list of, 186–188

Letter names:
  capital, 113–130
  lowercase, 130–142
Letter-sound association posters or wall strips, 146–148
Letter-sound associations:
  introducing, 142–154
  learning, 154–161
Letter-sound combinations, 194–197
Letter-sounds, blending, 178–181
Letters:
  capital: posters of, 115–117
    wall strips of, 117
  feelie, 134–136
  list of common words to associate with, 157–158
  lowercase, posters and wall strips of, 132–133
  plastic, 117–118
    lowercase, 133
Linguistic approach to reading, 33
Listen and Learn with Phonics (Watson), 36
Literature for Children (Arbuthnot), 137
Long before Forty (Forester), 27
Look-say (whole word) approach to reading, 32, 33, 91–94
Lowercase letter cards, 134
Lowercase letter names, 130–142
Lowercase letter posters and wall strips, 132–133
Luckert, D., 18, 93
Ludus (Roman private elementary school), 15

Macaulay, Thomas, 65
McCracken, Glenn, 47
McEathron, Margaret, 91
McKee, Paul, 85
Magazines and books, 119–120, 136–137, 148–149

Magic *e* word list, 184–185
Magic slates, 136
Mail as tool in readiness, 129, 141, 153–154, 161
Martineau, Harriet, 30–31
Massachusetts Bay Colony, legislation on parental teaching in, 20–22
Materials, home reading, 94–96
  ABC blocks, 118
  ABC posters, 147–148
  beginning-to-read, 163, 166, 168, 170, 172, 173
  books and magazines, 119–120, 136–137, 148–149
  capital letter cards, 118
  capital letter posters, 115–117
  chalkboards and chalk, 118
  for developing reading skills, 174, 176, 177, 180, 181
  feelie letters, 134–136
  in going ahead with reading, 183, 185, 189, 192, 194, 197, 200
  letter-sound association posters or wall strips, 146–148
  lowercase letter cards, 134
  magic slates, 136
  movable alphabet cards, 144–146
  plastic letters, 117–118
    lowercase, 133
  for readiness, 130, 142, 154
  wall strips: capital letter, 117
    letter-sound association, 146–148
    lowercase letter, 132–133
Mathews, M. M., 14, 15, 17, 22, 45, 46, 94
Mead, Margaret, 3
Media:
  reading instruction via, 34–38
  as tool in readiness, 129–130, 141–142, 154, 161
Mental age, 43, 44, 45, 64, 70

Metropolitan Reading Readiness Tests, 83
Metropolitan Reading Test, 54
Middle Ages in Europe, reading and writing in the, 17–18
Middle sounds of words, 168–170, 175–178
Mill, John Stuart, 24–25, 65, 98
Miller, Merle, 27, 28
Minton, Judith, 83, 85, 86
Mobiles, clothesline, 158
Montessori, Maria, 9, 49*n*., 58, 83
Montessori methods, 126, 137, 144–145
Montessori Motivational Toys, Inc. 37–38
Montessori preschools, 4
Montessori sandpaper letters and movable alphabet, 91
Moore, O. K., 49*n*., 83
Morphett, Mabel, 43
Morris, Ronald, 25
Morrison, Coleman, 50, 66, 71–73, 85
Ms. magazine, 137
Multi-Max teaching machine, 55
Murphy-Durrell Diagnostic Reading Readiness Test, 71
Murphy-Durrell Learning Rate Subtest, 72
Musset, Louis Alfred de, 65
My Early Life (Churchill), 20

National Education Movement, 31–32
National Geographic School Bulletin, 129
Natural Education (Stoner), 25, 31
New York City Schools, 8
New York Times Book Review, The, 9, 35, 137
Nonprofessional reading teacher, defined, 6

"Old Deluder Satan" ordinance of Massachusetts Bay Colony, 21
Olilla, Lloyd, 50, 52
1001 Valuable Things You Can Get Free (Weisenger), 153–154
"Osmosis" learning, 83

Paidogos (Greek pedagogue-slave), 14
Palmer, E. L., 75
Parental teaching, 20–26
  (*See also* Home reading instruction; Teaching reading)
Parent's Guide to Children's Reading, A (Larrick), 119, 136, 137
Parke, M. B., 94
Pennsylvania, University of, 74
Perlish, H. N., 66, 74–75
Phonic emphasis in direct teaching of reading, 90–91
Phonics:
  "back to phonics" movement of 1950s and 1960s, 32
  defined, 34*n*.
Phonics/look-say controversy, 32
Photo alblums, 150
Physical and psychological aftereffects ascribed to early reading, 59–60, 100–101
Pines, Maya, 9, 83, 98
Pirenne, Henri, 17
Plain Speaking (Miller), 27
Plastic letters, 117–118
  lowercase, 133
Pliny, 15
Politics (Aristotle), 14
Pop Ups film loops, 36
Posters:
  ABC, 147–148
  capital letter, 115–117
  letter-sound association, 146–148
  lowercase letter, 132–133
Precocity, infant, 31, 47

234 · Index

Preschool Reading Instruction (Blanton), 51–52
Preschoolers (*see* Children; Early readers)
Pressure as teaching device, 7–8, 9
Primers, 46
Prior, Mathew, 17
Private Education (Appleton), 19
Programmed Reading Series, 108*n*.
Psychological and physical aftereffects ascribed to early reading, 59–60, 100–101
Psychology and Pedagogy of Reading, The (Huey), 41
Psychology of Teaching Reading, The (Anderson and Dearborn), 53
Pupils (*see* Children; Early readers)
Pushing as teaching device, 8, 9, 51

Quintilian, 16

Read, Charles, 58, 165
Readers, early (*see* Early Readers)
Readiness (reading), 43–45, 113–162
  books and magazines for, 119–120, 136–137, 148–149
  capital letter names, 113–130
  games in, 126–129, 140, 151–153, 160–161
  introducing letter-sound associations, 142–154
  learning letter-sound associations, 154–161
  lowercase letter names, 130–142
  mail as tools in, 129, 141, 153–154, 161
  materials for, 130, 142, 154
  media as tool in 129–130, 141–142, 154, 161
  mental age, 43, 44, 45, 64
  own words, 125, 139, 151, 160
  reading aloud, 119, 136, 148, 158–159

Readiness (reading) (*Cont.*):
  sight words, 125–126, 139–140, 151, 160
  things to buy or make, 115–118, 132–136, 144–148, 157–158
  things to make together, 122–125, 138–139, 150–151, 160
  things to read, 159
  what to do, 114–115, 131–132, 142–144, 155–156
  working together, 150
  writing and scribbling, 120–121, 137, 149–150, 159
  writing together, 121–122, 137–138, 159
  (*See also* Reading)
"Readiness to Learn to Read" (Durkin), 48
Reading:
  as apprenticeship skill, 3
  early (*see* Early reading)
  home (*see* Home reading)
  independent, 200
  informal path to, 87–90
  origin of, 45–46
  paths to, 86–94
  as social necessity, 3
  Sumerian legends on origin of, 45
  teaching of (*see* Home reading instruction; Teaching reading)
  and writing: in ancient Greece, 13–15
    in Europe in the Middle Ages, 17–18
    among Hebrews, 12–13
    in Roman society, 15–16
    in Sumerian Culture, 11–12
  (*See also* Beginning to read; Developing reading skills; Going ahead with reading; Readiness)
Reading, Chaos and Cure (Terman and Walcutt), 87
Reading aloud, 119, 136, 148, 158–159
Reading and Writing Before School (Hughes), 93

Reading experiences, subsequent, of early readers, 98
"Reading in the Crib" (D. and M. Steinberg), 56
Reading Newsreport, 83
"Reading Readiness" (Durkin), 48
Reading readiness (*see* Readiness)
Reading Reform Foundation, 32
Reading skills, five basic, 5–6
Reading Teacher, The, 37, 48
Reading teachers (*see* Teachers)
Reading-teaching kits, 37
Reading without Tears (Bevan), 19–20
Research:
 formative defined, 75n.
 on home reading teaching, 49–83
  case histories, 52–62
  empirical studies, 66–75
  retrospective studies, 62–66
  reviews of, 51–52
   "Sesame Street" studies, 50–51, 75–83
Revolution in Learning (Pines), 9, 83
Rhymes, 163–166
Rhyming word lists, 166, 175–177
 magic *e,* 184–185
Rickover, H. G., 47
Rimmel, E. L., 70, 91
Rodgers, Norma, 45
Roman society, reading and writing in, 15–16
Run Away, Little Girl (Segal), 93

Sartre, Jean-Paul, 26–27
Scholastic Press Record/Book sets, 107
School experiences of early readers, 98
Scott, Foresman pre-primer, 55–56
Scrapbooks, 123, 138, 150, 151
 alphabet, 157–158
 poetry and quotes, 160
Scribbling and writing, 120–121, 137, 149–150, 159

Scripture, E. W., 93
Segal, Marilyn, 93
Sendak, Maurice, 47
"Sesame Street," 4, 35, 47, 83, 84, 86, 87, 106, 107, 114, 130, 132, 141, 154
"Sesame Street" books and magazines, 149
"Sesame Street" research, 50–51, 75–83
Sheldon, W. D., 100
"Short Cuts to Reading You Can Teach Your Child" (Beck), 36
Sight words, 125–126, 139–140, 151, 160
 common, 197–199
 master list, 198–199
Slates, magic, 136
Smethurst, Wood, 34
Smith, Mortimer, 47
Smith, Nila B., 26
Smith, W. A., 11–13, 15, 45
Social problems of early readers, 100
Socioeconomic status (SES) of early readers, 68, 69
 and their teachers, 96–97
Sounds of words:
 beginning, and decoding pairs of words, 170–172
 ending, 163–166, 174–175
  and decoding pairs of words, 172–173
 middle, 168–170, 175–178
 vowel, and consonant combinations, 185–189
 (*See also under* Letter-sound)
Sputnik, 47
Stanford Achievement Test, 71
Stanford-Binet IQ test, 54, 67
Stars and Stripes, 37
Steinberg, Danny, 56–58, 91
Steinberg, Miho, 56–58, 91
Stern, C., 108
Stoner, Winifred Sackville, 25, 31, 46
Strang, Ruth, 65, 99

Strickland, Charles, 30
Structural Reading (Stern and Gould), 108
Sumerian culture, reading and writing in, 11–12
Sumerian legends on origin of writing, 45
Swift, Jonathan, 64
Swift, T. H., 13

Tacitus, 15–16
Teacher (Ashton-Warner), 139n.
Teachers:
  of early readers, characteristics and background of, 96–97
  nonprofessional reading, defined, 6
  and pupils, teaching and learning evaluated by, 98–99
Teaching:
  home, defined, 6
  (*See also* Home reading instruction)
  parental, 20–26
Teaching devices:
  pressure as, 7–8
  pushing as, 8, 51
Teaching machines, 55
Teaching Reading (Hildreth), 65
Teaching reading:
  code emphasis approach in, 90, 91
  direct: with phonic emphasis, 90–91
    with whole-word (look-say) emphasis, 91–94
  linguistic approach to, 33
  look-say (whole word) approach to, 32, 33
  (*See also* Home reading instruction; Reading)
"Teaching Reading by Machine: A Case History in Early Reading Behavior" (Evans), 55
"Teaching Reading to the Under-Six Age: A Child Development Point of View" (Hymes), 42–43
Teaching Them to Read (Durkin), 47, 48
Teaching Young Children to Read (Durkin), 108n.
Terman, L. M., 8, 52–53, 62, 84, 99
Terman, Sybil, 47, 87
Texas, University of, 83
Thompson, J. W., 17
To Kill a Mockingbird (Lee), 28, 98
Tomorrow's Illiterates (Council for Basic Education), 32
Torrey, Jane, 30, 60–62, 85, 97
Trace, Arther, Jr., 47
Troubleshooting in home reading, 110–111
Truman, Harry, 16–28
Tutorial tradition:
  in ancient societies, 11–12
  aristocratic, 19–20
  among Hebrews, 13
  in the Middle Ages, 17–18
Two-syllable words and two-vowel combinations, 189–192

U. S. Office of Education, 51

Voltaire, 65
Von Däniken, Erich, 45
Vowel blends, word lists of, 191–192
Vowel combinations, 192–194
  word list of, 193
Vowel sounds and consonant combinations, 185–189
Vowels, two-vowel combinations and two-syllable words, 189–192

Wackernagel, Philip, 94
Walcutt, C. C., 47, 87

Wall strips:
    capital letter, 117
    letter-sound association, 146–148
    lowercase letter, 132–133
Walt Disney Productions, "read-it-yourself" books. 4
Warner, W. L., 69, 83, 101
Warner's Index of Social Class, 83
Washburne, Carleton, 43
Watson, Dorothy Taft, 36, 108
Webster, Noah, 22, 47
Weisenger, Mort, 154
Wesley, John, 25
"When Should Children Begin to Read?" (Durkin), 48
Whole word (look-say) approach to reading, 32, 33, 91–94
Why Johnny Can't Read, and What You Can Do about It (Flesch), 33–34, 90
Wide Range Achievement Test, 57
Wiener, Norbert, 98, 100
Word families, 166–169
    list of, 169
        rhyming, 175
Word lists:
    blending words, 179–181
    comparative endings, 190
    -*ez* ending sound, 191
    -*ing* words, 189
    l or *ll* with vowels, 195
    letter combinations, 186–188
    long *i*, 197
    magic *e* words, 184–185
    pairs of words, 171, 173
    qu words, 195
    -*r* after vowels, 194–195
    rhyming, 166, 175–177
    rhyming families, 175
    sight words, 198–199
    soft *c* and *g*, 196
    vowel blends, 191–192
    vowel combinations, 193
    word families, 166–169

Word lists (*Cont.*):
    word pairs and threesomes, 176, 178
    -*y* endings, 190
"Wordland Workshop," 74
Words:
    beginning sounds of, and decoding pairs of words, 170–172
    blending, list of, 179–181
    common, to associate with letters, 157–158
    ending sounds of, 163–166, 174–175
        and decoding pairs of words, 172–173
    middle sounds of, 168–170, 175–178
    own, 125, 139, 151, 160
    paired, list of, 171
    sight, 125–126, 139–140, 151, 160
        common, 197–199
        master list, 198–199
    two-syllable, and two-vowel combinations, 189–192
    vowel sounds and consonant combinations, 185–189
    (*See also* Word lists)
Words, The (Sartre), 27
"Write First, Read Later" (Chomsky), 58
Writing, 165
    and reading (*see* Reading and writing)
    and scribbling, 120–121, 137, 149–150, 159
Writing together, 121–122, 137–138, 159

You Can Teach Your Child to Read (Parke), 94

Zborowsky, Mark, 13